All Walks of Life (and Death)

A Behind-the-Scenes Look at 42 Years as a
Firefighter/Paramedic

By

John (Scooz) Spicuzza

All Walks of Life (and Death): A Behind-the-Scenes Look at 42 Years as a Firefighter/Paramedic

Published in the United States by BCG Publishing, 2021.

www.BCGPublishing.com

To my wife, Beth, my two sons,
Michael and Ryan, plus the
many great partners and coworkers I had
throughout my career.

Table of Contents

INTRODUCTION

My background spans forty-two years in public safety which includes being a volunteer firefighter, full-time firefighter, full-time paramedic, emergency room paramedic, hazardous materials technician/instructor, terrorism instructor, meth lab instructor, and fire academy instructor.

This book details the good, the bad, the ugly, and sometimes downright messed up world members working in the public safety arena face throughout their career. Dealing with and assisting people from all walks of life makes it a fascinating field to work in. I would not trade that experience for anything.

I will discuss how I got started as a volunteer and some of the experiences I had in the beginning. The stories are not in chronological order; however, they will be grouped together by category for the most part. I will get into more detailed and personal situations I encountered throughout my career, some of which I will never be able to forget, and some I would not wish on my worst enemy.

This book is intended for anyone who has an interest in a behind-the-scenes look at what the job entails, especially those of the civilian population who see the ambulances and fire trucks racing down the road with their lights and sirens blaring but for the most part do not know what happens at the other end.

For those starting a career in public safety or who are currently in the academy to become an EMT, paramedic, or firefighter, this will give you an idea of what you may experience once you get the opportunity to work in one of those fields. This behind-the-scenes look at this field will help you prepare for an exciting and challenging career.

This book is also intended for anyone who is well into their career as an EMT, paramedic, or firefighter or even retired, to compare notes, bring back memories, or even have a laugh at some of the similarities with your career. All the short stories and experiences noted are actual events that were experienced during my career. None of the names used in this book are real but they reflect real people.

All the experiences I share are typical of any department whether it be career or volunteer, large or small, urban or rural. The only differences one may experience would be due to geographic locations that may dictate some of the varied unique experiences related to that area. This would include responses related to earthquakes, hurricanes, mountains, mudslides, avalanches, large urban cites, small rural areas, older buildings versus newer buildings, and the like. The number of runs you make are not dictated by the size of the department you work at. My career consisted of working with small and medium-sized departments and ran as many as twenty-four runs out of one unit in a twenty-four-hour shift. Some large city departments may not run anywhere near that due to having many more stations that are available to respond. On the flip side, some rural volunteer departments may run very few calls, and some larger departments run twenty or so runs with one apparatus a shift.

Worth noting is that all fires are hot and dangerous no matter who responds to them or where, and all medical runs are typically similar in nature. This book will cover those personal experiences during my forty-two-year career along with a peek behind the curtain detailing what it is really like to work in public safety and interact with people from all walks of life.

Chapter 1

A CERTAIN DEGREE OF EXPOSURE

"A certain degree of exposure leads to a certain degree of contamination." That is a common phrase used by hazardous materials technicians. The quote is self-explanatory. It also defines how I eventually got involved in the public safety arena after a certain amount of exposure to the job.

❖ Neighbor Mechanic

My very first encounter with the fire department and emergency care was at the age of ten. A friend of mine and I were watching a neighbor work on his car. He was lying underneath a car up on four jacks with all four wheels off the ground doing some mechanic work. He and his wife were very friendly to the kids in the neighborhood and welcomed us to watch him work and ask all the curious questions we had at that age about working on his car.

As he was pulling hard on a wrench, he caused the car to move and fall off the jacks. When it did, the car fell onto his chest, causing him to make a horrible grunt sound. The undercarriage had him pinned under the car. I ran into his house and yelled for his wife to call for help, explaining to her what happened. My friend, his wife, and I tried to lift the car off his chest to no avail. When the fire department showed up, they used a floor jack that was nearby to raise the car and drag him out. They transported him to the hospital with multiple fractured ribs. Fortunately he recovered and did fine.

My New Sister

When I was around thirteen years old, I had my first family emergency. My father was at work and I was home with my mother and sisters. My mother was nine months pregnant at the time and went into labor. We called the local fire department (direct number, as 911 was not a thought yet) and they showed up with the fire department ambulance, which was a Cadillac that looked just like the one in the original *Ghost Busters* movie. My mom had her suitcase ready to go and I assisted her to the ambulance while carrying her bag, and off they went. I was intrigued with the firefighters at the time even though they only had first-aid training. They were very caring and helpful for my mother. The next day she came home with my dad and a new sister.

First Exposure to a Structure Fire

In my early teens, a neighbor's house caught fire and was fully engulfed when the fire department got there. I watched the firefighters from several fire trucks on the scene work hard fighting the fire and getting it under control. From close-up it looked like chaos, but what I remember when it was all over was how everyone knew what they were doing even though they were going in different directions and doing different tasks. I was impressed with the job the firefighters did at the time but did not think of it much more after that.

A Smashed Bug

Around the age of fourteen I was riding in a station wagon with my family when we came to an intersection and watched a Volkswagen Beetle coming from the opposite direction get broadsided by a car that ran a traffic light. We watched the little car fly in the air in front of us across the intersection and into someone's front yard. My father and sisters screamed and were visibly upset, and I yelled at my dad to stop the car so we could help.

He pulled over and I ran over to this tiny smashed car and saw two teenage girls slumped over, unconscious. I had no idea what to do other than try to wake them up and stay with them until the fire department got there. I felt totally useless, but I felt we at least needed to be there for them.

When the fire department showed up, I backed away and watched as they cut them out of the vehicle with pry bars and axes. They were very aggressive and determined to get them out of the little car with the hand tools they had at hand. There were no hydraulic rescue tools developed yet. I saw how caring the firefighters were when removing them from the car and placing them on a stretcher for transport to the hospital.

I started seeing a pattern of caring for total strangers and the teamwork required to accomplish their task. The next day, I read in the newspaper that one of the girls had died at the hospital.

Never Play with Matches

One morning when I was a sophomore in high school, one of the younger girls who typically came over and played with my little sisters ran over screaming that her house across the street was on fire and her little brother was still inside. We knew her parents had run to the store for a few minutes and she was watching her little brother.

I ran over to the house with my dad, and we found the little boy in the living room while the back bedroom was engulfed in flames with smoke starting to bank down from the ceiling. My dad took him out of the house and gave him to my older sisters to watch while I dumped out a trash can from the bathroom and filled it with water in the bathtub, ran to the bedroom door and threw it on the bed that was on fire. When my dad came back, I told him to dump out another trash can and keep filling them up in the tub and bringing them to me.

We had the fire out by the time the fire department showed up. I had no idea what we were doing other than it seemed like the right thing to do at the time. We found out the little boy was playing with matches under the bed and it caught on fire. The fire damage was limited to the bedroom and there was smoke damage in the rest of the house.

The parents come home to see fire trucks lined up in front of their house with their lights flashing and firefighters going in and out of their house. The firefighters were empathetic and supportive while assuring them the kids were fine and the house was repairable.

EMERGENCY!

When I was in my teens, like most kids around my age, I spent time watching the TV show *Emergency!* all the time. I was a senior in high school when I really got pumped about watching the program. Just like most my age, that is what got us excited about the job. There was nothing cooler than Johnny Gage popping the caps off medication before he administered drugs, fighting big fires, or facing challenging rescues.

That TV show introduced paramedics to the general public for the first time and highlighted how they worked hand in hand with the doctors and nurses in the emergency room. It also exposed the job of firefighters and the wide array of emergencies they responded to. It was a classic.

My First Exposure to a Disaster

In 1973 I had moved out of my parents' house and out of state with Jose, a neighbor I grew up with. We were next door neighbors from the time we were five years old up to high school. I came back to visit my family in 1974 and it just happened to be the same time a rash of tornados came through the region. I was on the way to visit a high-school friend with another high-school buddy of mine when we heard sirens everywhere.

There were fire department sirens, police sirens, and tornado sirens going off.

As we looked around, we saw in ahead of us what appeared to be a large dark cloud that covered the entire sky. We assumed it was a bad storm coming. As we got closer, we realized it was a tornado that was touching down in the city we were traveling to. It was an F5 tornado and was cutting a swath three-quarters of a mile wide on the ground. As the tornado passed it left devastation behind. We got a few miles from our destination when we could not drive anymore due to debris and trees all over the road. We got out and started walking down the street, and the devastation was unbelievable. I knew what street we were on, but it did not look familiar at all.

As we walked down the street, we realized there were no emergency responders anywhere in the area. All the responders were sent to the downtown area, which had been hit by the storm much worse than anywhere else. We decided to make sure there was nobody in need of help and started looking for signs of people. There were gas lines leaking, large trees smashed onto homes and vehicles, and it was eerily quiet. A three-story condo was now a pile of debris only about ten feet tall. We called out but didn't hear or see anything, so we kept moving. About a block farther we heard someone crying in the distance. We followed the sound to a house that had a lot of exterior damage and was completely missing its roof. We walked inside the house and followed the sound to what was a hallway closet and when we opened the door, we found a young mother holding her baby, sitting on the floor of the closet, crying. The closet was intact due to it being in the middle of the house and surrounded by framing, including the ceiling above it. She had no idea her roof was completely gone until we got her outside. A neighbor came over and stayed with them and we left.

I believe it was at that point that I started to become a little more interested in being a first responder , at least in the back of my mind. Some would say I might be a little slow in picking up the signs that this is something I would like to do, but it all worked out eventually.

Chapter 2

VOLUNTEER FIREFIGHTER

❖ The Beginning of My Journey

In 1975 I was driving down the road and saw a sign outside of a fire station advertising that volunteer firefighters were needed. It piqued my interest enough for me to stop and check it out. When I went inside and inquired about the sign, a grumpy old man in his sixties named Jason Isiki was sitting at the desk in the front office and smoking what appeared to be his second pack of cigarettes according to what I saw in the ashtray, told me that if I was interested, I should fill out an application and turn it in at one of their monthly volunteer meetings. I took the application and left, not knowing what would become of this first step into the world of being a first responder.

I showed up at the next meeting and presented my application, explained why I was interested in being a volunteer, and answered questions from a board of fire commissioners. I was then asked to step outside while the board and the rest of the volunteers discussed whether I should be accepted or not. A few minutes later they welcomed me and at the end of their meeting, I was issued my gear and equipment.

I was issued a pair of rubber "pull-up" fire boots, a cotton fire coat, a pair of bulky fire gloves and a plastic fire helmet. That was the extent of our protective equipment. A jumpsuit was ordered for me to wear when calls came in at night to make it quicker to get dressed. Blue jeans were the preferred pants to wear for fighting fires at the time.

I was then given a Plectron Fire Alert box to plug in at home. Pagers were relatively new, and our department did not issue them yet. A license tag denoting that I was a volunteer firefighter went on the front of my vehicle, then an application to use emergency lights on my vehicle was sent to the sheriff's office. Once he signed the permit, it was up to me to purchase a teardrop emergency light that would plug into the cigarette lighter and go either on my dashboard or on top of the car, just like on the TV show *Kojak*. If you are too young to know what that is, look it up. Funny stuff.

At this time, I was temporarily living with Jose and his parents. When I got home from the volunteer firefighters' meeting, I told Jose about the whole process and said I thought he would like being a firefighter as well."

He eventually had a full-time career and retired from the fire service as well.

The Process

I learned that two part-time firefighters took turns working at the firehouse during the day. This was because volunteers were not that reliable during the week when most people are working their normal jobs. Other than the two part-timers, the rest of the department was all volunteers. The firehouse had a system in which volunteers scheduled their time working the night shift at the station after the part-timers left. The system was typical of most volunteer departments in the area. There was no 911 system in place at the time and people in the fire district had to call the firehouse direct. We handed out phone stickers for residents to place on their phones so they knew what number to call for emergencies. Most people would dial "0" for the operator, but it would delay the call as the operator tried to figure out the location and what department to call.

When a call came in, the phone in the front office would ring along with an extremely loud Klaxon horn that was deafening. If the operator forwarded the call to the county dispatchers, they would pick up the Automatic Ring Down (ARD) phone that would automatically ring at the station, setting off the same Klaxon horn. This worked just like the ARD that Police Commissioner Gordon used to call Batman. When you picked up the phone, it automatically rang at the bat cave, or in this case, the fire station. Again, if you are of the age where you don't know what I am talking about, Google that as well.

The information was written down on a notepad, a button was pushed on a paging system that sent out a tone on a Plectron FM Transistor Radio Receiver Fire Alert box in the volunteer's home that set off a loud tone. The firefighter who took the phone call would then talk into a desk microphone and relay the message stating the emergency and the address. They would then flip a switch on the wall that set off a house siren that was mounted high above the fire station on a radio tower. It could be heard for miles around the fire station. This would alert the volunteers who were not in the vicinity of their alert box that there was an emergency. After all that, they would gather their fire gear, jump in the fire truck, and respond. Depending on the day and the time, it was not unheard of to be on scene all by yourself if nobody else was available or if everyone else was at work.

We were required to pull a certain number of "night duty" shifts at the fire station per month to remain an active member. We were also required to attend a set number of monthly meetings/trainings a year. Our responses to either the station or the scene were tabulated each month, and we were compensated $2.50 per response for the month. This was to help compensate for fuel used and wear and tear on our vehicles. Considering gas was around fifty-seven cents per gallon at that time, it was not bad.

To pull night shift at the station by yourself, you had to be cleared to drive the fire apparatus. This consisted of asking if you knew how to drive a stick shift, and if so, you were shown how to put the truck in pump mode to be able to flow water. You could officially become a driver/engineer in less than a week. Thank God we do not see that too much today.

Back to driving the fire trucks. For some of you younger readers, believe it or not, there was a time where power steering and power brakes were not so common. The first-out engine we used was a commercial cab and chassis with a hose bed, water tank with 500 gallons of water, a body with cabinets full of equipment, and a fire pump in the middle. The front tires were as high as my waist and it took a few steps to climb into the cab. It had a five-speed manual transmission with a stick shift on the floor and a steering wheel that was insanely huge.

Once you pulled outside of the garage bay, you had to stop and get out to manually close the bay door before responding to the call. Making any turns while moving at a slow speed was a challenge. You almost had to stand up from the seat to grab the wheel and turn it hand over hand with everything you had, which was virtually impossible at a standstill. When stopping you had to push in the clutch to take it out of gear and stomp heavily on the brake pedal. By the time you got on scene you were worn out from driving.

When it came time to put the pump in gear to flow water you had to push in the clutch, engage the emergency brake, move the stick shift to fifth gear, flip a lever for the pump to engage, then slowly let out the clutch, allowing it to engage with the pump and not the transmission. Once you heard it engage the pump, you could let the clutch all the way out; then you stepped out of the truck and moved to the pump panel.

A valve handle was then pulled out, allowing water to flow to the fire pump, a knob was turned counterclockwise to increase the rpms of the engine and at the same time a larger knob was turned clockwise, increasing the pressure in the pump. This was like patting your head and rubbing your belly. Then a valve handle was pulled out to allow water to flow to a certain discharge outlet and hose. A majority of the time we pulled the hose that was coiled on a hose reel at the top of the pump since it got water to it right away and was easier to handle if we were by ourselves, which was fairly common for the initial setup. The other reason for the hose reel was that it was easy to roll back up by pushing a button that operated an electric motor that turned the reel, allowing it to be stowed away very quickly.

My Volunteer Career

Is there such thing as a career volunteer? I was a volunteer firefighter for twenty-four years while working full-time with EMS and while working full-time with another fire department. Some in the business consider full-time firefighters as professional firefighters and volunteers as, well, volunteers. I can tell you from my forty-two years of experience that not all paid firefighters are professional, and many volunteers are very professional. That is a poor choice of words for a description. Some prefer to define it as career versus volunteer. My preference is paid or full-time versus volunteer. There are many out there who have had a long career as a volunteer firefighter. It is common to have a volunteer firefighter spend more years as a firefighter than a typical full-time firefighter. In many cases the only difference between the two would be that one gets paid while the other does not, or one department has a large tax base, allowing for the latest and greatest equipment and the other may not, or one may run more calls than the other. And note I did not mention which one is on which side of the equation. That is because it goes both ways. I know of full-time firefighters who spent their entire career without fighting one structure fire and volunteer departments that have numerous fires under their belt.

As I mentioned earlier, the one undeniable fact is that fires do not know or care if the firefighter is paid or volunteer. The fire reacts the same, burns just as hot, and kills firefighters indiscriminately. Almost seventy percent of all U.S. firefighters are volunteer. (U.S. Fire Administration, n.d.) There were 157 firefighter LODD (line of duty deaths) in 1977 with eighty-two being volunteers. In 2018 there were a total of sixty-four LODD with thirty-four being volunteers. (Fahy & Molis, 19). Nuff said.

Safety Be Damned

Back to my days as a volunteer. When we got a call while at the station, the routine was to kick off your shoes and put on your rubber fire boots. Keep in mind, these rubber fire boots were pull-up boots that were folded down to the size of a normal calf-height boot with handles inside to pull them up. We never pulled them up to our upper legs because it was not cool-looking. As long as you had on blue jeans, you were good. We would then jump onto the tailboard of the fire truck, throw our coat and helmet on the hose bed, and hang on for dear life to the bar that ran across the back of the hose bed. The truck would take off and with one arm around the bar, we took the other arm and put on our coat one arm at a time, followed by the the helmet, all while bouncing down the road at crazy speeds. It was common for both feet to bounce clear off the tailboard when hitting some bumps.

Being young and naïve, the excitement about this whole new world was addicting. You could not get enough of it once you started making runs. Imagine, standing on the tailboard of this speeding fire engine, hanging on for your life, sirens screaming, cars pulling to the side of the road to get out of your way, and seeing a column of smoke in the distance knowing that was where you were going...what a rush. Someone was having a bad day and we were going there to make it better for them. It gave you goose bumps.

If we got on scene and had to lay a supply line down while approaching the fire (forward lay), the truck would stop next to the hydrant, one of us would grab the "huge" 2½" line and a hydrant wrench, jump off the tailboard, and wrap it around the hydrant, yelling at the driver to go. The engineer would drive down the street to the scene of the fire and firefighters would pull a fire hose off the truck and start fighting the fire with the water that is carried on the truck. When the engineer was ready for water, we would open the hydrant and then run up to the scene to fight the fire. The engineer would then have a continuous supply of water from the hydrant for the crews fighting the fire. Riding tailboard is not an allowed practice anymore, and for good reason. Too many firefighters would be injured or killed falling off the tailboard.

Fire Hose and Nozzles

In our department the typical initial attack line was the ¾" rubber hose off the hose reel. The typical attack line used for a decent fire was a 1½" fire hose and big fires called for a 2½" line. Today the 1½" line is almost unheard of. It was replaced with a 1¾" line, which can move much more water and is easily maneuvered. The 2½" fire hose went from supply lines to attack lines in today's fire service, and supply lines are now typically a 5" or 6" hose.

In the '70s we had a reverse hose lay setup (from the fire to the hydrant) that we pulled off the hose bed of the truck as a skid load and it dropped to the ground. It had two 1½" attack lines attached to a gated wye that was attached to a 2½" supply line, and that was attached to a discharge on the fire engine. The engine was then connected to the fire hydrant. It gave us two attack lines at once with an established water supply. We thought we were moving some water back then, but not compared to today's fire hose and water supplies.

It was still a lot of work since most of the nozzles were brass and very heavy. A 2½" combination (fog or straight-stream) nozzle weighed sixteen pounds by itself, not to mention the brass hose connections, heavy double-jacket cotton hose, and the water. Now we have lightweight connections, lightweight nozzles, and lightweight hoses. And if a department uses a compressed air foam system (CAFS), even the water is lightweight.

Don't get me wrong, that's a good thing. There's enough work to do as it is. Almost every department had a huge, knuckle-dragging good ol' boy named Bubba back in the day just to be able to lug around all the heavy hose. I think it was a requirement that each department had one back then.

Smoke Eater

Just when you thought that we had it rough because everything was heavier back then, do not forget that we also had to be smoke-eaters. Was it a requirement? Some back then would think so, but there were a couple of reasons for that where I worked. One is the fact that we thought we had to be a badass to be a firefighter. Well, I thought it was true back then, and I still believe that to be true today. You must be in shape to do this job well. That will not change.

It was typical for us not to wear breathing apparatus for most fires. We had to learn to suck it up and learn that coughing up a lung was part of the job. We learned to breathe what fresh air we could get from just behind the nozzle where entrained air would be pulled into the water stream or catch some oxygen from the water by putting our face into a fog pattern of water.

To prove nobody was a sissy at the fire, when we got back to the station, we would have a "hocker" contest. We all leaned over and with one finger on one side of your nostril would blow out these nasty black boogers from our nose and compare who had the nastiest one. The winner would get a free soda from the machine in the bay. I know, pretty gross, and pretty stupid as well.

The second reason for eating smoke was all about convenience and money. Okay, some things have not changed over the years. We had a couple of boxes with breathing apparatus in them in the compartments of each truck. We even had a couple of spare bottles of air as well. The problem was we did not have an air compressor to refill any bottles in our department. As a matter of fact, nobody else in the county did except for a city department that was about twenty minutes away. We were strongly encouraged not to use the air because someone would have to drive to the city department, wait for them to be filled, and drive back to put it in service. Not very convenient if only a few volunteers showed up, and the day-shift worker who is unable to leave the station.

The money part of that involves another type of breathing apparatus we had that made no sense to me, but we had it on each truck as well. It was called a Chemox re-breather. This was developed for use by the U.S. Navy for shipboard firefighting during WWII. It used a canister containing a chemical that scrubbed the carbon dioxide from your exhaled air, allowing you to re-breathe the oxygen that was left. Yes, that is correct,

you would breathe oxygen while in a fire environment. On top of that, the canister would heat up during the chemical process and become uncomfortable after a while. The issue with using this equipment was the canisters were one-time use. We had to buy new canisters when they were used and as with most volunteer departments, we did not have much of a budget to constantly buy these. A vintage training video showing how it works can be seen on YouTube here:
https://www.youtube.com/watch?v=dUn2d41f-0Y

"Is it Always Like This?"

Here it was, 1975, and Jose and I were officially volunteer firefighters. We had our gear, our dashboard red lights, and a Plectron alerting station. At the time, if you were not home to hear the alerting station go off, the only indication of an alert was that the speaker stayed on and when you got home, you would hear all of the radio traffic until you shut it off.

One day Jose and I got home and heard radio traffic on the Plectron and were listening to what sounded like a rather large fire. We called the station and asked what was going on and they said there was a huge fire at the South Town Marina, and they needed help. We told him we would be en route right away.

We were a little pumped as we drove all the way to the marina with the dashboard red light flashing. Fortunately, there was not a lot of traffic at the time. Upon arrival we saw fire engines and ladder trucks everywhere. Water was flowing from multiple trucks, handlines, and ladder trucks from every direction. This was a 100' x 300' metal building that kept 300 boats in dry storage, and the entire building was burning with half of the building already collapsed. We were told by some of the first on scene crews that 55-gallon drums of fuel were exploding and shooting into the air like rockets, gas tanks on boats were exploding, and flames were everywhere. There were multiple mutual-aid departments on scene to assist.

Most of the work left was knocking down fires that remained, which was mostly boats still burning under the collapsed metal structure. I can remember working a handline trying to reach some of the buried boats still burning, and at times I would see it explode with sparks and increase in intensity. Most of the boats had magnesium engines and when you hit it directly with water, it would have a violent reaction. We were there for hours trying to get it all knocked down. Yes, we were having a blast at our very first fire. We thought that this was going to be awesome fighting fires like this all the time. Almost 300 boats were destroyed along with the structure and the damage was in the millions of dollars. Still to this day, it is considered one of the largest fires in the county's history.

When it was all over, back at the station we were getting things back on the truck, washing hose, rolling it out to dry, and cleaning other equipment. We excitedly asked some of the volunteers who had been in the department for some time, "Is it always like this?" They kind of chuckled and said it was not the norm and was the largest fire they had seen yet. It was still cool that we were a part of it.

Our volunteer fire department had a good group of firefighters who worked well together. Being a fairly progressive department at the time, we even had female firefighters who were just as good as anyone else. The department had one station with two engines, a Chevrolet truck with a utility body, and a chief's car that was used for running errands, and other odds and ends.

The call volume fluctuated like all departments in our area. We had waves of being busy to nothing for extended periods of time. The first out engine was the older truck with a 500 gpm (gallons per minute) pump and no power steering or power brakes. Our second out engine was a Ford cabover with a 750 gpm pump with power steering and brakes. A utility truck was used for brush fires and vehicle extrication. It had a manual stick shift on the floor and was pretty quick.

Porta-Power to First Ever Hydraulic Jaws

Our pickup with the utility body had tools for fighting brush fires and equipment for vehicle extrication. We had a set of hydraulic tools called a Porta-Power that was used to pry open doors and move metal away from people trapped in vehicle accidents. We had a four-ton and a ten-ton set of jaws along with an array of other attachments. These tools were primarily used in the auto body field and were used for pushing and pulling metal when repairing cars. The Porta-Power or hand tools were the typical tools used for extrication. One firefighter would maneuver the jaws where they needed it while another firefighter would push a hand pump that was connected via a hose to create pressure to open the jaws.

The Jaws of Life was invented in the early '60s by George Hurst and was originally invented for use at NASCAR racing events for freeing drivers from cars that were crashed. The tool took on the name "Jaws of Life" after someone commented that the tool snatched victims from the "Jaws of Death". The tool was patented, then put to use in fire departments in the early '70s. It was expensive, and nobody in the county had a set when I started in 1975. The term "Jaws of Life" is used generically for all hydraulic rescue tools, even though it legally refers to the Hurst tool only.

Around 1976 our department was one of the first in the country to purchase a set of the Jaws of Life, made by Hurst. The Hurst tool was enormously powerful but also extremely heavy and difficult for one person to maneuver. It came with a set of cutters that could be swapped out for the tips used for spreading, which was a hassle to change out. The original set weighed sixty-five pounds compared to an average of forty-eight pounds today. Extricating victims from vehicle accidents was much easier and faster with this new lighter-weight tool. Today, battery-operated extrication tools are popular as they are much lighter, easier to maneuver, and just as powerful.

My Turn in the Hot Seat

As I mentioned earlier, once the part-time firefighters went off duty, it was up to the volunteers to work what we called "night duty". We would work from the time they got off duty until morning when they came back in. Typically, you would be at the station by yourself all night, but at times another volunteer would stay with you.

My first time working night duty was very nerve-wracking. I had to prove to everyone that I was responsible enough to pull it off. After the part-timer left, I set up my gear by the driver's side of the first out engine and started doing an equipment check to refresh my memory of where equipment was located and to assure all was in working condition.

After I was done checking everything out, I set up the desk to make it easy for me to answer the emergency phone and to write down the information on a pad of paper. I also wrote out a list of things I needed to do in the correct order, in case I got a fire call.

It was difficult falling asleep that night, but I finally did. I woke up to the ear-piercing Klaxon horn. I was a little confused coming out of a heavy sleep but got up and answered the phone. It was the county dispatcher telling me there was a residential structure fire on North Hampton Circle. I wrote the address down on the pad of paper, looked for the location on a wall map we had in the office, pushed the button to activate the Plectron alerting stations and repeated the info I got from county dispatch over the radio. "All units and monitors, we have a residential structure fire at 3250 North Hampton Circle." I then flipped the switch to activate the house siren for fifteen seconds, then ran out to the bay and manually opened the heavy all-glass bay door in front of the engine. I then pulled on my boots and put on my fire jacket, threw my helmet on the front seat, and pulled the truck out of the station, parked it, went back to pull the bay door down, got back in the truck and started driving to the fire. And of course, I had to drive uphill both ways in the snow. You know, we had it tough back then.

Making a hard-right turn in a large truck with no power steering and huge wheels while moving very slowly proved difficult. It took all I had to turn the steering wheel and make the turn. Changing gears with this tall stick shift on the floor while pushing in the clutch was no problem until you go into third gear, which apparently is normal to grind a few pounds of teeth before sliding into gear.

As I flew down the road, I was looking for North Hampton Circle on the right. I knew it was not that far from the station, but I could not find it. When I knew I went too far I did a three-point turn onto another street and backed into the main road to go back. That was a chore in itself with the truck barely moving along and panic setting in. As I started back down the same road going the other way and looking now to my left for the road, I heard the fire chief on the radio asking where I was. I picked up the microphone in between shifting and told him where I was at the time, and he told me I had to take Argon Street off the main road to get to North Hampton Circle. I eventually located it and found the address with the fire chief already on scene. He had taken a hand extinguisher in with him and put out a small kitchen fire before I got there.

That was a little embarrassing, to say the least. In my excitement, I found the address on the wall map but did not notice that I had to take another street to get there. I was just focused on North Hampton Circle. The chief was not pleased, but he knew it was my first night shift and was watching out for me to begin with. And no, I was not able to go back to sleep when I got back to the station.

Medical Response (From the Fire Department?)

Medical training at our department was at a minimum at the time I started, and I felt we needed to be able to assist our residents better when they had a medical emergency. Other than responding to vehicle accidents and assisting the county Emergency Medical Service (EMS) with extracting and moving patients, medical calls were not responded to.

In February of 1976, I attended a Red Cross first-aid class, followed by a CPR certification and advanced first aid a few months later. I convinced the chief to allow the department to purchase some basic medical equipment and place it in the chief's car that was typically parked at the station. I got permission to respond to some medical calls with the chief's car when I was at the station, as long as someone else was there to respond to fire calls. Having someone at the station to respond to fire calls was the priority and it made no sense to leave the station empty to run medical calls.

In July of 1976 I took a class and passed the state certified Emergency Medical Technician (EMT) program. I became the first EMT in our department's history. It only made sense to now have more medical equipment available when responding to medical calls, so the chief agreed to purchasing more medical equipment for the Brush/Rescue Truck. The idea to use this truck to respond to medical calls and vehicle accidents became somewhat successful, so we used it for brush fires as well as a rescue truck. Of course, we thought it was cool since the television show *Emergency!* was popular then and our utility truck looked remarkably similar to Rescue 51.

<u>Ate Up with It</u>

One of the first volunteers I became friends with was Don Amps. Don was twenty-two years old, about 6'4" tall and thin, but muscular, along with huge mutton chop sideburns. He had been a volunteer for a few years. Don took me under his wing and helped me get acquainted with the equipment on the trucks, the routine when responding to calls, and led some of the training events with the other volunteers. He was very likeable and serious when it came to being a firefighter. You had to love his passion for the job. He lived alone in a nice house in an upscale neighborhood just around the corner from the fire station. His mother was rather wealthy and took care of him, but you would never know it by his work ethic. He worked hard with everything he was involved in. He was also an incredibly good mechanic who modified his really badass 1970 GTO with a beefed-up engine with a chrome blower sticking out of the hood and colored stainless steel connections under the hood. When he started his car, all you heard was BRUP, BRUP, BRUP, BRUP. It was as powerful as it sounded. Needless to say, he got to the station pretty quickly when the fire alarms went off.

Don was the captain on our firematics competition team and was extremely competitive. This is probably why we did so well and had trophies all over the station from various competitions around the state. Not only was it a source of pride and allowed bragging rights, but it also made us good at fireground skills.

Don and I became good friends and he allowed me to stay in his spare bedroom while I was looking for a place of my own. About a year and a half later he made the decision to move to Alabama. I helped him pack and load up a large moving truck, then drove to Alabama with him. It was just the two of us making the move and of course, he moved into an apartment on the third floor of a condo with no elevator. Believe it or not, we had a baby grand piano on the truck. I swear it took us all afternoon to get it upstairs. "One, two, THREE!" was called out one step at a time. All I remember was there were too many steps.

In short order, Don became a volunteer firefighter in the town we moved him to and became involved with the department. Every year on July fourth, the department sponsored a huge celebration fundraiser that included fireworks, games, music, and plenty of food. To start the festivities, the fire department had a tradition of setting off an antique cannon. When everyone heard the loud percussion of the cannon, they knew it was time to have fun. Don was part of the cannon team and after lighting the fuse, it did not go off. They weren't too sure what the problem was, but the cannon suddenly exploded, sending shrapnel everywhere. Don was killed instantly. Even though Don had moved away some time before, it tore the department up emotionally. He was too young and talented to lose his life so early.

Attic Rat

After a few months, I found myself hanging around the fire station quite a bit and was always at the top of the list of volunteer responses each month. I pulled night duty often and was getting some runs under my belt. The number of volunteers would fluctuate over time, and there was a period when they had a difficult time getting all the night duty shifts covered. I ended up there many nights in a row to assist and get some experience. It helped that I was single at the time.

While some of the fire commissioners were brainstorming how to increase the number of volunteers in the department and how to get night duty coverage, I made a suggestion that blew everyone away. I offered to move into the fire station and be there almost every night for coverage and if someone did pull night shift, I would be a second man on the first out engine.

It ended up being a win-win for everyone and they agreed to give it a try. The upstairs portion of the station was just storage. I rearranged the

23

storage area and remodeled the rest of the space into a bedroom area. My full-time job was as a carpenter, making the transition easy to accomplish. For almost a year, I lived upstairs, and they always had someone available if they had trouble finding night duty coverage, or I became a second man on the engine, or depending on the call, I would be able to respond with two engines at once. It was a pretty awesome deal since I got to respond to many, many more calls than was possible before. It was a great experience.

Another Marina Fire?

My very first fire as a firefighter was that huge marina fire that burned up around 300 boats. Three years later while at home, my alerting system went off stating there was a fire at the Harbor Marina. I was only a few blocks away and after jumping in my car and leaving my driveway I could see a large plume of dark black smoke just down the road. I was first on scene and the first engine was on scene right after me. This marina was about half the size of the other one I responded to, but still it was a large metal building with around 150 boats inside. The large sliding doors that went from the ground to just under the trusses was wide open with thick, dark black smoke billowing out.

Knowing this would be almost impossible to stop and would take an enormous amount of water, I motioned for the first engine to nose in at the curb facing a canal where the front-end loader typically lowers boats into the water. I told the firefighter on the engine that I would drop the hard-suction hose into the canal to draft for an unlimited amount of water while he pulled the 3" hose and set up a ground monitor to flow a large amount of water into the front of the building. This was a difficult task for one person, but I pulled both hard-suction hose lines down to the ground, one with a strainer already attached, connected them, connected the whole setup to the intake of the pump on the side of the engine, then swung it around and dropped it into the canal. The reason this is tough is the hard-suction hose is mounted high above the hose bed on two racks, and they are very heavy with large brass connections. Today's hard-suction hose is lightweight, with lightweight connections, and can easily be handled by one person.

I put the pump in gear, pulled the handle to activate the air pump that evacuates the air from the hose allowing water to flow into the water pump. As the motor was screaming, it never changed tones like it normally does once it gets a draft. It just kept screaming at a loud high-pitched tone. After trying several times, it never worked. The next in engine parked next to this one and we set it up for draft as well and it worked fine. The frustrating part was having the hose on the ground with the ground monitor on the end with a firefighter yelling for water and none coming. All this while smoke is pouring out the huge front doors of the building.

Pumping water from the water tank would have been a waste of time since it only carried 500 gallons of water, which would only have lasted one minute and therefore would have had no effect on the fire. This fire was going to need multiple engines from multiple departments drafting and flowing the big guns all at the same time.

There was no stopping this fire as it was similar to the first marina fire with multiple boats including magnesium engines and fiberglass bodies. There were at least four mutual-aid departments assisting and all were drafting from different areas of the canal and waterways. It was a total loss, to say the least.

After we got back to the station, we tried several times to figure out why we could not get a draft from the first engine. It worked fine each time we tried. A few days later we decided to duplicate it exactly, so we took it to the marina, nosed it in, and dropped the suction hose into the canal. It would not draft again. We discovered that there was a hairline crack in the intake section of the pump, so that when we bent the hose forward into the canal, it opened the crack just enough to prevent it from creating negative pressure in the line. In earlier tests we just dropped the drafting hose down to the side without making a sharp bend, which put no stress on the intake. It was a fluke that nobody would have known about unless we put stress on it. We had it repaired later that month.

Gasoline Tanker Overturned

A few months after that we responded to a gasoline tanker that overturned at a busy intersection. This semi-truck was carrying about 9,000 gallons of gasoline at the time. Upon arrival we saw the entire truck lying on its side with a huge gash in the tank and gasoline pouring out onto the ground. The entire intersection was already flooded with gasoline and it started to flow down the road toward a sewer grate about 100 feet away.

There was a condominium and golf course under construction at the time at that very intersection, and I noticed a huge front-end loader moving dirt. The first thing I did was run over to the operator and tell him I needed him to dump multiple loads of dirt just in front of the sewer grate along the side of the road so it would absorb the gasoline and keep it from going down the drain.

As the dirt was being dumped, we set up a hose line with high-expansion foam; I took the foam eductor at the end of the hose line up to the truck and started to lay down a blanket of foam, working my way back to the edge of the gasoline. The gasoline that was pouring out of the tank had slowed down to an easy flow by then, but the entire intersection had gasoline spread out at least four inches deep. I had my fire gear on with rubber fire boots but no air-pack. Keep in mind, it was a habit not to wear breathing apparatus due to the hassles of getting them filled, as I mentioned earlier. Since gasoline has a low vapor pressure, it was off-gassing with the fumes rising. This is the reason for using foam—to suppress the vapors that could easily ignite with just a small spark.

While I was standing in four-inch-deep gasoline hoping it would not catch fire, a young kid around high school age who worked at a gas station on one of the corners of this intersection was trying to start a lawn mower so he could mow the grass. I assume he flunked out of science class. When I heard him trying to start the mower, I screamed at him to stop it. A deputy on scene ran over to him and threatened him, telling him he could blow us all up. Needless to say, he ran away.

After about twenty minutes of laying down foam, I started to get light-headed and nauseous. I got a bad headache and asked my friend Jose to take over for me. I walked over to the engine and sat down on the tailboard, gagging and coughing when a medic from the county EMS came over to check me out. They ended up transporting me to the emergency room to be treated for gasoline fume inhalation. They put me on high-flow oxygen for an hour and then released me after my blood work came back normal. Yes, it was a dumb-ass move not wearing the air-pack. We started to value the use of the air-pack more over time.

Surrounded by Fire

I responded to a structure fire in a relatively poor neighborhood called Haram High. The homes were all small, older homes built with wood walls, ceilings, and floors that were supported about two feet off the ground by concrete blocks. Typically, the wood was what we called "lighter pine", which is older pine wood that had a high concentration of pine sap, which was very flammable. So when one of these homes caught fire, it was hot and spread rapidly.

Upon arrival I saw thick, heavy, dark smoke billowing out a bedroom window. The rest of the house had filled with smoke and had a defined smoke ceiling at about five feet off the floor. I entered the structure through the front door with a hose line and moved toward the back bedroom where the majority of the fire was located. I opened the nozzle and aimed for the ceiling to knock the fire down a bit. After I put out most of the fire, I entered the bedroom to hit any hot spots that were left. As I was standing in the middle of the room, I suddenly heard a loud cracking noise and found myself falling through the floor. The rush of feeling myself falling through the floor was stressful enough, but when I abruptly stopped falling where the floor was even with my upper legs, flames came up through the opening around me. I became aware very quickly that the floor under the house was also on fire and I had just made a nice opening for it to escape. As I yelled out a few choice words, I calmed down and aimed the nozzle downward, putting out flames that were shooting up all around my legs. I then laid the nozzle down and climbed out of the hole so I could finish putting out the fire.

Smoke Diver

In 1980, while a volunteer firefighter at another department, I had this sick and demented desire to become a "Smoke Diver". You were considered to be a certified badass if you made it through this week-long course that pushed you to your physical and mental limits. To this day I consider it the most difficult task I have ever challenged myself to get through.

Three other full-time firefighters from two departments wanted to participate as well, and the four of us made the road trip to hell. The course was held at the state fire training academy, and it had a reputation for thinning the herd in short order. Of course, we thought we were in great shape already and were aggressive firefighters to boot, so what could go wrong?

Day one we met in a classroom of approximately forty firefighters. The lead instructor introduced himself and walked up and down the center aisle barking like a drill instructor in the marines. He told us in a loud voice that we would lose a few after day one, and another bunch on day two, and a whole lot after day three. He called them "quitters" who were not tough enough to complete the program—they even had firefighters drop out on day four or five. He warned the group that we would not have time for late nights, drinking, partying, horsing around, or anything like that. He suggested we eat smart each evening so we wouldn't vomit up our dinner the next day, and that we needed to get as much sleep as possible each night if we wanted to make it to the end. He also reminded us that there would be some dumb asses who would not listen to him and would regret it.

Well, if you were a tough guy like we were, he wouldn't have been talking about us. Right? Day one consisted of mostly classroom work until lunchtime and the rest of the day was all conditioning exercises. We had to perform a ridiculous number of push-ups and pull-ups, duckwalk around a quarter-mile track, chop a log with a sledgehammer, then start all over again. All of this was done in our fire gear while wearing an air-pack and mask. Duckwalking in shorts and tee-shirt is tough enough, but in heavy fire gear and air-pack and mask, it was insane. Especially trying to breath out of a small hole at the bottom of your mask. Mind you, we were not connected to the bottle for nice, cool, clean air. That just wouldn't be fair. It kicked our butts, and we were sore and tired at the end of the day. We had to hang our fire gear and gloves outside to dry out since they were all soaked with sweat. Pretty intense stuff to start the week off, but hey, we were tough guys.

That evening we found a restaurant and ate reasonably, then drove around town to see what other restaurants or entertainment was out there. We went to a grocery store and bought a bunch of Gatorade and snacks for the week as well. We had the entire week planned. This was going to be some fun stuff.

Day two started out interesting in that we had already lost four guys from the class just like the instructor said. No more classroom time after day one. We were told we would be living in our fire gear and air-packs for the rest of the class. Each morning after that we had to go to class wearing all of it, including morning directions sitting at our desk each day. We spent the entire day going through drills of some sort, including search evolutions in the open field and in the fire tower on several floors. Our masks were covered with tape or opaque paper, limiting our vision. We had to do searches based on people calling out for help, feeling our way around obstacles, and finding items such as a quarter or a small trinket in the dark tower filled with smoke. While some were searching, the rest were beating on a huge log with a sledgehammer to simulate using an axe or climbing a ground ladder up to the fourth floor, crawling in the window, then finding a spare air-pack bottle in the thick smoke and swapping out bottles from the air-pack we were wearing. You had to be able to hold your breath for a good period of time or suck some smoke while you shut off your air tank, disconnect it from your air-pack, swap out into the spare, and turn it back on. It was a fun challenge, but we all sucked smoke at one time or another.

We all agreed it was a tough day, but we knew this would be a great time and great learning experience by the time we finished the week. After getting back to the motel, we hung out our sweat-saturated gear to dry, took showers, and headed out to eat. We worked up an appetite and ate well that night. Heck, we even found a huge nightclub that had three different bands playing in different sections of the club. We had rock, country, and disco all in the same place. We were obviously not having any difficulty getting through the class, so we decided to enjoy the music and hang out a bit. We got back to the motel later that night and tried to get a few hours of sleep before class started again.

Okay, day three was "challenging". After a few good hours of sleep and a heavy meal, we were pumped to get going. Or so we thought. Yep, right on cue, we had lost a good number of guys again. We had all agreed that if one of us got discouraged, the others would get on our case and encourage us to continue. The day started out like normal with a bunch of calisthenics in our gear, which was heavier than normal because they were saturated with two days of sweat and did not dry out. And they stunk to high heaven as well. And I forgot to mention, it was hot outside.

That day one of our rotations was to feed the beast. The fire tower was set up to burn wood pallets just under the first floor, allowing the heat and smoke to rise up throughout the entire tower. The mountain of pallets outside of the tower was a little concerning. Just standing outside in full gear and air-packs in the hot temperatures carrying pallets to the tower to be burned was exhausting alone.

The other rotation was to climb a ground ladder to the fourth floor, climb in the window, find the end of a fire hose lying on the ground and while on your hands and knees, follow it out to the entry door on the first floor. Sounded simple enough to me. However, the hose was thrown all over the place, all knotted up, went into various rooms, around corners and obstacles, then down one floor at a time doing the same thing. If you lost contact with the hose, you could end up going backwards and find yourself at the beginning. All of this was while you were breathing air from your air tank, of course. The kicker was making it out the door before you ran out of air. If you ran out of air, it was your problem. We had learned various techniques for emergency breathing if you ran out of air and one of them was to have a short section of garden hose in your pocket to use. If you run out of air, you place one end in your mouth and the other inside your fire jacket, typically under your armpit, to filter out as much smoke as possible. Yeah, it is as disgusting as it sounds, but better than pure smoke. And we all had to use the hose to breathe in order to get out.

The smoke was so thick you couldn't see your hand in front of your face. It was so hot that any uncovered parts of your body would immediately get burned. When we got to the first floor, just above the pallets, the water on the ground was boiling. You had to keep your knees and hands on the fire hose to keep from getting scalded. Not an easy task in zero visibility smoke and heat.

As we were going to round two and about to climb the ladder again, I told my partner that I had to tap out. I told him I physically could not do it anymore. It was embarrassing, but I felt like I would end up in the emergency room if I continued. Keeping to his word, my partner got in my face and pumped me up and told me I was not a quitter and to keep

31

going. He shamed me into continuing and not leaving my partner by himself. It worked, and I finished the day. I wasn't the badass I thought I was. It was humbling. Nobody blamed me for thinking about quitting; in fact, they all said they thought about it themselves. It was the toughest day yet.

We did our routine of hanging out our gear knowing it wouldn't do much good, but hopefully it would get rid of some of the stench. We all took showers before going out to eat, and every one of us noticed our knees were nothing but blisters from the heat and the friction of crawling so much. Knowing we were going to be crawling, we brought knee pads anticipating this, but they didn't prevent any of it. However, I cannot imagine what the damage would have been without them. We ate lightly that night and drank a lot of Gatorade, then went to sleep early.

Day four started like every other day. We were missing quite a few guys that morning. I was almost one of them. Nobody in class was talking trash or laughing and joking around anymore. Everyone looked beat. The instructor told us they were just getting started and to buckle up for a tough day. The day was similar with drills, smoke, heat, sledgehammer, searching, dragging hose lines, etc. It was very tough again, especially being so worn down. This time another one of our guys wanted to tap out. He said they were all a bunch of wanna-be drill sergeants abusing us with a smile. None of us had anything good to say about any of the instructors at that point. Of course, we all talked him out of quitting and explained that there were only two days left and that wasn't the time to quit. He hung in there and we all finished the course.

We were glad the course was complete, we now considered ourselves badasses again, and to be honest, we all learned quite a bit. At that point there was no situation in my mind that I could find myself in while working a fire that I could not handle including running out of air, getting lost, getting trapped, getting worn out with more fire to fight, etc. We were all more confident in our skills after that and we all felt it was worth the suffering.

Chapter 3

THE RIGHT FIT FOR THE JOB

Even though many aspects of the job of a medic or firefighter has changed over the years, the one thing that has not changed, or should not change, is the importance of being a good fit for the job. The most important aspect of being a good firefighter or paramedic is the ability to work as a team member. Both jobs require teamwork and the ability to rely on and trust everyone else on your team. During my tenure I have seen some of the most intelligent and highly educated medics and firefighters who were not necessarily a great fit for the job. I do feel that a great majority of firefighters and paramedics I have worked with are the right fit for the job. There are always a few outliers in any profession, including this one.

Compassion

I feel at the very least one needs to be compassionate to be a good fit for the job. Merriam-Webster defines compassion as "sympathetic consciousness of others' distress together with a desire to alleviate it". The key to that definition is the desire to alleviate others' distress. If you lack that desire, you are in the wrong business. I have seen firefighters and medics who were robotic in their motions, actions, and responses to those going through a stressful event. Mind you, the job got done, it was just missing the vital component of human compassion. The ability to be compassionate is beneficial to the person you are there to help as well as making your job more enjoyable and successful. During a time of distress people will respond much more cooperatively with the right approach, and being compassionate is a major component.

Professional

There have been some who strongly believe all that matters is how well you perform your job. They think the patient or victim does not care about how you look or act, as long as you do your job. I strongly believe professionalism is a rather important trait one should have to work in this field. The Merriam-Webster definition of professional is "exhibiting a courteous, conscientious, and generally businesslike manner in the workplace". Part of the definition is being generally businesslike, however, it also defines it as being courteous and conscientious.

A personal peeve of mine is showing up to assist someone in need with your work shoes or boots unlaced and opened. That is just lazy and unprofessional, in my opinion. Learn to tie your shoes quickly, use Velcro or pull-up boots, or just keep your shoes on. This is no different than wearing a greasy or dirty shirt, being unshaven or unkempt, or

34

having hair that looks like you were just in a fight. I agree that the bottom line is the quality of care given, but part of that quality is your appearance, professional or unprofessional.

Dedicated

Being dedicated to one's job does not necessarily mean working all the time, such as taking as much overtime as you can get. It does not mean kissing your supervisor's ass at every opportunity either. If you are truly dedicated to your job, you constantly strive to improve your skills at every opportunity available. This includes doing what you can on your own to become a better firefighter or paramedic. Take continuing education classes, both didactic and hands-on. Do not limit yourself to just those classes that your employer will pay you to attend. You will have to spend some of your off-duty time and your own money to take advantage of all the opportunities out there to help you be better at your job.

You should be committed to the profession and devoted to your current position at the time. It should be obvious to everyone that you feel this way. You show it by your actions on the job. This would include responding to an emergency, at the station, and when you are off duty. Represent yourself in a good way while in public, around your coworkers, as well as around your family and friends. You need to set the example.

Aggressive

When hearing the word aggressive, most people think of it in a negative tone. That is not what I am suggesting. I believe the best firefighters and paramedics are aggressive in performing their duties on the job. What I am referring to are those who are not afraid of getting out in front of a situation and competently handling it.

A firefighter who is aggressive will grab a hose line off the truck and deploy it all by themselves and not wait for someone to assist like you would do in a training scenario that would typically be done by two firefighters. Grabbing a ground extension ladder off the truck by yourself, carrying it to the scene, and deploying it by yourself because time is of the essence is being aggressive. Waiting for a partner to assist with removing the ladder from the truck, helping you carry it to the scene, and going step-by-step in a two-person raise, just like in the academy, is someone who just goes through the motions. An aggressive firefighter knows what needs to be done and does it. It is that simple.

An aggressive paramedic is one who is not afraid of getting dirty or initiating life-saving procedures when it is necessary. An example would be showing up to a vehicle accident in a ditch and climbing down the dirt embankment to get to the patient, do a quick assessment, provide life-saving procedures as needed while still in the vehicle, and assist in removing them from the vehicle and getting them up the embankment.

The contrast would be standing up on the road waiting for some firefighters to remove them from the vehicle, carry them up the embankment, place them on your stretcher, and load them into the ambulance, and then do an assessment and provide care in the back of the ambulance without breaking a sweat or getting dirty. Not acceptable in my book, but all too common.

Competitive

Firefighters, medics, and cops are typically competitive by nature. It is a similar adrenaline rush you get when you compete in sports. When the task is over, you may be worn out, but it is satisfying. The job itself is competitive in a way. A firefighter is competing against the fire itself, which is typically a time-sensitive event. A paramedic is competing against whatever medical issue your patient is experiencing at the time, and choosing your treatment in a timely manner makes a huge difference.

During my volunteer firefighter days, we had a competition team that competed throughout the state against other firefighters performing timed events such as hose lays, raising and climbing ladders, catching a hydrant, flowing water, etc. We had a great team and had a room full of trophies to show for it. Not only was it a lot of fun, but it also made us good at routine tasks when on a real fire.

Paramedic

A paramedic that can memorize procedures or protocols and perform them flawlessly but has no connection to the patient or their coworkers is missing a large piece of providing optimum care and being a productive part of the team. Most people in need of emergency medical care not only need someone who can provide competent and highly functional medical care, but they also need the personal compassion and caring at a time when they are going through one of the worst days of their lives. Being compassionate and caring will assist in providing medical interventions by giving the patient assurance they are being taken care of; this will at times have just as much of a positive impact on the patient by itself.

Looking at this from another perspective would be the very personable and caring first-responder who is particularly good at empathizing with a patient but is lacking in confidence or skills to quickly evaluate a patient with a medical issue and flawlessly provide important interventions. Holding a patient's hand and providing comfort and emotional support alone is not enough. A typical bystander can do this. A medic should not become emotionally attached to the emergency at hand, but should be able to provide competent, quality care and at the same time be compassionate and caring, even if it means holding their hand and reassuring them you are doing everything in your power to make the situation better for them.

By no means am I suggesting that a medic will not become emotional about certain situations. I am suggesting that this is fine if it occurs after you have completed your assignment. Becoming emotional while on scene or prior to completing your response is counterproductive and it takes a special mindset to separate the two. This also does not mean that this has never happened to me or that you are a bad responder if this occurs. I will respectfully say that when it does occur, your level of care or reactions to the emergency at hand will suffer. Later on as I recall various responses, you will see that I fell into that trap myself, and I can assure you I was not at my best.

The ability to get along with your coworkers and partners will make a huge difference in the level of care given and surviving years on the job. The best partner I ever had while I was a career paramedic was Don Jartel. We knew what each other was thinking at any given moment on a medical call and rarely spoke during the call. We typically ran a cardiac arrest without saying more than a few words to each other. We trusted each other, knew our skill levels, and knew what needed to be done and when. Everything we did was very fluid and in sync with each other. If you can find someone on that same level to work with, it will not only be good for your patients, but you will enjoy the entire shift and know you provided the best service to everyone you encountered that day.

Firefighter

You must be a good fit to be a firefighter as well. Dealing with structure fires, vehicle extrication, water rescues, hazardous materials, or any other emergency that a firefighter may respond to requires not only a good working knowledge of each aspect of the job, it also requires the ability to use common sense and to improvise and be flexible in your decision-making. Because most responses made by firefighters are dynamic in nature, situations can change rapidly, and the ability to think on your feet and make decisions that could be life-altering for other firefighters as well as victims that are involved is crucial.

Understanding fire behavior in different environments is one of those critical skills you must have. Recognizing when your actions are making things better, not having any impact, or making things worse is a learned skill that experience plays a large role in. As with emergency medicine, just having a formal education alone, or being someone who studies and takes exams well is not enough. Critical thinking and common sense will go a long way in this job. I have seen firefighters with a master's degree who promoted quickly through the ranks, requiring them to make critical decisions on the fireground, but they have no common sense or lack the respect needed from the ranks to be productive and safe.

On the other hand, there are experienced firefighters with lots of common sense and a track record of knowing how to perform their jobs well but lack a formal higher degree of education. I can tell you, that is who I want to be by my side and making decisions. It is not out of the ordinary to see a firefighter spend his/her entire career at the rank of firefighter and love doing that level of work. That is a noble position to take, and they are typically the tip of the spear as it relates to knowing and understanding the job.

It is more commonplace today to require college degrees to be company officers or above. This is a good thing if one would like to pursue higher-ranking positions in the department. But one must ask themselves if they would trust the decision-making on the scene of an emergency to someone who is experienced or to someone who has a college degree in their back pocket.

It is just as important for firefighters to have that compassion and empathy toward victims we encounter as it is on medical responses. Being able to communicate and comfort someone pinned in a vehicle due to an accident, while evacuating someone from their homes during a wildland fire or flood, assuring a victim of a fire in their home that you are doing everything in your power to save as much as you can, or to rescue a lost child or pet goes a long way. Not all responders are able to communicate or to assure them, but when you do it is more important than you would think. A robotic impersonal demeanor does not typically go over well with those who are suffering from a disaster of some sort.

Another aspect of being a right fit for the job of firefighter involves being able to be either a quick learner or having some experience dealing with tools. A large part of the job of firefighter is being able to work with hand tools, power tools, ladders, and various other equipment needed to complete a task. Fire trucks are large primarily due to the need to carry numerous tools and specialty equipment. Knowing how to use every tool available and knowing how to improvise as needed is critical.

Historically most firefighters had a background of working with tools. Mechanics, carpenters, and construction workers were a good fit because a lot of the equipment on a fire truck are the same or similar tools they use every day. I have seen several generations come and go in the fire service, and there are good and bad aspects to each generation. The latter part of my career I saw a larger number of new hires who have never held a screwdriver in their hands, never mind a power tool. Even if one did not work in the trades, most in my generation grew up learning how to work on cars, build things, work around the house, etc. To expect a majority of new firefighters to have experience using chainsaws, ladders, hand tools, sledgehammers, axes, etc. is not reasonable anymore.

The biggest disadvantage to this lack of experience is that it takes much longer than in the past to be competent in using these tools. The biggest advantage that the latest generation has is the drive to ask why things are done a certain way and the willingness to learn. This goes back to the ability to think creatively and improvise. They are constantly trying to figure out better ways to accomplish different tasks.

Having good communication skills and the ability to get along with just about anyone is an important aspect of the job. You literally must trust your partners and coworkers with your life and vice versa. You must be willing to risk your own life to save one of your coworkers. Getting along with them, being able to communicate well, and trusting each other is vital.

All Public Safety Personnel

To be a good fit for the job you must also work with everyone else in the public safety arena. This typically includes firefighters (FF), paramedics (PM), law enforcement (LE), dispatchers, and emergency management (EM). Having the ability to respect everyone else you work with in the public safety circle, and working well with them, makes life easy.

Dispatchers are involved in every emergency call, no matter the need. That being understood, I will not include them in these groupings that work together on scene. Fire scenes typically involve the main three (FF, PM, LE), crime scenes will involve all three, vehicle accidents will involve all three, medical calls will involve firefighters and paramedics, and larger incidents may involve everyone from multiple agencies. During my career I had the honor of training and responding to incidents with members of the local police, county sheriff's office, highway patrol, emergency management, SWAT teams, bomb squads, Urban Search & Rescue (USAR), hazardous materials teams, FBI, and National Guard.

Chapter 4

THE BROTHER/SISTERHOOD

Everyone who works in the public safety arena is considered family. This would include firefighters, paramedics, law enforcement, dispatchers, emergency room personnel, and emergency management. It was not uncommon that on our days off we hung out together, even if we'd just gotten off a twenty-four-hour shift working with them. This would include activities such as boating, camping, dinners, fishing, etc. We attended each other's kids' birthday parties over the years. We were in each other's weddings. We helped each other out whenever someone needed help with anything around the house. Unfortunately, we also attended many coworkers' funerals.

Tag-along

The fire service especially has always been a brother/sisterhood no matter where you were from. If you were to walk into a firehouse while on vacation in a different county or state you were welcomed inside, compared trucks and equipment, told war stories, and sometimes were invited to join them for lunch or dinner. I saw that wane a bit over the years, but my personal experience proved each department had its own personality and some are more welcoming than others.

I had the opportunity to do a ride-along with the Fire Department of New York (FDNY) Rescue 1 in Manhattan one year. I honestly expected to be looked down upon coming from a relatively small department compared to theirs. I anticipated some grumbling about being a tag-along or complaints of how many firefighters from around the world want to ride with them and pick their brains. I cannot emphasize enough how wrong I was. The crew I was with and all of my interactions with everyone in that department were overwhelmingly positive. I can say they treated me better than I have seen smaller departments in my area treat visiting firefighters.

My opportunity occurred when someone I knew who worked in New York City in emergency management had connections with FDNY, and I mentioned that we were taking a family vacation that took us through Manhattan. I asked about the chances of getting to ride with Rescue 1 while we were there, and he set it up for me. Now understand, this was a "family" vacation. Yes, I took one day out of my "family" vacation to ride with one of the most elite group of firefighters in the world. I will discuss how important family is and how having a spouse who supports you during your career is vital in a later chapter. Yes, I left my wife and two sons alone in Manhattan so I could go play. And yes, we are still married.

I took a cab from the motel to the firehouse that Rescue 1 worked out of, and of course they were not in their station. They're known for being busy. I was disappointed, but at least I got my first cab ride in New York City. That was exciting in itself. I decided to hang around the area to see if they came back so I could jump on the rig. It wasn't so bad since the weather was nice and warm. About fifteen minutes into my depression, I heard sirens everywhere. And all were loud Federal Q mechanical sirens and air horns. It all accumulated about three blocks from my location, so I walked over there expecting to see a huge fire downtown and anticipated getting hooked up with Rescue 1. There were no fewer than ten engines and ladder trucks along with a battalion chief on scene. It was a minor trash can fire in a high-rise. The only information dispatch got from the caller was that there was a fire and the location was in a high-rise. I got this information from the battalion chief on scene when I asked about Rescue 1's location. He said they were out on a boat dock fire and were too far away to respond. I thanked him then walked back to the station. I paced up and down the street in boredom waiting to see them return.

I watched as a blue pickup truck pulled in front of the station and a gentleman in jeans and T-shirt got out, punched in a code to the door and went inside the station. I walked closer and as he walked out to get in his truck, he asked if I needed any help. I explained I was there to do some ride time, and he said okay and started to leave as if he was in a hurry. He stopped before he got to his truck, turned around and punched the code in again, telling me to stand by. He said he just got off shift there and left something in his locker, and that was why he was there.

He got on the phone to dispatch and asked where Rescue 1 was. He looked over at me and said, "They are wrapping up from a dock fire and are going to do some dive-rescue training while they are there and won't be back for a bit." I thanked him for making the effort and started to walk away when he told me to "load up, I'll take you there." I politely declined, but he insisted I let him take me to the crew.

I jumped in the truck and while driving relatively fast down the road (none of which were familiar to me), he called his wife and said he was going to be a few minutes late as he had to take a friend of his over to Rescue 1 at the docks. He then introduced himself and asked where I was from, and we carried on a conversation like we knew each other. When we got to the dock, he walked me over to the crew and introduced me to the lieutenant and another firefighter on the dock along with other crew members who were in dive suits about to go underwater. They were testing out new communication equipment with their new dry suits. The lieutenant introduced me to them over the radio, and they waved back before going underwater.

I did not interfere with their training, as diving in a dry suit must be taken seriously and communication is critical. When they finished, I assisted in picking up their equipment and placing it back on the truck. We then jumped in the heavy rescue and started back to the station while they all introduced themselves again and we all started talking. When we got back to the station the first task was a review and critique of the dive training they'd just completed using a whiteboard and a copy of their dive protocols. Rescue 1 has special equipment on the truck just for dive and water rescue, and the crew member who oversaw the dive team did the training.

After the review we all went into the kitchen area of the station in the back and sat down at a table. A firefighter asked me what flavor ice cream I liked, and I told him chocolate. He pulled a couple of large containers of ice cream out of the freezer and started filling bowls. We all had a bowl of ice cream and were talking shop when they mentioned that one of their retired guys had bought an ice cream store with his wife, and he kept the freezer stocked with ice cream for them. As we talked further, they asked where I was from. When I told them, they all started laughing and one said, "You're kidding. Three of us own lots there and we all plan on building houses and moving there when we retire. It was amazing to me that they even heard of where I lived, never mind some of the local eateries and attractions. They were all excited about the day they could move to the area after they retired and just go fishing and hang out with each other. We all talked about how good the fishing was there and what their plans were for retirement. The rest of the shift was slow with nothing out of the ordinary. In the morning as I was leaving, they thanked me for being there and bringing them one of the slowest shifts of the year. That is typical when there is someone riding and looking for the big one.

This was all in August of 2000. On September 11, 2001, this same crew was the first rescue on scene of the terrorist attack on the Twin Towers. Everyone on the truck I rode with that day died during the building collapse.

Unfortunately, during a career in the fire or EMS arena you may have certain memories you will never forget for the rest of your life thats may even trigger an emotional response. This was one of them. Call it being human, call it PTSD, or call it being wimpy. Whatever.

The Family Album

If you look at the family album or digital pictures on the computer of most public safety personnel, you will see pictures of birthday parties, camping trips, fishing trips, etc. Most of them will have firefighters, paramedics, and cops who work together in the picture somewhere. There are pictures of my wife's baby shower with coworkers' families, emergency room physicians, nurses, and cops. Later albums will include some of the same people at their birthday parties, graduations, etc. If you looked at our wedding pictures, you would see all my groomsmen were firefighters, paramedics, and cops.

When we were building a new house, I asked a couple of my coworkers if they had the time to help one day as I had to install the lawn sprinkler system before the sod was to be laid. I told them I would supply the pizza and drinks. Understand, I asked two guys. That weekend ten guys showed up with shovels and work gloves and they all worked until the pipes were all laid in the ground and ready to go. When I asked what they

47

all wanted on their pizza, they all declined and thanked me for the offer but said they had other family plans to attend to and left. That was a typical response.

A fellow firefighter put out a call for help on short notice to help him move a house-load of furniture due to his wife kicking him out of the house. We also found out they were planning on getting a divorce. It was a little awkward as we knew them both well and were just as upset as if we were seeing a family member go through a divorce.

The next day around fifteen of us showed up with pickup trucks and trailers lined up down the street. We all got directions from the couple as to what was being moved. We quickly organized and moved almost all the contents of the house to a rental in about two hours. Nobody asked questions, no digging for information, and no taking sides. We moved it all and we placed everything where he wanted it and then we all shook hands and left, wishing him luck.

It was typical during my career that we would all become friends, which made it even easier to work on the scene of an emergency. I mentioned earlier that our wedding party consisted of firefighters, paramedics, and police officers. My bachelor party was held at a popular discotheque (I got married when disco was popular, okay?). It was a good thing we all knew the cops who responded to a disturbance that night. It was not as bad as it sounds, just helpful.

Putting Off Some Heat

One of the more enjoyable tasks is setting up hands-on training on an acquired structure where we can pull hose lines, flow water, force open doors, pull ceiling, etc. It takes a bit of prep work, but it's all worth it. Now, if we can get permission to set the structure on fire, that's a whole new ballgame. This is like taking a kid to Disney World. Not only do we get to see real fire behavior, get competitive with the fire, and work with some tools we don't get to use all the time, but just the feel of the heat and the crackling of the fire gives you an adrenaline rush. This is what it's all about, after all. And we can make it safer to deal with as precautions are taken to make it safe and have other measures in place to keep it that way. On an actual structure fire, things happen fast, as you are trying to stop the spread of the fire and search for victims as quickly as possible.

I got permission to burn down an old wood frame house made of pine. I knew it would burn hot, so we set up a few "protection lines" to prevent causing any unwanted damage. One would be used to keep a vinyl fence belonging to the next door neighbor wet so the heat would not cause it to melt. Another was to be a backup line to keep the firefighters safe while fighting the fire. The fence was closest to the burn house and the neighbors' house was another fifteen feet from the fence. I figured it would be a safe distance from the burn house.

We ran a multitude of simulated fire attacks, did some fire behavior studies that got published, and got some hose time and heat exposure for some of the rookies. It all went well. For a finale, we agreed to burn the house to the ground for the homeowner who gave us permission to burn. It's cheaper for the homeowner than hiring a demolition company, and it gives the fire department great training.

We went through the house setting multiple rooms on fire and exited out the other side and let it burn. We had a few hose lines in place to keep it in check. The fire got so hot that it started melting one of the plastic emergency lights on the back of one of the fire engines. We moved the truck farther away to prevent further damage when I noticed the vinyl siding on the side of the neighbor's house was starting to melt. The fence was fine since a firefighter kept water on it the entire time. We immediately pulled another hose line to water down the siding, but it was too late. A good portion of the siding had melted. I felt horrible and took full responsibility. The neighbors were extremely nice to us during three days of training and making noise. They even made chocolate-chip cookies for the firefighters each day and sat in lawn chairs to watch us train.

After everything was picked up and everyone left, I went over to the neighbors with my head hanging low, feeling like a real loser. I could not apologize enough. I told them that we would take care of the problem and the department would pay for any damages. Of course, I knew I was about to get my ass handed to me when I tell the Chief, but it had to be taken care of.

The neighbors were way too nice about it and walked me over to a shed he had and told me he had boxes of vinyl siding underneath that he planned on using to re-side his house anyway. He said we can use that to save some money. Like I said, they were unbelievably understanding about the situation.

Since I had been in the construction business for many years on my days off when I wasn't working on shift, I told him I would be back in the morning with my truck and tools to replace the siding. The next morning, I did just that and started tearing down the siding. The neighbors had enough siding to complete the entire side of the house. About two hours into the job one of our engines showed up with Lt. Justin Marlin and his crew, with the intention of talking about the live-fire training they'd participated in a few days before. When he saw what I was doing, he asked what was going on. I told him the siding needed to be replaced and it was my fault, and I was making the repairs. He was a little upset that I didn't call him and ask him to come over to help. I told him that I knew he was on duty and he didn't need to worry about it. He and his crew told dispatch that they would be tied up for a bit, and all four of them jumped in and helped me finish putting up the siding. He gave me a hard time for not letting him know that I needed help, but that's just the way he was. He was always willing to help someone out. The repairs didn't cost the department a dime, but I got my tongue-lashing anyway. Yeah, I deserved that.

The Funerals

The one time you see an outpouring of support for each other is when a coworker dies. It doesn't matter if it was job-related or not. We did everything we could for the family and showed up in force offering our support. This happened more often than I would have liked. It is like losing a family member.

If you have never attended a funeral for a firefighter, it is one of the most emotional and heart-wrenching events you will ever experience. There are tears and goosebumps throughout the event. The sheer number of people who attend is mind-boggling. Services held at a church that can hold a thousand people have all the seats filled and the walls lined with those standing.

The parking lot will be filled with fire apparatus from the entire region. Ladder trucks, engines, staff vehicles, police vehicles, ambulances, and more will be packed into neighboring parking lots or empty fields. To see so many tough firefighters, police officers, and medics having a difficult time emotionally is heart-wrenching. The toughest time is when the pipes and drums play "Amazing Grace" on the bagpipes and drums. Not a dry eye in the place. Then, to make it more emotional, the county dispatchers set off emergency tones calling for the deceased to respond to the radio but get no answer. This is noted as their "last call" to service.

The funeral procession following the service is jaw-dropping. Some processions have taken thirty minutes to pass. Along the route, engines that could not attend are parked along the side of the road or on overpasses with their crews standing at attention in their dress uniforms saluting as the engine with the deceased drives by. Police drive ahead and have all intersections blocked off for the procession and salute as they drive by along with bystanders stuck in traffic. It will give you goosebumps.

51

Throughout the book I will explain in some detail the individuals who had a distinct impact on my life. I will summarize others who are not meant to be minimalized, but unfortunately, I can fill a book will all the coworkers' funerals that I have attended.

To be exposed to death on a routine basis throughout your career is tough enough, but to experience so many losses of brothers and sisters in the fire, EMS, and LE community during your tenure eats you up inside a little bit every time it occurs.

The sad part is that it seems to be the only place where we run into friends and coworkers we don't work with every day. Every time we attend services it feels like a family reunion of sorts, just more depressing.

Dr. Kurley

We were lucky to have had some of the best emergency room physicians in the state in the early '80s. I will cover that in more detail when I discuss my time working in the ER. Dr. Kurley was one of two ER docs who started working as emergency room physicians around the same time I worked there part-time as a paramedic. They graduated from one of the first emergency medicine residency programs in the country. Up until that time, the ER was typically staffed by family physicians or others who would fill in part-time for extra money. Their expertise in emergency medicine would vary depending upon their specialty.

Dr. Kurley and his friend, Dr. Mess, were aggressive in treating emergency patients and highly educated in emergency medicine. They were quick to diagnose and treat anything that came through the doors. They also loved paramedics since emergency medicine was also paramedics' specialty, and they spoke the same language along with having the same aggressive approaches to treating patients.

When a patient was brought in while Dr. Kurley was on duty, after you gave your report, he would ask you what you thought the diagnosis was and how you would treat it further in the ER. He made you think and challenged you every time you walked in the door. Most times he would have you stay with him in the treatment room for a bit (much to the dismay of the EMS supervisor or dispatcher) and allowed you to administer treatment under his guidance that was sometimes out of our scope of practice. Of course, we thought that was awesome even though dispatch was irritated that it took so long for us to become available for another call. Some of the nurses would get upset because most of the procedures were not allowed to be performed by them either, or they couldn't perform them even if under the watchful eye of Dr. Kurley. Things were more strict with nurses, while paramedics and emergency medicine docs were a bit on the maverick side. Since both paramedics and emergency medicine were still in their infancy, we got away with doing things out of the norm quite often.

Dr. Kurley was so good, he was asked to be the county EMS medical director. The position would dictate what protocols were followed, procedures allowed in the field, training requirements, and included the sole power to allow a paramedic to perform those procedures or not. He was so excited to fill that role, he was like a kid in a candy store. It was the best thing to happen to the county EMS in history. He loved his EMTs and paramedics. He stood up for them, trained them, and treated them like they were family.

Classic Dr. Kurley came out when another emergency room physician was being very arrogant and nasty to one of the paramedics after he brought a patient to the ER and had performed a procedure that he thought was out of the paramedic's realm of practice. Dr. Kurley got a call from another medic who witnessed this verbal scuffle. In short order Dr. Kurley was there, stomped into the ER and demanded that the ER doc go outside. When Dr. Kurley got an earful from the obnoxious ER doc, he proceeded to jump to the paramedic's defense, claiming he was more than qualified to perform that procedure and even threatened to kick the ER doctor's ass. After things calmed down and the ER doc was convinced the paramedic had been properly trained by Dr. Kurley himself, they shook hands, and the ER doc went back to work. Dr. Kurley became every paramedic's hero that day.

We became good friends since we both were involved in EMT and paramedic training, and I also worked with him in the ER. We both had the same passion for emergency medicine and were similar in personalities in that we were both workaholics. We were at each other's weddings, celebrated each other's birthdays, and rode bikes together. I had the utmost respect for him.

In 2002, Dr. Kurley became sick and was eventually diagnosed with Parkinson's disease. This was a horrible thing for him to go through. To be so intelligent and knowledgeable and have difficulty communicating or using his hands drove him crazy. He was forced to retire way too early in his career. While on a family vacation he tripped and fell, hitting his head on the concrete walkway and suffered serious head trauma. He deteriorated quickly and eventually passed away at the age of fifty-five. His death impacted so many people in public safety, it is hard to quantify. He was a mentor for other physicians, nurses, EMTs, paramedics, firefighters, and law enforcement. His death had a permanent impact on the community and emergency medicine alike.

Ronny

Ronny was one of the nicest and kindest firefighters I met throughout my career. He was a lieutenant whom everyone wanted to work with. He was in his late thirties and in good shape. One day in 2005 I got a call from him while I was at another station asking if I could find the time to come by so he could ask me a medical question. He was very vague, but it sounded important to me, so I drove over to the station as soon as I hung up.

Ronny met me out in the apparatus bay, and he said he had noticed over the last few shifts that he had some tingling and loss of sensation to a particular side of his face and felt like he had a difficult time speaking clearly. He said he was concerned about the possibility of having had a stroke. Ronny was a good EMT and knew enough about symptomology related to strokes, so he was concerned. I did a more detailed exam and asked a lot of questions, not only to get specifics of his concerns, but also to evaluate his speech. I did notice his speech was a little slurred and not as clear as normal. I went and talked to his crew and they conveyed the same feeling that his diction had not been as clear over the past few shifts.

It didn't appear to be a stroke as not all his symptoms fit, but I was concerned. I explained that it was some sort of neurological problem and that it may well be Bell's palsy. I told him that without a detailed exam by a neurologist, it was difficult to diagnose. I was concerned enough that I made him call his primary doctor and get an emergency referral to a neurologist. Ronny went off duty and got in to see his doctor that same day with a follow-up with a neurologist.

He never went back to work with his crew again. After some extensive testing over a few weeks, he was finally diagnosed with ALS, or Lou Gehrig's disease. Ronny was devastated by the news. He was determined to fight it for as long as he could, not really knowing there was no chance of him getting better.

While hanging around at the station one day after a doctor's visit, we got banged out for a structure fire at a condo with flames showing. He was with me in my office talking and I could see the excitement on his face. I told him to load up and I would take him with me. I assisted him into the passenger side of my staff vehicle, and we went en route to the fire, along with the other engines and ladder truck.

On arrival there were flames blowing out from the balcony of a second-story unit. It was a tough, working fire that lasted for hours as it ran through a common attic space and spread to three other units. We called mutual aid from another department for another ladder truck to be put into operation.

Ronny spent most of his time sitting in my vehicle or by one of the engines and felt helpless, knowing he could not help. That was Ronny's last fire.

Later, he was told he would not live much longer. It was horrifying, to say the least, to watch him rapidly deteriorate and lose his ability to walk, and eventually he couldn't talk. To see a physically fit firefighter quickly become totally dependent on someone else to assist with normal daily functions was upsetting to the entire department. Crews took turns going to his house to run errands for his wife and kids, mow his lawn, make repairs on the home, etc.

Ronny was loved so much by the department that it was decided to honor him while he was still here with us. There were some big hoops to jump through in a short amount of time, but the department made it happen. Ronny showed up by invitation one afternoon to a massive turnout of support from the department, other agencies, and family. We wheeled him outside in his wheelchair to the intersection in front of the station and his brother-in-law and I supported him from each side and assisted him to his feet. We slowly walked him over to the corner with a huge crowd around him. He was no longer able to stand on his own, was not able to speak anymore, and had a difficult time holding his head up.

When we got to the corner someone pulled a cover off the street sign and he saw that the street name was changed to Lt. Ronny Heckler Way. As difficult as it was for him to show emotion, it was obvious he was overwhelmed and appreciative. That street will always be there to remember a great man, a great firefighter, and a great husband and father.

<u>Raul</u>

Raul was that guy all firefighters wanted to emulate. He was kind, hard-working, dedicated, and knowledgeable. He taught at the local fire academy for many years and was also the training officer with his department. I was lucky enough to have worked with him at the fire academy, taught fire classes with him, and responded to calls with him. Even though he was at a different department, when there were large wildland fires in our region, other agencies would assist by being a part of a pre-designated task force or strike team. Raul and I were both on rotating call as one of the supervisors on the team.

Our last fire together was a rather large wildland fire in an area that was extremely difficult even for four-wheel brush trucks specifically designed to maneuver through that. We both were on scene as supervisors and we spent quite a bit of time troubleshooting how to free numerous trucks that were stuck in the sugar sand. While we did that, forestry tractors and planes dropping retardant kept the fire in check.

Most of the crews were relatively young rookies and did not have a lot of experience with wildland fires or handling the trucks. It wouldn't matter who was driving, it was impossible to drive in that terrain. Raul and I sat on the bumper and were talking to the crews and setting up strategy now that all the trucks were free. We asked them what they thought could be done to finish putting out the numerous spot fires and tree fires that were left in the burn area.

We got blank stares, suggestions that we try different brush trucks or more air drops. We each walked over to a brush truck, pulled out some shovels and sat back on the bumper. "Well, do you guys remember how to use one of these?" Raul asked. Once again, blank stares and confusion as they stared at shovels and rakes. Raul stated, "All we got left is to go old school." All the young guys started moaning and crying while Raul and I started laughing. Raul said, "Okay, that is sad. Are two old guys going to have to show you how it's done?" We both enjoyed the physical work and wanted to rub it in that a couple of old farts were going to lead the way. We took off and walked the entire perimeter of the fire, digging up sand and throwing it on the spot fires that were left. After about two hours of exhausting back-breaking work, we worked our way back to the truck where these youngsters were all sitting around, drinking water and talking trash.

Of course, we went from two steps away from collapsing to standing up straight with our chests out and laughing as we got back to the trucks. "You guys are pathetic," Raul said. "Let's go home so you can see your mommies and make you feel better." Of course, he was laughing as he said it. Of course, we both got back and cried to our wives about being so sore, but we loved every minute of it. During the entire two-hour walk putting out spot fires, we had great conversations about everything but firefighting.

At the end of his career and just days from officially retiring in 2015, Raul went on a hunting trip with his son for some one-on-one time. He was a big family man. Rumor had it that in all his years of hunting, he never once pulled the trigger to shoot anything. He just loved being in the middle of nowhere with friends or family. He was sitting in a tree stand and slipped and fell a good distance to the ground, landing on a pointed tree stump sticking out of the ground. He was impaled on the stump and died instantly at the age of fifty-eight. Even though this happened in a different county, the responding firefighters knew him. They called his department and asked if they wanted the task of removing him from the scene themselves. His department sent a crew to the other county and they removed him from the scene and transported him to the Medical Examiner's Office themselves.

The funeral was the largest I have ever attended and the procession from the church to the gravesite took almost forty-five minutes to pass. It was incredible to see the outpouring of love and support for such a great man who never saw his first day of retirement.

Mitchell

I worked alongside Mitchell at the fire department as well as the local fire academy. He was the son of a firefighter who went to the fire academy around the same time I did in 1976. It was awesome that they worked at the same department at the same time. His dad was so proud of his son following in his footsteps and being so good at it and so determined to be as good as his father. He had big shoes to fill and was always pushing himself to make his dad proud.

I enjoyed being around him because of his enthusiasm for the job. He kept me pumped and excited every time I was training with him at work or at the academy. His dad was a lieutenant with the last department I worked at and was looked up to by not only his son, but everyone in the business in the region. Mitchell was an only child and made his father proud every day.

One morning getting ready for work he had a sudden-onset severe headache that was debilitating. He was a paramedic himself and knew that was a bad sign. He called his dad, who was close by in the neighborhood, told him what was happening, and his dad came right over. His dad called 911 and the medics who showed up knew them both well—it's always tough taking care of someone you know. His dad followed the ambulance to the hospital, and when he saw the lights and siren turn on and the ambulance picked up speed, he knew it was bad. Mitchell had a cerebral bleed and passed away at the age of thirty-seven.

It happened in 2018, and I had just retired and moved out of state with my wife. It was a tragic ordeal having just left months before and going back for a funeral of a good friend's son whom I had worked with and was just getting established in his career. Mitchell had just passed his test to be promoted to engineer and was given the official title prior to his funeral.

This death hit close to home with me on several fronts. I have two sons and the oldest is also a firefighter, and Mitchell and he were about the same age and knew each other. My son took it pretty hard as well. Watching Mitchell's father, who is a good friend and brother firefighter, hurt as much as he did, wore me down a bit.

Never Routine

I have been to coworkers' funerals way too often. No matter how many brothers or sisters died during my tenure it never got routine. It also grounds you a bit and reminds you of our vulnerability, but it stays fresh in your mind when you pronounce someone dead while on a run, not allowing your decision to become routine, no matter how often it happens. Someone is always grieving and that is why being compassionate is an important trait to have in this business. I will summarize with other brothers and sisters who died during my time in the business.

Rick went to the fire academy around the same time I did, which was in 1976. He initially worked at a different department than I did in the same county for his entire career. He was a lieutenant for many years, and everyone loved working with him. Rick had this very animated, infectious laugh and was always in a good mood. He loved practical jokes and loved talking to just about anyone who would listen. My two sons played baseball with Rick's son for several years and we got to know him, his wife, and his son outside of the job. They were a great family that did everything together.

When Rick got cancer, there were fundraisers of all kinds throughout the county. A bunch of guys at their department shaved their heads in unity after he lost his hair due to chemotherapy. He fought it hard as expected, but eventually succumbed to cancer. Rick passed away at the age of forty-four.

I worked with Bob at one point, as I changed shifts at times. He was one of the first paramedics in the state and was a mentor to many. He died in a vehicle rollover crash not long after he retired and was thrown from the vehicle because he was not wearing his seat belt.

Nannette was a popular paramedic supervisor who knew almost everyone in the public safety arena. She was married to a city cop, was a paramedic instructor at the local college, and got along with everyone. Out of nowhere, she became ill and was eventually diagnosed with cancer and passed away in 1999 at the age of fifty-seven.

Another paramedic named Byron was one of those guys whom everyone in the business knew and admired. This guy seemed to have a photographic memory. He would listen to a lecture and would retain it right away. While everybody else was cramming and studying for an exam, he was hanging out at a sports bar drinking beer. He would then come to class and ace the exam every time.

He played on a rugby team that competed statewide. He was a large, tough, muscular guy who was always the nicest, most caring person around. He became sick in 2000, and about a month later was diagnosed with cancer. He quickly deteriorated and was in hospice care in short order.

To see this once huge, strapping athlete lying in bed weighing 110 lbs. at best, wasting away, made you sick to your stomach. I stopped by hospice to visit one evening. He could only talk at a whisper by then. After talking about some of the funny incidents during work, and him trying to laugh, he asked me to come closer, and I leaned in to put my ear to his mouth to hear him better. He said, "I have always loved your work ethic. Don't ever give up the fight." This was a personal message that we both understood. I shook his hand then gave him a hug and we said our goodbyes. He knew it was time. You could see in his eyes that it was over. He passed early the next morning at the age of forty-two.

Stefan was a paramedic supervisor I had worked with for many years. Right after he retired, he continued to work part-time as a security guard at a local hospital and I got to work with him again when I set up hazardous materials training for our hazmat team to coordinate with hospital staff during a hazmat mass-casualty event. One day while teaching at the fire academy another instructor asked the rest of us if we heard about Stefan being in the hospital. Nobody was aware of anything at the time. He showed us a picture of him lying in a hospital bed, about fifty pounds lighter and wasting away. He had late-stage cancer and was not doing well. A few months later we were attending his funeral as well.

I worked alongside Dabney as a paramedic for several years. When she was a rookie, she was assigned to work with me when I was a Field Training Officer (FTO) at the time. She was one of those female medics who was physically and mentally tough. She would not take any crap from anyone, especially when it came to a guy pandering to her. If a guy tried to lift a patient or a stretcher for her, she would shove him aside and do it herself. I loved that.

She eventually got hired with a local fire department as a firefighter/paramedic and did a great job. She worked her way up to engineer over a short period of time. After going in for a routine checkup, they found something they needed to follow up on. They eventually found she had cancer and had to start treatment. She took off work during her treatment phase and never came back. She passed away from cancer in 2015 at the age of forty-nine. It was just like losing a sister.

Dom was a fire inspector at our department for many years. He suffered from gout later in his career, making it difficult to traverse stairs at construction sites that needed fire inspections. Dom was one of the nicest guys in the department. Even though he was in pain, he never complained about it and kept a positive attitude. He was always smiling or joking but was serious at the right times. He loved his job. Dom was out sick for a long time and most of us assumed it was from his gout. The next thing I knew, he was not doing well, then shortly after that he passed away.

Tucker was the best dispatcher I have ever encountered in my career. He was already an accomplished dispatcher when I started as a volunteer firefighter in 1975. Most would say he was a legend. Not only did Tucker have a very deep, distinguishing voice over the radio waves, he also knew every street in the county. This guy was amazing. Nobody was ever as detailed as he was.

Tucker gave you directions such as, "Make a right off Evergreen Road, the address will be the fifth house on the left, the mailbox is black with the number three missing, with flowers planted around the base." And he was right. Tucker came over the radio with a certain tone that was louder than normal and spit out, "We have a structure fire, totally involved with flames through the roof at 284 Riverside Drive. All occupants are accounted for, a dog is missing inside the house, and the closest hydrant is 200 feet to the south." He could get more information from a caller than a police detective. It was amazing and helpful.

In 2009, shortly after retiring from thirty-two years dispatching fire and EMS, he passed away. Everyone in the county had talked to Tucker at one time or another and he had a great turnout for his funeral.

Early in my job as a paramedic I responded to a school bus accident with multiple injuries. One of the older kids on the bus, named Neff, took charge and helped direct kids out of the bus including his younger brother, Tim. Neff ended up working as a firefighter in a county just north of us and Tim became a firefighter at the same department where I worked.

In 2014, at the age of fifty, Neff died of an aortic dissection right after getting off work at the fire department. I had the privilege to recount the bus story at his funeral explaining how Neff was destined to be a firefighter due to his heroic actions as a student on the bus that day.

Sadly, four brothers and sisters I worked with committed suicide. Three while still on the job and the fourth just after retirement. There seems to be a trend of increased suicides in the EMS and fire community in recent years.

A study commissioned by the Ruderman Family Foundation revealed that first responders (policemen and firefighters) are more likely to die by suicide than in the line of duty. In 2017, there were at least 103 firefighter suicides and 140 police officer suicides. In contrast, 93 firefighters and 129 police officers died in the line of duty. PTSD and depression rates among firefighters and police officers have been found to be as much as five times higher than the rates within the civilian population. (Ruderman Family Foundation, 2017)

According to the Journal of Affective Disorders, 46.8% of firefighters in a study reported career suicide ideation, compared with the 5.6–14.3% lifetime prevalence of suicide ideation found among the general population of U.S. adults. This same study showed 15.5% of firefighters reported having made at least one suicide attempt during their time in the fire service, in contrast to the 1.9–8.7% of U.S. adults estimated to have attempted suicide at some point in their lives. Both categories are two to eight times higher than the general population. (Stanley, Hagan, Hom, & Joiner, 2015)

First responders, including EMS providers, experience high degrees of workplace stress. Traumatic calls, poor sleep quality, long shifts, lack of downtime after difficult calls, low salary, and low job satisfaction combine to make EMS one of the toughest jobs around. For these reasons, EMS providers are at high risk for burnout, anxiety, depression, PTSD, and suicide. (Lulla, Tian, Moy, Mueller, & Svancarek, 2020). According to a report in Money Talks News, in 2014 an EMT or paramedic was ranked the fourth most stressful job in America. (Cooper, 2018). A study by CareerCast.com listed firefighting as the second most stressful job in 2018. (CareerCast.com, 2017)

Chapter 5

THE GOOD

B eing in this profession is a constant adrenaline rush. The experience is a mix of emotional and physical challenges that include great positive highs, depressing lows, and either a feeling of accomplishment or failure. There always seems to be something that toys with you on a physiological and psychological level, and how you handle it will define your time in the business.

I will recapture numerous short stories involving responses I have made as a paramedic, a firefighter, and a paramedic working in the emergency room at a local hospital. Most of these incidents will never be forgotten, while some I wish could be erased from my memory.

There are many positive or feel-good stories I can relate throughout my career; unfortunately the tragic events outnumber the good. That is to be expected, as when someone calls for emergency help from a firefighter, paramedic, law enforcement, etc., something is typically not going well for someone. Even in those situations, I can say from the responders' perspective that there are some good stories that come out of them.

Emotional Reunion with a Stranger

While setting up some training for paramedics to practice administering medications via an umbilical cord for newborn medical emergencies, I had a chance encounter with a family I did not recognize. I was walking into a local hospital heading to the OB/GYN floor to retrieve a bucket of umbilical cords the staff had been saving for me. I would take these cords back to the station and have paramedics practice finding the proper blood vessel in the cord and place a catheter inside, calculate a medication dosage for a newborn, and practice administering it via a syringe. Hands-on training for something that is critical but not common is invaluable and the hospital was more than willing to assist.

As I was walking through the double doors, I saw a family of four coming in behind me. I held the door open for them, letting them go ahead of me. I was on duty and in uniform at the time. When they were in the vestibule area, a woman in her forties stopped in her tracks and looked at me like she knew me from somewhere. She stated, "You were at my house a few days ago when my father had a heart attack and went into cardiac arrest." I told her I remembered that call and mentioned what neighborhood it was in. She broke down crying, came over and gave me a hug, stating, "You saved my father's life. I remember you shocking him and giving him drugs and getting his pulse and breathing back before you transported him to the emergency room." I distinctly remembered that call and apologized for not recognizing them, as we were focused on her father and nobody else on scene.

First, I was not by myself the entire time, two paramedics on a rescue truck and two paramedics on an EMS ambulance were also on scene. She just remembered me because I got there in a staff vehicle prior to the others, then we all worked together when everyone else showed up.

She excitedly introduced me to her mother and her two children, and I shook their hands and gave them hugs. She said they were going to visit her father in the hospital and that he was going to be discharged in a few days. I told them I was happy for them and we went our separate ways.

For the record, that is a rare situation. It is rare to know the outcome of most of the patients we deal with in the field, never mind getting the update from family members. That encounter was one of the most positive experiences I had in my career. You know you made a positive impact on an entire family.

Electrocuted!

I was working with a seasoned EMT downtown when around noon we received a call for a fall. Upon arrival we found a gentleman in his thirties lying on the floor of a business, unconscious and not breathing. There were pieces of broken ceiling tile lying on the floor around him. We found out that he was an electrician and had fallen through the ceiling while working on some wiring in the attic. His coworker believed he'd been electrocuted as he heard him shout out and at the same time the power went out in the business. I noticed a burn mark on his hand that indicated an electrocution as well.

My partner started breathing for him with a bag-valve-mask, and I would intermittently administer CPR along with attaching the heart monitor. The monitor showed he was in ventricular fibrillation, which would be indicative of an electrocution; this rhythm also has a better chance of converting with defibrillation, or an electrical shock to the heart.

I squirted conductive gel onto the paddles, charged them up and placed the paddles on his chest, then pushed the button. The patient jolted from the shock and after checking for a pulse, it was determined that it did not work. I charged the paddles to a higher capacity and shocked him again. He jumped from the shock and this time we felt a strong pulse, so we loaded him up on the stretcher to rush him to the hospital. While en route he started breathing on his own and before we left the ER he was sitting up and talking. The fact that we got on scene in about a minute, plus he was young and healthy and he was electrocuted, all played a role in his surviving. He ended up going back to work a week later.

Welcome to The World

My partner and I responded to a yacht club for a possible childbirth. There was a young couple who lived on a sailboat that was in dock, and the husband met us outside to guide us to his wife. We climbed down the three steps and went through a hatch to the very back of the boat where the bedroom was. We walked through a small door into an area that ended up being all bed with no room to walk or stand. His wife was nine months pregnant and in labor with contractions about two minutes apart and her water had already broken.

I crawled over to her on the bed's foam mattress to examine her, and she was crowning already with contractions becoming more intense. We brought in our OB kit that had all the supplies we needed to assist with childbirth, so we set it all up to prepare for delivery. Mom let out a loud straining noise and a little boy came sliding out into my hands. I suctioned his nose and mouth, wiped him clean, wrapped him up in a small blanket and placed him on his mom to hold and keep warm.

I told her that we would wait for the placenta to deliver before leaving to make sure there would be no complications. This was when she told me that we could just go and thanked us for our help. I was a little confused, so I explained that we needed to take her to the hospital so they could both be evaluated and make sure the baby is healthy.

She told me that it had been their plan all along to have the baby naturally and not in a hospital. They called 911 when the contractions got more intense just to play it safe. She agreed to allow us to stay until the placenta delivered and make sure everything was alright. All went well and as we were about to put the placenta in a bag from our OB kit, she told us not to worry about it, as they planned on eating the placenta and they would take care of it. Bon appetit.

Headache

While at EMS, we had one of our crazy busy days where the entire county was busy. It was raining, and car accidents were occurring everywhere along with the typical medical calls. It didn't happen very often, but this day, there were calls waiting in the queue to be responded to. We had emergency calls coming in, but no ambulances in the entire county were available.

We brought a stable heart patient into the ER and we'd just finished giving a report to the nurse when we were told we had to wait for a stretcher to become available. The ER was just as busy as we were and had no empty stretchers.

My partner and I told the nurse that there were no ambulances available in the entire county and we needed to get out of there. She said she had asked for spare stretchers and wheelchairs from other units in the hospital and was waiting for them. Just then, dispatch came over the radio and dispatched an ambulance that had just cleared a hospital on the other side of the county to a lightning strike to a child. The location of this call was only a few blocks from us.

We told the nurse that she had to take control of the patient we brought in and that we were going to leave our stretcher. We jumped in our ambulance and told dispatch we would take the call. This was the only time I can recall responding without a stretcher in the back. I figured we always had a portable stretcher and backboards we could transport on, if necessary.

We got on scene in just a few minutes to find a twelve-year-old boy lying on the ground in the middle of the street. A witness stated he was riding his bike down the street when he saw a bolt of lightning hit the boy in the head, throwing him about ten feet. He was unconscious but breathing. He had a burn to the top of his head and to his right hand, where we assumed the electricity traveled.

We placed him on our portable stretcher and transported him on the bench seat of the ambulance to the same hospital where we'd just been. His heart rhythm was fine, so all we did was administer supplemental oxygen and start an IV on the way. He eventually became conscious and started talking in the ER before we left. His only complaint was a headache. I would have told him to buy a lottery ticket, but we didn't have a lottery yet.

That Made My Day

While instructing at the local fire academy, someone in the recruit class was having difficulty with one of the required evolutions. The students were required to go through a three-level maze that was built in a single-wide mobile home. The objective was to enter through one door and exit through the other with full fire gear and air-pack on.

This was a difficult maze, as it was totally dark inside with multiple dead-end tunnels and small passageways that required you to take off your air-pack and push it in front of you while staying on air. To continue with the class, all students were required to complete this task. On the last day Mitch was having a lot of difficulty going through the maze, becoming disoriented and panicked. He had backed out multiple times already and the day was coming to an end.

I tried talking him through the process, keeping his mind off the issues, but he was about to just give up and quit, feeling like he could not complete this task. Everyone in the class had already left for the day and he was the only one left, along with another instructor and me. We tried yelling at him to encourage him, talked nicely and calmly to relax him, and even reminded him that it was make it or break it today.

All had failed and he decided to just drop out of the class. I encourage him to try one more time before quitting. As he got about halfway through the maze, he started to get panicky. I had crawled in from the other direction without him knowing, and when he started to freak out, I started talking to him in a normal voice, telling him that I was in the maze just in front of him but breathing nasty, smelly, sweaty, hot air while he was breathing nice, clean, cool air from his air-pack and that he was better off than me at the moment. I was wearing my gear but no air-pack. I told him I was lying down and chilling, and he should do the same for a few minutes to get his composure.

Mitch calmed down and I told him that I would be just in front of him if he had any problems as he continued through the maze, so he had nothing to worry about. As I backed up, I quietly exited the maze through an escape hatch without him knowing it to let him complete it on his own. When he got to the end and came out the exit door, I was there to greet him and congratulate him on completing the maze and that I would see him in class the next day.

Fast forward, Mitch was already a paramedic when he took the class, and after he became a state certified firefighter, he got a job with a department close to his home. Ten years later I was putting on a class for firefighters at the academy and Mitch was in attendance. The class was primarily for other fire instructors and team leaders to take the information back to their respective departments, and Mitch was now a training captain in his department.

During a break before lunch, he pulled me aside and thanked me for getting him through the maze ten years before when he was about to give up, and now he was a training officer and doing well. He was a little emotional as he was talking about it, and he said he owed his career to me helping him get through the day. We shook hands and I told him I was glad he was doing so well. Made my day.

Turning Tragedy into a Positive

My partner and I responded to a motorcycle accident about five blocks from the station, so we arrived on scene quickly. A young man in his twenties laid down his motorcycle and slid approximately fifty feet, then hit his head on a fire hydrant. He was not wearing a helmet and had significant head trauma, which included a fractured skull with brain tissue showing.

He had agonal respirations and a weak pulse when we arrived, and by the time we got him packaged on a backboard and placed him on a stretcher, he stopped breathing and lost his pulse. Under similar circumstances, along with other life-threatening traumatic injuries, we would pronounce him dead on scene.

While quickly glancing at his driver's license, I noticed he was an organ donor. Since he was twenty years old and his only injury other than some road rash was serious, non-survivable head trauma, I told my partner that I would intubate him, and we would ventilate for him and do CPR all the way to the hospital to keep his viable organs alive.

I contacted the hospital via telemetry and explained to the ER physician that this was not a viable patient and why we were bringing him in with ventilations and CPR being performed. The nurse who oversaw organ donations just happened to be in the hospital that day and was paged to meet us in the ER. When we arrived, he was taken to the trauma room and placed on a ventilator, then ER techs took turns doing compressions to keep him viable for possible organ donation. The organ donor team had already been paged and were setting up the operating room. When his family arrived, they were told the situation and as difficult as it was, they agreed to honor his wishes to be an organ donor.

About a month later I ran into the nurse who oversaw the whole process, and she was excited to tell me that the young man had saved many lives and that fifteen recipients received various organs. She was happy that we took the effort to keep him viable for the process to occur since it is typically overlooked and not even a thought. I have been an organ donor since I started driving and have never felt more committed to the program since that call.

Santa Saves the Day

In the early '90s I was fortunate enough to lead a task force of two ambulances, a fire engine, a rescue truck, and a command post bus from Emergency Management to an area devasted by a Category 5 hurricane. I will give more details about that response later in this book but will talk about the aftermath here.

We witnessed some of the worst devastation one could imagine from this powerful hurricane, and what struck us most was how traumatized so many little kids were. They were totally confused about what just happened and scared, due to having no home or sense of normalcy. This storm came late in the year and the holidays were just around the corner.

My wife and I decided we should try to coordinate a toy drive to help the kids from the area we took care of during the storm. This process progressed from putting out a few emails to other firefighters and medics and their families to a full-blown county-wide effort that involved some amazing people from the community. Just about everyone from EMS assisted in some way, along with numerous citizens from the area and multiple businesses.

The news media was a huge help in getting people to donate and assist. A local business donated a warehouse for us to use to gather, sort, and wrap gifts for the kids. We filled the huge warehouse to the max and had to find another location for the overflow. It was amazing. A local moving company donated two semis and drivers to help us caravan to the city that we assisted following the storm, and the owner himself dressed up as Santa. Yes, we had two moving semis filled completely with wrapped gifts when we left.

I contacted the Assistant City Manager to let him know what we were doing and the day we were coming. He got the word out to the entire city that Santa was coming to town on this day. As we pulled onto the road that city hall used to be on, the street was lined with hundreds of kids and families. This was a relatively poor city and most of the residents were bad off prior to the storm. Just seeing all the little kids packed along the sides of the street screaming and clapping with huge smiles on their faces brought tears to our eyes. Their lives were turned upside down with almost everyone still living in shelters or tents, and Santa still remembered them.

Our two sons spent all their time off from school and weekends helping us sort and wrap gifts, so it was special to take them with us to assist Santa. We spent almost all day there handing out gifts to all the kids, and what was left we had the Assistant City Manager hold on to for those who could not make it. It was a very uplifting and emotional trip that we will never forget.

It's Hot in Here

We had a working structure fire in a duplex that was abnormally hot with flames everywhere. The right side of the duplex was completely full of smoke, and flames filled the living room and entryway. The front door and the door frame were burning. That was very odd. They usually act as a fire break for a good amount of time.

An elderly gentleman who was on oxygen twenty-four hours a day had just escaped the fire but had left two oxygen tanks in the living room. The fire was close to the tanks, causing one of them to explode and spreading pure oxygen throughout the living room, thus causing the fire to intensify very quickly and burn extremely hot.

As the attack crew made entry, they had to put out fire on the door and door frame just to get inside. They said it was abnormally hot, and it

75

took some time to get it under control. Once the rear door was opened, most of the heat and smoke started to leave.

I was the Safety Officer on scene at the time and as I was walking around the perimeter of the house doing a size-up, I looked inside the window of the bedroom and saw a cage just under the window. I looked closer and saw a puppy inside shaking like a leaf and moving around like he was on a hot plate. There was no floor in this crate and the metal cage was hot and burning his feet. I broke out the window, reached inside and pulled the cage out through the opening. I laid it on the ground and opened the crate door and pulled him out. The door was hot even with my fire gloves on. I held him close to my chest telling him it would be alright and walked to the front of the duplex toward an engine. We had a cooler of drinking water on the truck that we used to cool down his hot feet and allowed him to get a drink. We had dog oxygen masks as well, so we administered oxygen to him for a while since he had been breathing smoke.

All went well and the owner was happy to see him. He was crying, thinking he had lost his puppy, but when we placed him in his lap while he sat in his wheelchair, he gave him a big hug and smiled.

A Christmas Miracle

Around the middle of December, we responded to a residential structure fire in a two-story home that had flames showing through the roof upon arrival. The fire was mainly on the second floor but had burned everything to the point that it was all unrecognizable; charred material was literally about a foot deep. You could see the metal frame of the bed in the master bedroom and two burned-up lumps of char that used to be nightstands on each side.

The elderly couple who lived there came home from a trip to the store to see their house burning. They were obviously upset but grateful nobody was home at the time, and nobody was hurt. Luckily they had taken their dog with them on a car ride to the store.

I talked to the couple to get more information about what may have caused the fire, and they had no clue. The wife suddenly realized that they had Christmas money set aside to buy gifts for their grandkids and it was in the nightstand on her side of the bed. I explained to her that there was nothing left and everything had burned up, and she was more upset about not being able to buy gifts for the grandkids than anything else.

After the fire was out, I walked upstairs to the bedroom to see if anything could be found for the couple. It was difficult walking up the stairs, as they were covered in charred debris. When I got to the master bedroom I looked up at the sky—the entire roof was gone and lying in a charred pile of debris on the floor.

I walked over to where the nightstand was and saw what was left of a drawer. Nothing but charred items in a burned and smashed drawer were visible. I took my gloved hand and started to move some debris around and miraculously found a stack of money under a phone book that had been burned beyond recognition.

I grabbed all that was salvageable and took it downstairs to the owners, and they were as shocked as I was that none of the money was burned at all. She counted out one thousand dollars while I was standing there, and she told me it was all there. They both broke down and started crying happy tears.

Chapter 6

THE BAD

———————

As I mentioned before, most of the calls we respond to are not a good thing and someone is having a bad day. I do not want to come across as a negative Nelly, but that is the real world of public safety. I had a difficult time separating the "bad" calls from the "ugly" calls, but you will understand as you read along.

❖ I Am Having a Bad Day

Sometimes we have bad days along with those calling for help. The first day I was working as a paramedic by myself was a nightmare. It was stressful enough knowing that everything fell on my shoulders during a medical call. There were no firefighter/paramedics at the time and my partner this day was an EMT. I was the lone paramedic for the first time, and no, I was not out "saving the world".

Other than a few basic calls for service in the morning, it was uneventful. Just before lunchtime we responded to a cardiac arrest on the second floor of an office building. The patient was an employee in her fifties and in cardiac arrest. The only way up to the office she was in was via a winding staircase. A rescue truck from the fire department and our medic unit arrived on scene at the same time, and we carried all the necessary equipment we needed up the stairs.

An oxygen tank, drug box, heart monitor, telemetry unit, and a backboard were hauled upstairs, and I started my patient assessment. She collapsed in front of a coworker and they called the emergency number right away, so she was not in cardiac arrest for long. Nobody was administering CPR or ventilating her when we got there, and she was cyanotic (bluish color) due to a lack of oxygen.

One of the firefighters started chest compressions, another started to ventilate with a bag-valve-mask and my partner attached the heart monitor leads to her chest to see what rhythm she was in. The rhythm was Ventricular Fibrillation (V-Fib), so I applied some conductive gel onto one of the paddles and rubbed them together, then charged them up. I told everyone to "clear" away from the patient and I administered an electrical shock. Her body jolted and after checking the monitor she was still in V-Fib. I repeated the process and shocked her again. This time we got a Normal Sinus Rhythm on the monitor and a strong pulse, but she was still not breathing.

I got out my equipment and quickly intubated her, making it more efficient to ventilate her. I started an IV with no problem and gave her a bolus of lidocaine to help prevent her from going back into V-Fib, and then started an infusion of lidocaine.

Hey, I am a badass paramedic, and my first cardiac arrest is going to be a save. Hold that thought. We strapped her on the backboard and carried her down the stairs with one person on each end and one guiding the firefighter walking backwards downstairs, while I was ventilating via the endotracheal tube with a bag-valve-mask, holding the IV fluid in my teeth with the heart monitor slung over my shoulder and wires flung everywhere. Things were clicking and all was going well until I started to drop the IV bag from my mouth. I instinctively reached to grab the bag and was still holding onto the bag-valve-mask. I yanked so hard on the tube that it became dislodged from her airway (I know, not a great tape job on the tube) and when I reached down to pull the IV bag back up, the tubing got caught under the backboard and I pulled the IV out. I went from looking cool and competent to looking like an idiot.

When we got to the bottom floor and placed her on the stretcher, I re-intubated her and started a new IV. While en route to the hospital she started to breathe on her own, so I assisted her breathing with the bag each time she inhaled. All went well and before we left the ER, they removed the breathing tube, and she was awake and alert. It all ended well for her but was embarrassing for me.

Zombie in the Roadway

In the '80s, PCP was getting popular. This stuff made people crazy. They would hallucinate, be violent, and it would make them many times stronger than normal. PCP stayed popular for about five years then faded out, but it is making a comeback as I write this.

Responding to a call for a person crawling in the median of a major four-lane road with heavy traffic was weird to begin with. We found a female in her twenties in the grass median crawling near the roadway. We blocked the road with the ambulance with the emergency lights on, so nobody got hit by a vehicle.

She was talking incoherently and there was blood all over her. When I put my hands on her to get her attention and to get her to stop crawling, she pulled her arm away and started yelling at me that the bugs were inside her body. She then started chewing on her own arms trying to pull out her blood vessels with her teeth. My partner and a firefighter assisted in restraining her so I could evaluate what was going on, and they had a difficult time keeping her down due to her unbelievable strength. You could see her skin was missing, with tendons and blood vessels exposed. Her mouth was full of blood and skin tissue from biting at her arms. She was freaking out believing she had these bugs and worms under her skin, and she was trying to remove them.

We placed her on a stretcher with restraints to her wrists and ankles and some extra straps to her body. She fought all the way to the ER and all I could do was wrap her arms in bandages to slow the bleeding down. Before we left, we found out she had a history of PCP overdoses and was well known in the ER. The nurses cleaned out the bugs and worms before she was transported to a mental health facility for evaluation.

"Do You Know Who That Is?"

We ran a call at the local pizza pub at lunchtime for a possible mental patient. Dispatch told us a police officer was on scene with him. As we walked in the door and scanned the area, I saw a family with two small children eating pizza to the left of the dining room, and at the back of the dining room I saw a police officer, who I happened to be friends with, sitting with a rather large gentleman across from him at a table, talking. My cop buddy, Mick, was of small stature, wore glasses, and weighed about 120 pounds. The man sitting across from him was about six feet, four inches tall and weighed around 240, all solid muscle.

Mick saw us walk in and waved at us to come on over. I took one step toward him and stopped in my tracks. The guy he was sitting with was a well-known mental patient by the name of Harris More. He had a reputation of taking on six cops in a fight and winning. There was a story about him breaking handcuffs he was in to escape at one time. The problem was that Mick had never seen him in person. He had no idea who he was talking to.

I motioned to Mick to come over to me instead and when he came over, I said, "Do you know who that is?" He said all he knew was that the man told him his name was Harris. I said, "That is Harris More, THE Harris More!" The color drained from Mick's face and he had a look of horror on his face. Then he asked what we should do. I had run on him before and said we needed a lot of backup before we could even approach him, so Mick called for some help.

We went out and got our stretcher and in addition to the three straps already in place, we added two more and attached leather restraints to the side for his wrists and at the bottom for his ankles. When we had three more cops in the lobby, I suggested two of us go up to him to talk calmly to him and convince him to walk to the stretcher and lie down so we could take him to the mental ward to see his doctor.

My partner and I walked up to him and talked for a few seconds, explaining that we were there to help him and were willing to take him to see his doctor. He complied and stood up, towering over both of us, and we each grabbed an arm to escort him to the stretcher. The other cops waited in the lobby in case we needed them. As we were walking through the dining room slowly and calmly, Harris suddenly stopped, and it felt like I was trying to move a statue. He looked at me and in a soft and calm voice, said, "I am going to kick your ass!"

A second later he threw his arms up in the air to release our grip on him, hitting me in the face and knocking my partner over into a dining booth. It was game on.

I grabbed Harris around the waist and tried to take him down, and my partner tried pulling him down by his arms. We crashed down onto a dining room table and flattened it as broken pieces of chairs flew everywhere. It was a barroom brawl at its best.

Three cops jumped into the fray, then it was assholes and elbows everywhere. Suddenly I felt a handcuff go tight around my wrist. Then a cop yelled, "I got him cuffed!" Yeah, he had Harris cuffed to me! I started screaming like a little girl begging him to take the cuff off me. The cop was panicked (not as much as I was) and was shaking as he tried to put the key in the cuff to release it from my wrist. He finally got it off me and placed it on Harris' other wrist. It took all six of us to wrestle him onto the stretcher and place him in restraints and straps.

I glanced over to the family that was eating, and they were wide-eyed in shock as to what was happening right in front of them and were afraid to move. They got entertainment along with their meal that day.

If that wasn't enough, after we put him in the ambulance and started to transport him to the mental floor of the hospital, things got crazier. My crazy partner, who was just as much of a practical joker as I was, stirred the pot. You see, the ambulances had two-way voice communications between the driver and the medic in the patient compartment. This was so the driver could monitor what was going on in the rear in case there was a need, and the medic in the back could just talk out loud telling the driver to get to the hospital quicker, slow down, ask for help, and the like. The driver's voice came over a speaker that sounded like a pilot on an airplane.

I'd just gotten Harris to calm down a little bit and we were talking back and forth when I heard, "Hey Harris, your momma wears army boots! That medic in the back says he can kick your ass!" I yelled at him to stop it as I slid down the bench seat in the back toward the door with my hand on the handle. I knew this guy might be able to bust out of his restraints, and I was not going to hang around if he did.

I was legitimately concerned for my safety but at the same time I laughed, as it was a great practical joke, and I told him that paybacks are hell. We got him to the hospital without my having to bail out and all went well. They medicated him prior to us releasing the restraints and we left with a great story about the barroom brawl.

Road Rash

Road rash is a term used for the injury sustained by sliding along the road causing your skin to abrade away like it was rubbed with sandpaper. This can occur from a fall from a bicycle, a motorcycle accident, or when you are thrown clear of a vehicle in a car accident.

While working as a paramedic in the emergency room, a teenage girl came in by ambulance; she'd been involved in a motorcycle crash. The medics who responded told me that she and her boyfriend were on the way home from the beach and rear-ended a car at a high rate of speed. They both flew over the car and landed on the roadway, sliding and tumbling at least fifty feet beyond the car. He was wearing a swimsuit and she was wearing a bikini. Not a good mix.

I took care of most of the trauma and cardiac patients in the ER and I was assigned to her. Remarkably, she did not have any fractures. But she had road rash on every part of her body. One side of her face, both shoulders, back, chest, hip, both legs, and both feet were covered in road rash with lots of embedded tar and tiny gravel from the asphalt roadway.

The medics that brought her in gave her some morphine for pain and I gave her more. It was not enough. I had to take a betadine sponge and brush to scrub all the gravel, dirt, and tar from her wounds. I felt horrible every time I started scrubbing as it was painful the entire time. I would coat her wound with lidocaine gel before starting to assist in numbing the pain as much as possible. It was not enough.

After about thirty minutes of scrubbing and seeing how much misery she was in, I went to the ER doc and told him we had to find another way to clean her wounds. He looked at her again and agreed that it was torture for her to have this done and I was not making much headway yet.

He decided to call in the plastic surgeon on call and have him put her under in surgery to clean her wounds while under anesthesia and to see what he could do to help her wounds heal the best they could. Imagine being that teenage girl and having to deal with visible scars all over her body for the rest of her life. The only thing I knew about her outcome was that the surgeon said she was going to be seeing him for a long time to address the scarring.

In Your Face

A semi driver traveling on the interstate at around 70 mph got the shock of his life when a large tire came flying through the windshield and into his chest, pinning him in the cab. Somehow, he was able to stop the truck in the middle of the highway without losing control.

When we got on scene a huge tire and rim was found embedded in the windshield of this semi, pinning the driver in the cab. It was difficult reaching him to assess him due to the height of the cab. A pickup just happened to be driving around the accident when I asked the cops on scene to see if he would be willing to assist us by letting us use his truck as a work platform. He graciously offered his truck and we had him pull up next to the cab, allowing us to stand in the bed of the pickup to evaluate the driver.

He was conscious and alert but having difficulty breathing. He had an obvious broken leg and I suspected fractured ribs. His head had cuts from the windshield. A firefighter and I operated hydraulic spreaders and cutters to release the tire from the truck and then to free the driver from the truck. It was difficult to maneuver him, but we were able to lower him to the pickup, and he was then transferred to the stretcher.

Okay, you're wondering how this happened. You cannot make this stuff up. A concrete truck was traveling the opposite direction down the interstate when one of his rear tires just came off and rolled off the road, down into the median, then came back up the slope of the median and went airborne, slamming into the cab of this semi. What are the odds of that happening? Never seen anything like that before or since.

Here, Hold My Wallet

My partner and I responded to a possible spinal injury at a local motel pool. Upon arrival we found a male in his thirties floating face-up in the pool being held in place by a bystander. Thank God this bystander had the wherewithal to recognize a possible spinal injury and keep him from moving. He was conscious and breathing and there were no other injuries.

This gentleman dove into the shallow end of the pool headfirst and hit his head on the concrete bottom. His buddy who was holding him in the water saw it happen and jumped in to help. Spinal injuries were my specialty, and I knew that we had to keep him immobilized from this point forward to the ER. I handed my wallet to my partner, got in the pool, and had them pass a backboard down to me in the water. Working with the bystander, I pushed the backboard underwater and allowed it to surface directly underneath the patient. I then had him hold on to the board while I immobilized the patient on the board with straps and a head immobilizer. We floated him over to the side of the pool and slid him out to the deck.

We carefully moved him to the stretcher, and I had my partner drive slowly and carefully down the road to the ER, avoiding any bumps on the way. We got him to the ER without him being moved at all after getting him out of the water. We then drove the ambulance to my home and went out of service while I took a shower and changed into another uniform. It was not uncommon that we had to get wet, muddy, or dirty from various situations to get to a patient. Unfortunately, we found out later that day that he was permanently paralyzed.

"Do Not Step Here"

While working a fully involved fourplex fire, we started to put out some of the hot spots that were still smoldering and had about a foot of debris on the ground due to the roof collapse and all the contents that had burned. It was a hot fire that had two units fully involved upon arrival. As I was dragging a hose to get to a hot spot on the wall, I stopped in my tracks to get a closer look at something in the debris.

It was what looked like skeletal remains of a person in the debris. It was difficult to see at first, but I was able to see the outline well after examining it closer. I asked for two traffic cones from the crew outside and I placed one at the head and one at the foot. I told everyone on the radio this was marking the location of the body and to avoid stepping in this area or dragging hose over it so as not to disturb what was now a crime scene. I thought I was doing the right thing.

About thirty minutes later the state fire marshal showed up due to the death, and he proceeded to chew me out for placing the cones there. He explained that the plastic cones would contaminate the immediate area around the body and make it difficult to test for accelerants. At the time it was the only thing we had to mark the body and it made sense to me. We started using a metal wire with a flag on top from that point on. Lesson learned.

A Mother's Worst Nightmare

Most responders will tell you that dealing with children is always tough, especially if you have kids. The best way to be able to handle emergencies involving kids is to be well trained and competent in treating kids. This allows you to focus on treating them properly while at the same time keeping your mind off the emotional aspects.

We went to a call that dispatch described as a possible child Signal 7. This was a code used over the radio for a dead person. We responded as quickly as we could knowing that most kids are typically viable, as they normally do not have a lot of underlying medical conditions that would make it difficult to revive them.

Upon arrival we were led into the master bedroom by a hysterical mom yelling that her baby was not breathing. As we entered the room, I saw an infant that was only a few months old lying face up, not breathing, without a pulse, and cyanotic. When I placed my hands on the baby to move her to a location to administer CPR, I noticed that she was cold to the touch and already had rigor mortis.

There was nothing we could do. It was too late. One of the more difficult jobs is telling a loved one that someone has died. It is more difficult if it is a child or a baby. I told the mom that her baby was dead, and she totally lost it. Understandable. She started screaming that she was responsible and that she was a horrible mom. That comment caught my attention, so after we got her calmed down to the point that she could talk, I asked her what happened.

Mom was a large, overweight lady and the bed had a soft mattress. She explained that she decided to sleep with her baby that night and lay down next to her. Sometime in the middle of the night she had rolled over onto the baby and suffocated her without knowing it. When she woke up the baby was partially under her and that was when she noticed the baby was not breathing. There was no telling how long the baby was dead, but the autopsy confirmed it suffocated to death. You do not see that level of agony very often, and it was horrible.

The Tunnel Rat

We arrived on the scene of a possible overdose at a familiar address. Upon arrival we found a gentleman whom we had run on before for overdoses of various medications. He was a Vietnam veteran whose job was that of a tunnel rat. He crawled through the tunnel system that the North Vietnamese were famous for, looking for enemy fighters. He told us stories before about it being so dark that you were unable to see your hand in front of you. He would bump into the enemy and typically had hand-to-hand combat or a close-up firefight. Apparently, this job caused a lot of mental issues for veterans. It sounded like pure horror to me.

This guy had his top dresser drawer filled with various medications scattered about and three levels deep. He was on multiple psychotropic meds, pain meds, anxiety meds, and others. I'm sure some of these meds had bad interactions with each other.

We found him sitting on the edge of his bed slurring his words but able to talk to us. His eyes were bloodshot, and his pupils were pinpoint. His sister was with him and she had called 911. I told him we would take him to the ER for treatment, but he refused. He was getting agitated every time we suggested we go to the hospital, to the point of wanting to fight.

His sister didn't understand why we couldn't just force him to go. I explained that we cannot kidnap someone and take them to the ER against their will. He was awake and alert and knew what was going on. He had all his faculties and refused our service, to his sister's angst.

We knew that he was not in good shape and needed to go to the ER, so we told the sister that we would leave the house and sit in the ambulance outside and for her to wait for him to go unconscious. We knew it was going to occur quickly based on the medications he took, so we did not wait long before she waved us back in.

We found him unresponsive but breathing with a pulse, and we would be able to take him to the ER. This is considered informed consent. We put him on oxygen, started an IV, placed him on the heart monitor and took him to the ER. We didn't run on him any more after that and assumed that he did not make it out of the hospital.

I'm Outta Here

Working for the fire department, we responded to a structure fire in a duplex just down the street from the station. Upon arrival there was thick black smoke pouring out the front door along with some flames at the top of the door.

A lieutenant and a rookie who had been on the job for only a month made entry through the front door with a 1¾" attack line. They disappeared just past the door frame into the thick smoke. Suddenly the sliding glass doors at the rear of the duplex shattered due to the heat, and we saw more dark smoke and flames shoot out the front door.

We then saw the rookie come out the front door on his knees, and when he stood up, his face shield on his helmet had melted and was sagging all the way down to his chest. His bunker coat was smoking and when we looked closer, we saw that the mask on his air-pack was damaged from the heat. He stood there in a daze not really knowing what was happening.

I quickly took his helmet and air mask off along with his bunker coat to cool him off and asked where the lieutenant was. He said he was still inside. The lieutenant came out at that moment cursing and yelling at the rookie, asking him why he left without telling him.

The lieutenant was old school and believed that you should not flow water until you saw the fire. He explained that to his rookie, who he had placed on the nozzle, which is why he was not flowing water yet. This is not true, as if it is that hot, it needs to be cooled down before advancing.

They explained that as they had moved forward in zero visibility smoke and heat, every few moments, they felt what seemed like a blowtorch hitting them on the neck for a second. The smoke was so hot that at times pockets of smoke would ignite, and when it ignited near the firefighters, they felt it for a second. They had tongues of flame directly hitting them and it freaked out the rookie, so he dropped the nozzle and bailed out without the lieutenant knowing this while still holding onto the hose line backing him up. Lessons learned for them both.

Follow the Leader?

In the late '70s I was assisting some fire instructors in the county just north of us with teaching fire behavior and fire attack on commercial structures. We were lucky enough to have had acquired multiple large open buildings that at one time were hangars for planes on an old air base. The hangars were built of heavy timber lumber with timber roofs and thick roof sheathing.

91

We would take two crews of six into the structure from the entryway rollup doorway and pull a hose line all the way to the back of the hangar, which was 200 feet away. There were two windows on each side of the building, otherwise the only way out was the way we entered.

I had a crew to the right side of the fifty-foot-wide structure, and someone else had a crew to the left. The lead instructor from a larger department was coordinating the process of starting a small fire at the front of the building, allowing us instructors to explain fire behavior from the incipient stage to the rollover stage. This stage allowed the smoke to roll over our heads and bank down until it escaped from the large garage door at the entrance. As this smoke heated up to ignition temperature, it turned to flames rolling over our heads.

This was fascinating and educational, and everyone was loving it. The smoke started to bank down closer to the ground and got hot. I told my crew that if it got too hot, they should lie flat on the ground to get away from as much heat as possible and have the nozzleman flow water out in front of him aiming toward the ceiling to cool everything down.

The smoke banked down and got hot in a matter of seconds. The crew did exactly as I said but the lead instructor freaked out, stood up, and ran to a side window. He threw himself through the window, crashing to the ground on the outside. His gear was smoking, his air-pack face mask was charred, and he suffered severe second-degree burns.

Our crews cooled it down as instructed and in short order allowed us to back safely out of the structure. Most of us were shocked to see this seasoned firefighter panic and bail out, leaving us all in there by ourselves. You never know how everyone will act when conditions change so quickly, and the key is to have a plan and know how to react to the quickly changing fire behavior.

One of Our Own

Relaxing and watching TV one evening at the station, the tones went off telling us to meet an ambulance from another department just down the street, as they needed assistance and were five minutes away. We jumped in our ambulance and went to the intersection we were told and sat with our lights on so they could see where we were.

We suddenly saw lights in the distance and heard the siren wailing. The ambulance pulled up and the first thing I saw was blood pouring out from under the back doors to the patient compartment. I jumped in the back to see what they needed, and I saw blood everywhere as well as a medic, sweating and full of bloodstains on his uniform, ventilating a patient with an Ambu bag through an endotracheal tube. He had a look of horror on his face, and he said in a worn out, pleading voice that he needed more IV fluids because he had no more left in his ambulance.

As he was telling me this, I looked down and saw the uniform. It was that of a deputy, and he had been shot in the chest and abdomen. He was still bleeding profusely from his wounds, but the blood was very thin and watery. They had run so much fluid into him that he was bleeding out IV fluid since he had little blood left.

My partner came back with an armful of IV fluids and I replaced the two empty bags that were hanging and wished him luck. He thanked me and I got out, then told the driver to keep going on to the ER.

The deputy was pronounced dead on arrival to the ER. He was working a detail providing security in a parking lot for a local park and was ambushed. And I later find out this deputy was a good friend of the medic who was taking care of him in the back of the ambulance. I felt horrible for him. The park was later renamed in his honor and remains that way today.

"Do You See That Column of Smoke?"

Later in my career I became part of the county Incident Command Response Team. When a large incident occurred that would overwhelm a local fire department and mutual aid is called in, the team would respond to assist. We would fill rolls such as operations chief, safety officer, division supervisor, strike team leader, and the like.

During the dry season we had an increase in large wildland urban-interface fires. The county has a lot of thick woods and brush with houses scattered throughout. This was the most common type of response the team had as it got overwhelming quickly, especially when it was dry and windy with low humidity.

We had two strike/task force teams pre-assigned each week—one from the geographic north and one from the south part of the county. When there was an exceptionally large incident or multiple incidents occurring at the same time, tying up both teams, members of the command staff would call others on the team who were not on call that particular week to put together a backup group of responders.

I was aware of a rather large wildland fire occurring in a section of the county that was prone to large fires. They had already utilized the North and South teams of engines and brush trucks and listening to the radio, it sounded like they were having a difficult time getting it under control. It was abnormally dry with low humidity along with strong winds.

I got a call from the command post at the Emergency Operations Center (EOC) asking if I could be a task force leader for a backup crew if needed. I obliged and he told me what engines and brush trucks I would be responsible for if we got deployed.

It was only about fifteen minutes later when dispatch set off the tones asking our backup task force to respond to the incident. I responded in my staff vehicle and gathered the crew of firefighters from the fire apparatus I was to oversee once I arrived on scene in the staging area. I walked over to the Incident Commander and asked what he needed. This guy was a seasoned Incident Commander and was good at his job, and when I saw that he appeared a little overwhelmed, I knew it was going to be a long and arduous deployment.

As I was talking to the Incident Commander, I looked out in the distance and saw a huge column of smoke that was spreading quickly. I assumed we were going to supply support to the crews already there. When he got a break from talking on the radio to various division supervisors, he looked at me and then pointed in a different direction and asked me, "Do you see that column of smoke?" I swung around about forty-five degrees from the main fire and saw a column of smoke in the distance that was getting larger as we spoke.

In a disappointed tone (I thought I was going to the big fire) I told him that I saw it and asked where it was. He told me it was near one of the fire stations and that our team would be the first ones to respond to it. All the other crews were having a difficult time handling what they had and then they started getting calls from neighbors stating the woods were on fire near the fire station on the other end of the district we were in.

I knew where that was, so I led a crew of three brush trucks and two engines to the area and found heavy smoke showing from behind the fire station. As I turned the corner, I saw a pickup truck fully involved in fire and another car next to it smoldering and about to catch fire along with heavy brush burning and spreading quickly. I then noticed mulch in the landscaping of the fire station was also on fire from hot embers floating in the air and starting to burn up the outside wall of the fire station.

I directed a crew to attack the vehicle fire and keep it from spreading, another unit to stop the spreading brush fire, and another unit to put out the mulch fire spreading to the fire station. It went from zero to one hundred in a matter of seconds of arriving. The crews did a great job of putting out all the fires.

During overhaul we found out the pickup truck belonged to one of the firefighters who came on shift and temporarily parked in the grass until the other crew went home. Both shifts ended up staying and fighting the main fire at the other end of the district. Inside the truck we found all his books and papers from the paramedic school that he was attending. Not only did he lose a brand-new truck, but also all his schoolwork.

The fire station lost a bit of mulch and just had some charring to the side of the building, but it was a good thing we got there when we did, as it could have been devastating. But then things took a turn for the worse.

As we were mopping up hot spots, a car pulled up with a neighbor in a panic telling us that his house was in danger of catching fire due to the woods burning toward it. I turned around and saw a large dark column of smoke getting larger and larger.

I had all the crew members with me throw their hoses on the trucks and told them to follow me. As we went down the road, just a few blocks away we saw heavy fire in thick woods growing and moving quickly toward this gentleman's house. We set up the engines in front of the house and the brush trucks on the perimeter to make a stand against the approaching fire. As it got closer we could feel the heat intensify, and at the right moment the crews hit the fire with handlines and with water from the onboard tanks.

It worked, and the fire basically split in two, went around the house and kept going at breakneck speed. The brush trucks were overwhelmed with the size of the fire and could not stop it from going by them. We then threw the fire hoses on the trucks and started chasing the head of the fire. Literally. It was moving as fast as we could drive with limited visibility from all the smoke. I went ahead to survey the situation in front of the head of the fire. Houses were scattered everywhere in the thick brush and woods.

Some homeowners were diligent enough to make a break in the brush and woods by cutting down the brush or trees close to the home for just this type of scenario. Others had brush and trees right up to their houses. I had to quickly do structural triage and decide which homes we could protect and which ones we had no chance of saving. One of the more difficult decisions to make was to write off some homes and protect others. That was exactly what we had to do. Remember, we were all we had as Command was trying to put together another task force for backup.

When I came across a home that had created a barrier to fire, we stood our ground between the house and the head fire and were successful in stopping the fire from burning the house. The fire kept going either around both sides or winds would send embers over the house to catch the brush on fire on the other side and kept going.

Even though some of the firefighters didn't like giving up a fight when I told them to pass one house to protect another, it was the only way to save the most homes possible and also didn't put them in danger of harm to themselves. Firefighters are always looking for the fight and are willing to give it a go, no matter the circumstances. I told them that the decision was on me and to move on and protect the ones we could be successful with.

As everyone was busy protecting a few homes, another vehicle pulled up and said a neighbor's house is about to catch fire and it is three blocks away. Since all the brush trucks and engines were busy, I followed him over to his neighbor's house and saw brush burning up to the house and starting to burn up the outside of the wall. I carried multiple fire extinguishers and basic tools on my staff vehicle, so I carried my water extinguisher up to the house and put the fire out that was crawling up the wall and pulled all the mulch and dry grass away from the house with my fire boots.

I noticed smoke was still present in the eaves of the house and told the neighbor that I had to break into the house to make sure the fire was not spreading inside. I forced the garage door open and saw smoke coming from the ceiling near the exterior wall through some cracks. I found a step ladder in the garage and climbed up to the ceiling and started tearing into drywall on the ceiling. Sure enough, there was fire on top of the exterior wall, so I grabbed my water extinguisher and put it out.

As I stepped down from the ladder, I saw a large dog cage sitting in the middle of the empty garage with a large German Shephard inside. He was noticeably scared of all the commotion, and I opened the garage door from the inside to get fresh air to him. Not knowing what might happen when I left, I did not want to leave him inside the home alone. I dragged the cage and dog outside to the driveway away from any possibility of fire or smoke causing him any problems. I called for animal control to come and take the dog to get him out of danger. The neighbor agreed to stay with him until animal control showed up. I then went back to my crew a few blocks away and continued.

As soon as I got back to my crew, the Incident Commander called on the radio and said that dispatch told him a gentleman in a wheelchair was trapped inside his home with fire impinging on his home. I grabbed one of the engines away to go with me, but it was difficult seeing street signs with the thick smoke everywhere. It was frustrating knowing someone needed help and that we were moving as fast as we could to get to him but had great difficulty navigating to his address.

When we got there, fire was starting to go up the outside of his house, so we had one firefighter try to stop the fire from spreading while I and two others went inside the home looking for the wheelchair-bound man. We found him sitting in the middle of the living room scared to death. We wheeled him out to the driveway and as we got there, a relative showed up to assist in putting him in his van and then took him to their home for safety.

This went on all day long until the evening when the winds died down and we were able to get the fire under control. Even though I was initially disappointed about not going to the larger fire, we ended up having the larger of the two fires and eventually had multiple crews assisting by the end of the day. Crews stayed on scene for three days putting out spot fires and smoldering brush or trees.

Could You Pass the Potatoes?

We had a lot of elderly residents in our county, and it was not uncommon to have medical emergencies in a restaurant. Choking on food was not uncommon, nor was diabetics having issues with their blood sugar levels.

This day we responded to "a man down" in the middle of a popular all-you-can-eat restaurant in town. I wasn't quite there yet, but apparently when you reached a certain age, these events became quite competitive. It could be like walking into a bar frequented by a rival gang. It was going to get ugly.

We found a man lying on the floor in cardiac arrest in the middle of the line to get food. We started to evaluate and treat him with CPR, IVs, intubation, medications, defibrillation, and the like. Talk about a challenge. We had people stepping over us to fill their plates back up, stepping or tripping on the IV line, yelling at us because we were in their way, spilling food on top of us as we worked on this poor guy who had not had his first serving yet.

It was unsettling and humorous at the same time. We had to escort people back to their tables to make room for the stretcher to get in so we could transport him to the ER. We were in a bit of a hurry as we continued CPR and pushing medications, but as people shuffled along to get out of our way, it was like rush-hour traffic on an interstate.

We always wanted to try eating there one day as we figured the food must be surprisingly good since the patrons took it so serious trying to get seconds.

Chapter 7

THE SAD

There are many calls for help that are neither good, bad, nor even ugly. Some are just sad and if you are not emotionally upset, at least internally, you have a heart of stone. We deal with every situation you can imagine and some just hit you in a way that is upsetting for various reasons. This does not mean that we show emotions while on scene or even back at the station, it just tugs at your heart a bit.

❖ True Love

While working a condominium fire that burned up four units, I noticed an elderly lady sitting on the ground against a tree, sobbing. The fire was still burning, but just in spots, and the other firefighters were knocking them down. Since it was not as hectic as the first phase of the fire, I walked over to her and asked if she was okay and if there was anything I could do for her.

She looked up at me with a sad face, wet from tears streaming down her cheeks and said she needed her suitcase. I asked her what suitcase she was referring to and where it was. She told me it was in her condo in a closet. She said she needed her suitcase and that it was green in color and inside the hallway closet. Firefighters were still on the upstairs of her condo putting out fires with water flowing through the ceiling into the first floor.

I told her I would go look, but her entire unit was destroyed by either fire or water and I could not promise her anything. She pleaded for me to please try anyway. Just ten feet into her front door I looked in a small closet and there lay a green suitcase. The closet was not destroyed by fire but it had a lot of water damage inside.

I grabbed the suitcase and brought it out to her, asking her if this is what she was looking for. She openly sobbed and gave it a hug, thanking me for retrieving it for her. I told her it was my pleasure and I stood back to watch. She slowly opened the suitcase, reached in and pulled out a large framed painting, hugged it and started crying again.

Out of curiosity, I asked her if everything was okay, and she said that the only thing she cared about in her condo was this painting of her husband who had died only six months before. She used the suitcase to protect the painting when she moved from their house into this condo and was too emotional to hang it up yet. Of all the personal items she had lost that day in the fire, all she cared about was this painting. She excitedly told me about her late husband and how much she missed him.

I don't know what happened to this wonderful lady after that fire, but I'm sure she had her painting with her no matter where she went. She missed him sorely.

"My Life is On That Computer!"

At that same fire as above, a neighboring tenant was in the same situation—the fire destroyed the entire second floor and water from the firefight rained down onto the first floor. The fire had burned through the roof and the upstairs was completely involved in fire. There were several hose lines attacking the fire from the ground and from aerial apparatus.

A young man in his early forties stopped me as I was walking toward one of our fire apparatus, and he was crying. He told me he needed to go inside to retrieve his computer as his entire life was contained on it, and he was told he wasn't allowed to enter his condo with the fire still burning. He quickly explained that he owned a small business, and it was run entirely from his computer and he couldn't afford to lose everything if the computer got damaged from the fire.

I saw the desperation in his face and I told him that I would take care of it for him. I grabbed another firefighter who was nearby and told him to grab a few salvage covers and come with me. I explained that we needed to unplug the man's computer and I wanted him to help me bring it out to the owner, or at the very least cover it to prevent any damage from the water coming from above.

Keep in mind, the second floor was on fire but was separated by a solid concrete slab between the floors and the only concern was water damage. As we started walking to the gentleman's condo one of our chiefs stopped us and asked us what we were doing. I explained what we were about to do, and he said he was not going to allow us inside.

We both looked at him with a puzzled look and reminded him that there was no smoke, no fire, and no danger going in and this was important to the owner. He told us the condo was considered a total loss and that was it. We argued with him for a few minutes and he put his foot down and refused to let us go in.

I explained this to the owner, and he fell to his knees and bawled. We felt horrible about the situation and later told him that when we were given permission to make entry again, we would check his computer for him.

Once the fire was knocked down and hot spots were being doused, I went inside to his computer and everything downstairs was soaked in water, including his computer and desk. There was no smoke or fire damage at all. I brought it out to him, and he was devastated when he saw how much water damage had occurred.

To this day I feel that was a bad decision not to allow us to at least throw salvage covers over items downstairs that were not damaged yet by water. Good salvage operations occur while the fire is being fought in the early stages just for that reason alone. I am not aware of what happened to his files or his business after we left.

Family is Not Always There

My partner and I got on scene of a choking patient and found an elderly lady in her late 80s lying on the kitchen floor not breathing and without a pulse. My partner started CPR right away and I got out my equipment to intubate her so I could breathe for her.

As I placed the laryngoscope blade in her mouth to visualize the vocal cords, all I saw was a mouth full of peanut butter. It was odd that so much peanut butter was in her mouth. I thought to myself that I would not eat that much peanut butter at once for fear of choking.

I shouted out to family members in the other room to ask what had happened. All I got in response was that she was sitting at the kitchen table eating a peanut butter sandwich and started to choke, so they called 911 right away.

I reached in her mouth with my fingers to try to pull out as much peanut butter as possible but still could not see her airway. I pushed an endotracheal tube into her mouth toward the back of her throat and pulled it out with a large plug of peanut butter clogging up the tube. I repeated this at least five times, pulling out a tube with a plug of peanut butter in it before I was able to finally see her vocal cords and pass a tube into her airway.

We continued working the cardiac arrest for thirty minutes that included starting an IV, pushing medications, and continuing CPR. Her initial heart rhythm on the heart monitor was asystole (straight line) and it never changed. We pronounced her dead and started to ask questions as to what had happened. It was unsettling when we told them we did all we could do and pronounced her dead that nobody was upset at all.

Going back to us arriving on scene it was odd that nobody was in the kitchen with this lady, but her daughter, son-in-law, and two grandkids were in the living room watching TV and not in the least interested in what was going on. As I looked around the kitchen, I noticed there was no glass of water, milk, or any fluid in the kitchen. I looked on the table, the floor, and the sink. Nothing.

This whole situation was starting to look odd. I then took notice that when I scooped peanut butter out of her mouth and when I plugged up the endotracheal tubes, there was no bread to be seen anywhere either. Just pure peanut butter. I don't know about you, but when I eat peanut butter, I have something to drink right next to me to wash it down and typically don't eat it straight from the jar either.

We gathered the information we needed from family members and then called the Medical Examiner's Office and asked for law enforcement to respond. When the officer arrived, we told him we were suspicious about the situation and what happened. He said he would wait for the ME's office to comment.

When the ME's office called us back, they told us the lady's doctor was willing to sign the death certificate and would release her to a funeral home and decline an autopsy. I went into detail as to what happened and told him my concerns, but it was not taken seriously. She was released to a funeral home and we left.

This elderly lady was living with family members and was a burden on them based on my discussions with the son-in-law. I believe that this poor lady was murdered, and they got away with it. Nothing ever added up or made any sense.

Family is Important to Most

We responded to a possible drowning in a canal near a spillway, and upon arrival we saw a few people waving us down in a panic. A father and his young pre-teen son were fishing together while sitting on the concrete wall overlooking the canal. His son fell in and was struggling because he didn't know how to swim. His dad jumped in to attempt to save him. Unfortunately, he didn't know how to swim either.

His son was pulled from the canal first and pulled up on the grass. We administered CPR, initiated ALS procedures while en route to the emergency room, and they continued to work on him in the ER for a long time. They pronounced him dead prior to us leaving the ER. The father was not found until about an hour later and was pronounced dead on scene.

Not only was this a sad situation where a father and son both lost their lives while having a good time together, but it affected me as well. I had a son the same age, and what bothered me most was that my son and this little boy were both wearing the exact same shirt and shoes that day. It was a kick in the gut.

It is common to be more aware of the anguish family members are going through when a patient you're taking care of reminds you of a family member of your own. It's easy to get distracted at times when this occurs.

A Broken Heart

I'm sure you've heard about someone dying of a broken heart. Usually, it's said in a caring way about a person who is close to someone who passes, and the surviving person ends up dying as well. In my opinion, this is not an old wives' tale. I believe that this happens. I can safely say I have seen it multiple times.

It was not uncommon to run on an elderly person who has died on scene and to see the spouse completely break down and feel lost without their soul mate. Commonly, these are couples who were married for sixty-plus years and neither can function without the other.

After going through all the procedures necessary following a death on scene, we had already spent a good amount of time with the surviving spouse by asking multiple questions about the deceased so we had a detailed report we could pass on to the Medical Examiner's Office. You get a feel for how someone is going to be able to cope in the aftermath, and sometimes you get a bad feeling.

I have responded multiple times to a number of homes for a second time within a week or two of pronouncing someone dead to find the surviving spouse dead as well. It didn't matter if they had serious underlying medical issues or not. They had just given up and could not survive without their spouse. I believe one can die of a broken heart, and I have seen it.

Nobody Noticed

I responded with our rescue unit and dive crew to a popular fishing pier for a possible drowning. Upon arrival we were told that a young girl jumped into the water and never came up. We had two divers quickly get dressed in their dive gear and one of them submerged right away. I ended up being a line tender for the operation while the other firefighter was the backup diver.

The first diver tugged on the rope in a sequence telling us he found the victim. We made sure everyone was cleared from the pier and when he brought her up, we had difficulty getting her out of the water onto the pier due to weight. She was only about 120 pounds but seemed heavier than that.

After we got her on the pier, we found that both her pockets were full of rocks. A bystander told us that he saw her filling her pockets with rocks but thought she was just keeping them for mementos. He then watched her walk from the beach to the end of the pier and just step into the water, never coming up. She obviously filled her pockets to keep her down underwater. A relative later told us that she had been depressed but didn't think it was this bad.

This girl quietly and slowly filled her pockets with rocks, walked up the pier, jumped in and killed herself in front of about fifty people. This was a popular fishing pier that was always busy, but everyone was too busy to pay any attention to what was happening in front of them.

That is Not a Good Idea

During the time I was a training officer I got a call from the city police department asking me to attend a briefing on a SWAT operation. I had been a hazardous material technician/instructor for about fifteen years by then, and I'd set up a lot of multi-agency training in the past with local law enforcement.

I got to police headquarters and was part of a meeting that included the officer in charge of the SWAT Team, a bomb squad technician with the Sheriff's Office, an undercover detective, and a senior officer with the police department.

They invited me to the meeting since they knew I was on the department Hazmat Team and did the department training. They explained they were planning on raiding a meth house and asked that the fire department be on stand-by during the operation. I quietly listened to their plan and after they all put in their two cents' worth, they noticed I was squirming around in my seat wanting to say something. The lead officer asked me what I thought and if we were okay with doing the stand-by.

I told them that of course we would assist in any way that was needed, but I had some concerns about their plan. Meth production had not been a huge problem in our county and when it was encountered, it ended up being personal use production in small quantities. No lab of any size had been found or to be overly concerned about. This raid was based on the premise that they were operating a lab and selling the meth, and they had been under surveillance for about a month now.

The plan was for us to stand by about four blocks from the scene; the SWAT team would bust in the door and throw a flash-bang in the door to startle the residents, then take them down and arrest them. This was a married couple that was supposedly manufacturing meth and had a routine for selling and using. They also had two elementary school-aged kids who were in school. They set up Child Protective Services (CPS) to meet them at the bus stop, intercept them as they got off the bus, and take them away from the scene.

I told them that I thought it was a bad plan and too dangerous to implement that way. Of course, they looked at me like I was stepping on their party and questioned me as to why I thought it was a bad plan. They were all good guys and I'd worked with them before, so they respected me enough to let me have my say.

I told them that if meth production was in fact going on, there would typically be a lot of highly flammable and explosive chemicals present that are used in the production of meth. Therefore, throwing a flash-bang into the home could possible cause a major explosion, leveling the house and injuring or killing the occupants as well as the officers going in; at a minimum, it would cause a rather hot fire. Bad idea.

I also asked them if they were going in with their favorite firearms. I got a confused look from them, and I told them that most of the chemicals used are also highly corrosive as well, and if there are corrosive gasses in the air, it may very well corrode and damage their weapons beyond repair. I suggested that if they go in with weapons, they should instead go in with those they have no problem destroying.

I suggested that the bomb technician send in their robot that was equipped with a camera and speaker, and then they could remotely view everything from the back of their van. I also suggested we strap a gas monitor to the robot so we could see the readout as it went through the house to see if the atmosphere was toxic or explosive. It would also allow us to know if there was any meth in the process of being produced, as this would be the most unstable time in the process. This would allow us to make decisions from there.

If the couple was inside, they could communicate with them via the speaker and have them come out of the house. In this case, they were not inside and there was no meth production going on. The only thing found was some meth that had already been made on a table in the garage along with syringes and other paraphernalia.

I then suggested we send in our hazmat team in their hazmat suits, with gas monitors in hand for protection, to clear the atmosphere by opening doors and/or ventilating with our fans. Our team also has waterproof and chemical-proof portable cameras that they took in to photograph things for the officers.

Once the atmosphere was cleared, the officers could go in safely and do their investigation and gather evidence. We stayed to assist in handling some of the chemicals found inside along with the meth.

The couple was found at a store just a few blocks from their home and arrested. The sad part of this story was watching the two young kids being met by CPS as they got off the school bus. The CPS caseworker bent over to talk to them and then placed them in her car. I suggested they go to the hospital to be evaluated as they had been in the house breathing many chemicals for as long as their parents had been manufacturing meth. This could have had long-term effects on their health. Both of their parents were in jail and the kids were without a home.

Seeing Your Family/Kids in Patients

Even though it is not helpful, at times you see your family members or kids in patients you treat. Fortunately, it's a rare occurrence, but it always seems to take you away from rational thought, and that isn't good for patient care. I mentioned earlier about the young boy who drowned in a canal with his dad and how he was the same age and wearing the same clothes as my son that day. It didn't affect how I handled the call, but it bothered me. This is another instance when I compared a patient to a family member, and this time it affected my thought process.

At the time, my son was an infant and we responded to an infant not breathing. Upon arrival I met a firefighter, who happened to be a good friend of mine, at the door. This firefighter was known to get a little nervous on some medical calls and could get a little shaky. He told me that an infant had died and there was nothing we could do. Keep in mind, this guy had been on the job for many years, always had good judgement, and always had a kind heart for every patient he saw. Even though he was an excellent firefighter, he was not very comfortable with some medical calls.

I gave him an angry look and yelled at him while walking past him, "Who do you think you are not working an infant! We always work an infant!" I saw an infant about three months old, the same age as my son, lying on the couch, not moving, not breathing. "Start CPR, now!" I yelled at my buddy as I opened my medical box to get my equipment to intubate the baby.

The firefighter picked up the baby and started CPR, nervously started shaking like a leaf, thinking he let me down. I grabbed my equipment to intubate, and when I tried to move the baby's head into a sniffing position to intubate, I realized the baby had rigor mortis. The baby had been dead for some time and the firefighter was right, there was nothing we could do.

I was horrified that I treated this guy the way I did and didn't trust him or evaluate the baby on my own to confirm his suspicions. I couldn't apologize enough to him and it has haunted me to this day. I took pride in my ability to keep my cool in just about any situation I came across, but this time I lost my composure, as all I thought about was my son at that time.

Yes, you always give a child the benefit of a doubt and attempt to resuscitate, as they typically don't have chronic medical issues that would impede the resuscitation. But even in this situation, there was nothing anyone could have done at that point.

I still feel bad about that call. It happens. I'm just not happy that I let it happen to me.

Not the Way to Start Your Life

Being in this business you will run into such an array of people who come from all walks of life, a wide spectrum that spans from the most loving to downright evil and everything in between. This was one of the most uncaring individuals I saw during my career and it took all I had to remain professional.

Even though our winters were never horrible, it did occasionally get to freezing and typically got pretty darn cold on occasion. One winter evening we responded to a childbirth in a rundown section of town. As we walked up to a dilapidated shack of a house and knocked on the door announcing that we were paramedics, a female voice from a distance yelled at us to come on in.

Entering the residence, I noticed that it was a tiny two-room wooden house with a wood floor. Most of the house was living room and the only furnishings inside were a recliner facing a large flat-screen TV and a small metal kitchen table next to what I would assume was the kitchen that consisted of a fridge and a sink with two cabinets. It was very cold inside as there was no heating on in the house.

I saw a newborn lying on the floor, face up, not moving or crying. I asked the lady sitting in the recliner watching TV what was going on as I approached the infant. She said I just needed to take it away. The newborn was barely breathing, had blue skin, and was not moving or crying at all. The umbilical cord was still attached to the placenta, which was lying next to him and not tied off. If it had not coagulated, the infant would have possibly bled to death.

We had our childbirth kit with us thinking we might deliver a baby, so I immediately wrapped him up in the provided sheet and asked my partner to go grab a blanket from our ambulance. I suctioned out his nose and mouth, causing him to respond and started crying. I tied off the umbilical cord with the provided clip in the kit and wrapped him in the blanket my partner brought in.

He opened his eyes and looked up at me as I hugged him to get him warm. I whispered to him, "Buddy, you deserve better than this." He had a normal heart rate for a newborn and was breathing fine and looking around.

Knowing we had to get this situation taken care of, and to assure the mother was fine, I told her that we needed to take them both to the hospital to be checked out. I walked over to the mom as she sat in the recliner in a robe and slippers and told her we would get the stretcher for her. She was defiant and told us to just go away.

She just kept watching TV and ignoring us, so I decided to play the game. I told her that she had no choice but to allow us to take her to the hospital or legally she could be in a lot of trouble and we did not want that for her (all a lie, but we needed to get her in). She finally complied and we put her on the stretcher to take her to the ambulance. I asked if she wanted to hold the baby and she declined.

As my partner and a member of rescue loaded her into the back of the ambulance, I got on the radio and asked for a deputy to meet us at the hospital as well as a Department of Children and Families (DCF) member. When we got to the ER, I discussed the situation with the deputy and told him that I felt this was child abuse, abandonment, disgusting, evil, or whatever he could charge her with. My partner and I were disgusted with this evil, heartless sub-human.

The deputy later came by the station for a written statement and told me that the baby was under the protection of DCF, and that mom was arrested and taken to jail after being cleared in the ER. We just hoped that this little guy would get a good foster home.

Not Always Welcomed with Open Arms

In the middle of a particularly hot summer, my partner and I responded to an unknown medical complaint at a house in a typical residential suburb at around 3 p.m. As we knocked on the door of the caller, a woman in her thirties answered the door with a concerned look on her face and said she called us for her husband. She asked us to follow her up the stairs to their master bedroom, and when we get there nobody else was there. We heard the shower off the master bedroom shut off, and the wife nervously told us that he didn't know we were there.

We were confused as to what was going on, and she said her husband didn't want her to call 911, but she did anyway. She said he was working out in the yard and when he came in, he was unusually short of breath and never stopped sweating, even in the air conditioning. She said she tried to convince him to call us to check him out but he refused. She said he was going to be mad. Great. We were in the middle of a domestic that was about to happen.

As her husband walked out of the bathroom with a towel wrapped around him, he saw us and yelled for us to get out of his house. He then started yelling at his wife for calling. I tried to calm him down, explaining that she called because she cared, and we cannot force him to do anything or go anywhere. After some yelling back and forth between the two, I convinced him to let us just check him out by taking his blood pressure, pulse, and placing him on our heart monitor to convince his wife that he was okay, and we would leave.

He sat on the bed and his vital signs were within normal limits, but when we placed the heart monitor on him, we noticed an abnormality in one of the leads. The abnormality pointed to a cardiac event, but we would need to hook up more electrodes to do a 12-lead ECG to confirm. I explained this to him, but he refused and kicked us out of the house. The wife apologized and we convinced her she did the right thing and to call back if there were any more issues.

We got a call back just before going off duty at around 6 a.m. to the same residence. We found her husband lying in bed not breathing and without a pulse. He had lividity, or pooling of blood after one is dead for a period of time. We pronounced him dead, as he had died sometime in the night and there was nothing we could do. The wife was very emotional, going from upset to mad at him for being so stubborn the day before.

We run into a lot of stubborn people in this business and it usually ends up badly for them.

Chapter 8

THE UGLY

S ometimes the type of emergency responses we are exposed to are difficult for civilians to fathom. Sometimes it is downright disturbing. But they all need to be handled in a professional manner. I will outline some of the more graphic calls I have responded to throughout my career.

❖ Is That What I Think It Is?

There is a long, dark two-lane state road that has a lot of traffic that includes many semitrucks. Most accidents are head-on and involve fatalities. Late one evening we responded to one of those head-on accidents involving a fully loaded semitruck and a Corvette Stingray. Most of you know that the Corvette is all fiberglass and sits low to the ground compared to the semi.

Upon arrival all we saw was debris scattered down the road for as far as we could see. We stopped the ambulance and got out to assess the scene. The semi was on the side of the road not far from us, but we could not see a car anywhere. After doing an assessment on the semi driver and determining that he had no injuries, aside from being visibly upset over the situation, we started walking down the highway looking for the car.

As we walked, we had to step over pieces of debris at every step. Occasionally we would identify a car part, such as a part of the door, the hood, pieces of engine, a tire and wheel, etc.; the largest part we ever found was that tire and wheel. There was no car left. It had completely disintegrated upon impact and was spread down the highway at least five hundred feet. No body had been found yet.

We had crews walking down the side of the road with flashlights looking in the ditch and the weeds for a body. As we walked farther down the road, I hesitated and pointed out an arm lying on the road all by itself. This was not going to be good. As we walked a few more feet, I froze in place and commented to my partner, "Is that what I think it is?" He agreed that it was what it looked like, so we got up close to confirm it. It was a pair of testicles all by themselves lying in the road. It made you weak in the knees. This gentleman suffered a catastrophic accident that had mangled him beyond recognition.

His decapitated head was found farther down in the ditch along with other body parts. We didn't see many more parts and assumed they were either completely destroyed or flew far out into the open field on each side of the highway. Once the medical examiner got on scene, we left and heard later that not all of his body parts were ever found. I never saw a body so completely destroyed any other time in my career.

Rats Gotta Eat Too

In the early '90s my partner and I responded to a possible Signal 7 (dead person) in a rundown neighborhood that had a lot of crime and drugs. The dispatcher told us the 911 caller said he had not seen his neighbor for a few days and there was a bad smell coming from his house.

Upon arrival, we met a deputy who had just arrived on scene as well, and as we walked up to the house, we smelled it. The smell of rotting human flesh is unmistakable. It didn't help that it was in the middle of the summer.

We opened the front door and all we saw was waist-high garbage throughout the entire house. The smell of rotting human flesh along with rotting garbage was a treat. We could not stand there longer than a few seconds before having to back out so we would keep from vomiting.

The fire department was on scene and we convinced them to let us use their air-packs to go in and find the deceased person and pronounce him dead for the deputy. Sadly, we didn't have anything to protect our pants or boots from the nastiness. As we waded through the garbage, working our way through the house, we heard rats scurrying about. We would see some garbage moving about, then a huge rat would jump over the pile into the next room. I didn't know rats got that big.

We worked our way to the bedroom and saw a set of bunk beds with a body lying on the bottom bunk that was obviously rotting, and when we looked at the top bunk, we found another body lying there in similar condition. The one on the bottom was an elderly gentleman and the one on top appeared to be in his thirties. Both had rotting flesh, full lividity, and rigor mortis. The interesting part was seeing that their eyes, fingers, and toes had been eaten away by the rats. They were having a feast.

We were eager to pass this on to the Medical Examiner's Office so we could go home and throw away our uniforms and shower. We later found out that the elderly gentleman died from medical complications from diabetes, and the young man died from an overdose. I assume they tore this house down and did not rent it out again.

The Day the Grim Reaper Rode Shotgun

While working with EMS, my partner Juan and I had the most traumatic shift of my career. Absolutely nothing was positive that day, and it continued for the entire twenty-four-hour shift. One could be convinced the Grim Reaper was riding shotgun that entire day. The following occurred during one shift.

That Was Hard to Turn Down

The morning started out with a possible suicide in a nice, upscale neighborhood. Upon arrival a lady in her seventies met us at the door crying and visibly upset, and at the same time, mad. She walked us to the master bedroom, and we saw her husband lying supine in bed with his head propped up on several pillows, a shotgun lying on his lap aimed toward what was left of his head. There was blood on every wall in the bedroom with pieces of skull embedded in various sections of drywall on the walls and ceiling along with scattered brain matter. Needless to say, the scene was horrific.

As I pronounced him dead, his wife came in and went on a rampage about how she never wanted him to have all these guns around the house to begin with, and that he had been depressed for some time. A deputy sheriff arrived on scene at that time and the wife pointed to a large wooden cabinet and said she didn't want any of the guns around the house anymore and to take them away.

The deputy opened the cabinet door and on display were multiple rifles, shotguns, numerous handguns, and plenty of ammunition. The deputy explained to her that he didn't have the jurisdiction to just take someone's property away. Examining a little further, he noticed most of the weapons were very collectible, including many vintage guns, and worth a lot of money. The deputy explained to the wife that they were all very collectible guns, and she could sell them and make a lot of money to assist with expenses she may incur after her husband's passing.

She didn't want to have anything to do with that and told the deputy and me to take them and keep them for ourselves if we wished. Our eyes were wide with shock, and I quickly told her we couldn't do that. I swear the deputy started sweating and stumbling with his words while telling her he couldn't do that either. I think he was pondering if it would be possible to do such a thing. He finally came to his senses and told her that the only option was for him to confiscate all the weapons and place them in evidence, and they would eventually be destroyed. His voice was shaking when he said that out loud. To see that many collectible, expensive guns destroyed would be a shame. After calling the Medical Examiner's Office, we cleared the scene and never found out what happened to them.

Thank God He Didn't Suffer!

Just before noon we responded to an industrial accident at a forklift repair shop. Arriving on scene we saw multiple workers either vomiting just outside the work bay or crying and shaking their heads in disbelief.

We were led into the work area about twenty feet past the roll-up doors to find a male in his thirties lying face down (literally) on the floor in a pool of blood with two forklifts next to him. One was on its side and the other next to him with the forks over his head.

As you know, forklifts can lift a lot of weight due to the heavy lead rear end that keeps them from tipping over forward. This gentleman was making a repair on the forklift that was lying on its side and had lifted it off the ground with the forks of the other unit. Yep, one forklift holding another up in the air so he could work on the underside of the other. Apparently, there was a slight hydraulic leak on the one doing the lifting and the forks slowly started to dip down, causing the unit being worked on to slip off the forks and crush the worker to the ground.

The awful part was the only part of his body that was crushed was his head. The heavy lead rear end flattened his head to the concrete to the point where his head was about two feet in diameter and no more than an inch thick. One eye was staring straight up but was flat, and it actually looked like a flounder on the ground. It was a horrible sight along with the trauma many of his coworkers were going through after witnessing this event.

Grilling 101

Around lunchtime we responded to an unconscious person in a van on the beach. It was a popular beach for people to go to so they could get away from the crowds, and some would stay all day. We parked in the parking area since the sand was too soft in most places and would not allow us to drive there. After walking over a boardwalk and down the beach for about 100 yards carrying all our medical gear, we finally got to the van. I had no idea how he got there without getting stuck. It was a typical van with a camper top that raised up when camping. We looked inside the dark interior to see a middle-aged man lying unconscious on the floor of the camper section in the back. The doors were locked, so we had to force our way in by breaking one of the windows to open the door.

When we opened the door, we were knocked back from the stench of an overheated dead body and the strong smell of charcoal. His body was extremely bloated, with mottled blue skin. There were burgers on a small charcoal grill inside the camper that were burned, and the charcoal was already cold to the touch.

This gentleman had been there for some time and nobody paid much attention to the van most of the day. It was obvious that he succumbed to CO (carbon monoxide) poisoning while trying to use a charcoal grill inside a closed van. He probably passed out from the lack of oxygen and the fire eventually burned out.

The medical examiner and the Sheriff's Office took care of the scene from there and we left. It should be obvious to most people that you do not cook or light a fire in an enclosed space for this reason.

Too Close for Comfort

We were responding to a possible suicide attempt in a rundown neighborhood with a lot of single-wide mobile homes. The caller stated they had talked to the occupant of the home, who had said she was going to kill herself.

We arrived on scene and stepped inside the mobile home yelling out to see if anyone would answer. Nothing. I went in first and took slow steps shouting out for someone to answer me. I walked down the very narrow hallway and looked inside each room for someone; we had to walk sideways to get down the hall while carrying our medical equipment.

Small single-wide mobile homes have tight quarters and are very claustrophobic. I came to a spot with doors on both the left and right of me, so I opened the door to my left and looked inside a small bedroom but saw nobody. I opened the other door to an extremely small bathroom and looked inside; as I opened the door, I saw a toilet to the left and a small shower next to that. I pulled the shower curtain back and was face-to-face with a girl in her twenties hanging in the shower with an extension cord wrapped around her neck. We were no more than a foot apart from each other and she was looking in my direction, almost as if she were staring at me.

It startled me and I jumped back and probably let out a few choice words. When I composed myself, I stepped back in to evaluate the situation better. It was obvious she had been there for some time and I pronounced her dead at that point. As we looked around, we found an empty bottle of sleeping pills on the floor, and it was apparent she took them prior to hanging herself.

Keep in mind, years later we would not go in by ourselves but would wait for law enforcement to arrive on scene to ensure the scene was safe. In the early days of my career, it was common never to see someone from LE due to them only having three deputies covering the entire county at times.

This Should Never Happen

Later that same day we responded to the juvenile detention center. It was not a nice place and not in a nice neighborhood. It was depressing seeing so many kids having so many issues to deal with.

We were dispatched to a hanging at this location and already knew it was not going to be pleasant. Upon arrival, staff members were screaming and freaking out, pointing to one of the rooms the detainees stay in. As we entered the room, we saw an unconscious nine-year-old male lying on the floor with a belt around his neck. Upon examination, it was determined he had been dead for a long enough time to have rigor mortis setting in. When we told the staff that he was dead and that there was nothing we could do for him, they became very emotional again.

We called for the Sheriff's Department and called the Medical Examiner's Office to respond as well. Once LE showed up we cleared the scene. It is never a good day when someone that young commits suicide. By this time, my partner and I were getting a little depressed and did not speak much for a while after that call. We just kept it inside and moved on to the next call.

This is Mutiny

In the middle of the night, we responded to a stabbing on a commercial fishing boat. Upon arrival we were told that the victim was down inside the berth of the boat. We had to jump from the dock to the boat while it was rocking back and forth from the waves in the water and while carrying our medical equipment.

Once we were on deck, we made our way down a few steps to a galley and then down some more steps to get to the berth. We could barely get down there ourselves, never mind with our equipment. When we finally got to the patient, we saw a middle-aged gentleman lying on a bed in a pool of blood with multiple stab wounds. Upon examination, it was determined that he had bled out and we pronounced him dead. Apparently, he had an argument with a shipmate along with some heavy drinking that led to a fight.

We waited for LE to arrive on scene and turned it over to them, then went available for God only knows what next, as it had been a horribly trauma-ridden day of death so far.

You Cannot Make This Stuff Up

My partner and I got back to the station at around 5 a.m., and we were exhausted from numerous calls and a day full of traumatic deaths. We had enough and could not wait to get home.

As we were sitting at the kitchen table at the station waiting for the relief crew to come in, we were watching the news on TV and could not believe what we were seeing. Someone was found hanging under the bridge going to the boat docks that we had responded to that morning. It was determined that he had hung himself around midnight and was found that morning at 6 a.m. by a passerby.

Yep, he was hanging from the bridge as we drove over it to get to the stabbing on the fishing boat. That was creepy.

Well Done

I know. I know. You will not like the title of this story, but it is accurate. In the middle of the summer at around 4 p.m., it was still extremely hot, and we got a call to a little getaway cabin on the beach.

When we started to approach the cabin, we noticed a familiar stench in the air. Yep, the smell of death on a hot day is unmistakable. As we walked inside, we saw an elderly but rather large gentleman lying face-up on the floor. He was extremely cyanotic (blue) and very bloated. Gasses build up inside the body, causing the corpse to expand, the eyes to bulge out and the tongue to be forced out of the mouth.

Decomposition of a body is accelerated when it is exposed to high temperatures over an extended period of time. It was unknown how long

125

this person was lying dead on the floor, but we guessed it was at least a few days.

During this early time in my career, we were responsible for transporting the dead to either the funeral home or to the morgue, depending on the situation. We carried a supply of body bags just for this type of scenario.

The body was so bloated and to the point of decaying, it became difficult to roll it to the side and then roll it back into the body bag—he kept slipping from our hands as the skin sloughed off. I grabbed his wrist to assist in pulling him into the body bag when suddenly, his arm came off at the shoulder. It came off just like baby back ribs that were smoked to perfection where the meat just falls off the bone. There is a lot of anatomy that holds the shoulder in place, but it was all deteriorated to the point that it just came apart.

We finally got him (and his arm) in the body bag and had to make a note on our report as to what happened, to let the medical examiner know the situation. It took until the next shift to get the smell completely gone from the back of the ambulance even though we disinfected it to the nth degree.

Sometimes You Just Cannot Tell the Whole Story

One of the worst times for vehicle accidents is when it is dark and rainy. Not only does it contribute to accidents, but it makes it miserable for those of us who respond to them. Add to that distraught family members who are not thinking straight while in the middle of a roadway, and it becomes that much more difficult.

About fifty feet from a large intersection an elderly lady decided to walk across an extremely busy roadway to a donut shop at a point where it was six lanes wide plus there was a turning lane in the middle. And remember, it was dark and raining.

A driver did not see her among all the traffic and hit her. Upon arrival we found her lying in the turn lane along with a rather inconspicuous smear of blood stretching from her head for about twenty feet. At the end of the twenty feet was a small blob of bloody tissue.

We immediately called her a Signal 7 due to significant head trauma, as her head was crushed from a tire rolling over it. Our hearts skipped a beat when we saw the small bloody item not far from her, initially thinking it was an infant. Upon closer examination we found what was her completely intact brain. Now that is unheard of since the brain by itself does not stay together well outside of the skull. I learned this after spending all my time in the morgue and handling the brain for weighing in scales, etc.

Again, this sounds messed up, but the best way to describe this was that her brain had popped out of her skull like a zit. The patient's skull was crushed and when the wheel ran over her head, it squeezed her brain out of her skull exactly right to keep it intact. I did not think this would be possible, but that is what we saw.

Keep in mind, there was a lot of traffic and the uh-oh squad (bystanders) and the looky-loos (drivers looking out their windows staring and driving slowly) were plenty. We immediately covered her body up with a paper sheet and used another to cover up the brain. Unfortunately, that made it appear exactly like our first impression, that there was an adult and an infant.

To make matters worse, a young man in his thirties came running up screaming, asking if that was his mom. He said she was going to walk over to get some donuts, and when he heard the sirens, he got concerned. I asked if he knew what she was wearing, and he confirmed to me that it was his mother based on the bag of donuts and her clothing.

He became very distraught and started screaming and tried to uncover the sheet to see her. I grabbed his arm and told him that he couldn't do that and that he should walk over to the side of the road so we could ask him questions in a few minutes. He started to freak out and with his hands to his face while walking backwards, he almost stepped on his mother's brain. I couldn't imagine explaining *that* to him. He then almost stepped into traffic as the drivers were playing looky-loo and not paying attention. Needless to say, it was a little stressful for a while.

Why Would You Carry a Scalpel on an Ambulance?

Some people do not understand the need for paramedics to carry scalpels on the ambulance or rescue truck, but there are times that invasive procedures are required. Our protocols allowed us to perform a cricothyroidotomy to assist a patient in breathing.

I responded to a rock quarry in a supervisor's vehicle that carried extrication equipment for a vehicle accident. When I arrived, it turned out to be a large front-end loader and a dump truck. There were many large piles of rock around the quarry that were several stories high and dump trucks and loaders traveled around them.

Everyone was in a hurry since time is money. Both a dump truck and a large front-end loader were traveling extremely fast for the conditions, and they both happened to come around a large rock pile from different directions at the same time. The bucket of the loader was leveled off and about six feet off the ground, and it struck the front of the dump truck just above the engine and drove it into the passenger compartment.

The blade of the loader had cut through the hood, knocking off parts of the engine and went through the firewall into the driver. It had pinned the driver in his seat with the blade severing his left leg almost completely off.

I got there before anyone else and the driver of the loader had already backed off the dump truck, exposing the driver's leg wrapped around the firewall and dangling into the engine compartment.

This was in a remote location and it was a long drive to the trauma center, so I called for the medical helicopter for transport. As an ambulance and the fire department showed up, I had already gotten out my extrication equipment and set it up. I crawled on top of the engine of the dump truck and used the jaws to move metal away from his legs to get him free. It was difficult getting the right angle to completely untangle him, but I got the right leg free quickly. As I looked closer to his left leg, I saw it was crushed severely and he had lost a lot of blood, but the crushing injury helped slow the bleeding down.

By then the helicopter had arrived and we were still working on freeing his left leg. The driver was now unconscious with the helicopter waiting, so I decided to ask for a scalpel from the medical kit and I finished cutting off his left leg. Now keep in mind, all that was holding it together was a bit of muscle and tissue. Once I cut the leg free, we were able to maneuver the driver onto a backboard and onto a stretcher to move to the helicopter. The crew put a tourniquet in place, and I was then able to more easily free the left leg.

As they loaded him into the helicopter, I handed them his leg to take with him. They were not able to reattach his leg, but he did survive.

A Family Tragedy

A family of six including two children was on their way home from church one Sunday morning and it ended up being a horrible tragedy for the entire family. They were sitting in a small four-door sedan at a traffic light with nobody behind them when an older beefy Volvo hit them from behind while traveling at a ridiculous rate of speed. The cops estimated he was doing at least 70 mph according to witnesses.

The impact was so great that the rear wheels of the sedan ended up touching the back of the driver's door. You do not see this amount of damage very often from a vehicle accident. The car was pushed completely through the intersection and the Volvo was in the original position of the sedan. The Volvo had extensive damage to the front of the vehicle with the driver pinned in and unconscious.

I was in my supervisor's vehicle with extrication equipment, and I arrived at the same time as the fire department. We agreed that they would extricate the driver of the Volvo and I would work on the sedan.

The initial assessment revealed four adults in the sedan. The driver was unconscious with head trauma, the front passenger was conscious with severe injuries, the rear passengers were unconscious and crumpled up on what was left of a floorboard in about twelve inches of space total.

Another supervisor had already called for a total of four ambulances, and we manually extricated the driver and loaded him into the first ambulance, and they left for the trauma center. The front passenger was easily removed from the sedan and put into the second ambulance . The rear passengers were pinned in due to the rear doors being severely crushed. I used the jaws to remove the rear driver's side door and was finally able to access the first patient in the rear. The female in her thirties was dead, and I had to remove her to get to the second patient in the rear. As we removed her from the car, it was unnerving to see and feel that she was just a bag of crushed bones. I do not believe there was a bone in her body that was not crushed.

I was then able to reach the other patient for the first time—she had a pulse but was unconscious, with head trauma and multiple fractures. It took a few of us to be able to pull her out of what was left of a rear seat and onto a backboard. As we were waiting for another ambulance to arrive, I started an IV and put her on some oxygen. The driver of the Volvo was pulled out about the same time and had to be intubated and have IVs started; he was put into the next ambulance for transport. Once we found out that it was going to be awhile before the fourth ambulance arrived, the crew decided to take both patients together.

As we were cleaning up our equipment and trying to determine what had happened, a bystander asked what happened to the kids. We had no clue what they were talking about. I told them that there were only four adults in the car and no kids. That was when an officer with the police department told me she put two kids in the back seat of her car to keep them out of harm's way after they were pulled out of the car.

Apparently, the kids were sitting in the rear between the two ladies, who cushioned them from the impact. Bystanders helped pull them through the window since they were crying and trying to get out. The officer said they had no injuries and did not see a need to bother us during the commotion, but I insisted they be transported to the hospital for evaluation due to the degree of trauma from the accident.

Sadly, the kids and the driver of the sedan were the only ones who survived. Even the driver of the Volvo died at the hospital and was found to be heavily intoxicated.

I Could Have Sworn He Was Dead

As you can figure out by now, we came in contact with a lot of death. We were always responsible for making the quick decision to treat and transport a patient or pronounce them dead upon arrival. Sometimes it was unquestionably obvious and other times it took some quick examination skills and quick questions to be asked of relatives or bystanders. It was never an easy call and was never easy to tell a loved one that someone had died and there was nothing we could do.

While we're on that subject, let me be clear about another one of my pet peeves. I am a firm believer in telling a family member that when we pronounce someone dead, he is actually dead. I have seen some tell family, "I'm sorry, there is nothing we can do." That is not telling them they are dead. I have seen family members, who are in a confused state anyway, then ask, "Then who can? Can the doctors at the hospital save him? Are you taking him to the hospital?"

Or telling someone, "I'm sorry, he is gone." Then a family member says, "Okay, where did they take him? Who took him?" Kinda get my drift? You have to be blunt but caring and professional in making it clear that someone has died, and here is what happens next.

Back to the story. We responded to a possible Signal 7 in a poor neighborhood that was rundown with houses falling apart and trash all over the place. As we approached the house, we noticed the front door was making a "humming" sound. That was weird, but when we got closer, we realized it was a screen door completely covered with flies trying to get inside. And based on that all too familiar smell, we figured they were trying to get to something dead.

After knocking away as many flies as we could, we walked in to see an elderly gentleman lying faceup on the floor, motionless and smelling like death. His mouth was gaped open and there was no obvious breathing. Suddenly, a cockroach came crawling out of his mouth. Nice. As I reached down to feel for a carotid pulse, the man let out a loud groaning sound, causing me to jump as I was not expecting that at all. This guy had a pulse and had shallow breathing.

My partner and I looked at each other in disbelief and then went into medic mode and started working on him. We intubated, started an IV, checked his blood sugar and then transported him to the hospital. His blood sugar was so low that the test kit we used would not read it. We pushed some glucose with no response.

All we know is he ended up in the ICU for unknown causes. Just when you think you can anticipate an outcome, you get thrown a curve ball.

Treated Like Trash

We responded to a possible Signal 7 in a remote part of the county off a dirt road in the brush. When we get on scene, we saw the body of what appeared to be a young female, completely naked, rotting flesh, bloated, and her head obviously crushed in. She had clearly been there for some time as her torso appeared to be gutted out and was full of maggots, and the area of her head that was crushed in was also full of maggots.

We backed out until LE showed up to conduct a crime scene investigation, but it did not last long. We gave them our statement and did our report, and then she was released to the Medical Examiner's Office. At the time, we were still responsible for transporting Signal 7s to the morgue, so we had to wait.

The disturbing part was that maggots were escaping out of the body bag we put her in while transporting her to the morgue. We had to take the ambulance out of service for the rest of the day to be completely deconned.

The sad part is they eventually found out that she was one of two young females who had vanished from the mall on two separate occasions over a two-month period. She was eighteen years old and had multiple stab wounds to her torso. The other seventeen-year-old girl was never found.

"Are You Serious? We Need to Talk."

As I mentioned, I worked in the emergency department as a paramedic for ten years as one of my part-time jobs. During the early years working there, we had a few physicians who would rotate through from out of town, working like traveling nurses do today. They would typically work at a couple of hospitals certain days of the week. Some of the physicians were amazingly sharp emergency room docs, some were genuinely nice but moved awfully slowly, and others were, uh, well...dicks. Yeah, those guys would treat the nurses like garbage, treat the patients rudely, and sometimes were good at their job, but you hated working with them.

One doc in particular had a cocky attitude and thought he was a ladies' man. He would strut his stuff around the ER, talking trash to any nurse who would listen to him, and sometimes even flirt with patients. He was annoyingly obnoxious to be around.

We had sections of the ER that were set aside for trauma/cardiac, general injuries, and another for medical issues, etc. These areas were separated by curtains that each had stretchers in them to provide what little privacy you could get between curtains. Once a patient would be discharged, we would pull the curtains back and strip the stretcher of the sheets and pillowcases, clean and disinfect the stretcher and place new linens on them.

One evening when I was working, we were slow for patients. I pulled a curtain back where a discharged patient had been so I could do my routine of getting it ready for another patient. As I did, I saw this traveling doctor sitting on the stretcher sideways with one foot on the floor and a latex tourniquet around his upper arm while injecting something into his vein, just like you would see a junky doing. I knew exactly what was going on and he had a look of horror on his face that he had been caught.

He immediately got mad and told me to go away and it was not what I thought I was seeing. I leaned into him and told him I knew exactly what was going on and that we needed to go to the doctor's lounge and talk. I knew the patient who was in that room had been given some morphine for pain and this doctor was shooting the rest of the unused drug into his vein.

I will not get into the chain of custody of a controlled substance, but this doc put a kink in it by telling a nurse he would administer it to the patient himself and dispose of it properly. That is not typical as most know, and it should not have happened.

Since it was slow, we went to his office and sat down. I told him that I had to call the charge nurse who managed the hospital at that time. He started telling me he had a problem. I told him I understood and that it needed to be addressed but that I would have to notify the administrative nurse on duty at that time. Even though nobody liked this guy, it was obvious he had problems. The administrative nurse showed up and called in another doctor to cover the rest of his shift, and she did the paperwork for him to resign. She later told me that they set him up for rehab somewhere near his hometown. I hope he took advantage of the break he got.

Fish Filet

Another night working the three-to-eleven shift in the emergency room, we had a fisherman come in by ambulance. The boat he was on had the boat motor in the middle of the boat. It was my understanding that the motor was situated there so it would avoid the fishing nets he used when deploying or hauling in.

Apparently, the steering cable broke and rendered the steering wheel useless. The fisherman decided to give the engine a bear hug and maneuver it manually to get him back to the dock. As he got closer, the water got shallow and the prop hit some rocks on the bottom. This caused the engine and rotating propeller to kick up through the space in the middle of the boat. The propeller ripped this guy wide open from his knees all the way up to his abdomen.

Imagine what it would look like with a propeller cutting you from your knees to your abdomen. Yep, that is exactly what it looked like. There were not only bones exposed on both legs, but intestines and other organs completely ripped to shreds. The medics who brought him in had two IVs going and supplemental oxygen via a face mask. They had administered morphine for pain, but I don't think there was enough morphine on board the ambulance to dull the pain.

What do you do? Not much, other than to call a surgeon or two and get him to the operating room. We covered him with multiple large trauma dressings and kept them moist with saline to hopefully keep what was salvageable in good enough shape to repair. The ER doc gave him medication to sedate him and we intubated him to protect his airway. I transported him to the OR on our stretcher and left. The story was that he was required to have a colostomy bag for the rest of his life and had a few organs transplanted later. He apparently survived but was disabled forever.

Chapter 9

DIFFICULT SITUATIONS

Most of the stories I have mentioned already are difficult situations. Some of the incidents in this chapter don't fit in any other category, other than that they were just difficult situations. The one attribute you must have to be a good firefighter or paramedic is to be innovative, flexible, and not to think too deeply into a situation. Sometimes you just act, based on your experience and your gut.

❖ "I've Got Your Back"

There are many instances where you rely on your partner or other first responders to have your back when needed. This includes LE, medics, or firefighters. As I mentioned before, the beginning of my career as a paramedic had us respond to many calls by ourselves without backup from rescue or law enforcement.

My partner, Mick Roid had many years of experience and was very road-smart. He could read a scene better than most. For a little background on Mick, he was in a motorcycle accident years ago and had permanent injuries to one of his arms. He had a difficult time bending it at the elbow and keeping his hand oriented. We affectionately called him Flipper, referencing his flailing arm. Even though it was injured, it was strong as an ox.

We responded to a medical call in one of the rougher neighborhoods that had a lot of crime and drug issues. We got to the tiny three-room house set on concrete blocks and we opened a rickety, broken-down wooden screen door to get inside. We found an elderly lady having difficulty breathing and we started our assessment. Her son was someone we had run on before who was always in trouble with the law with drugs.

As I was treating this lady with my back to the door, the wooden screen door flew open, and her son came in screaming. He did not like anyone in a uniform. Mick was assisting in patient care and as I stood up to look at Mick, he appeared to be taking a swing at me. His open hand went just over my shoulder as if he tried to punch me in the face and missed, and all I heard was a loud "Umph" sound behind me. As I swung around, I saw the patient's son flying through the screen door backwards and onto his back on the ground. Mick yelled at him to go away or he would call the cops, and he obliged.

Mick told me that her son had been in motion to attack me from behind and he just reacted and punched him out of the house. We took care of the mom, loaded her into the ambulance, and did not see her son the rest of the call. That is having your partner's back.

"What Are You Thinking?"

We were responding to a call in a remote part of the county but were coming from the city. There was the typical heavy traffic and plenty of traffic lights to maneuver through, but I noticed a car riding my bumper through the traffic lights and around vehicles that had pulled off the side of the road to let us through.

Once we got through all the traffic and were traveling down a long two-lane road with very few cars, I noticed this car was still following us closely. As we went through one more traffic light and he followed us through, I slammed on my brakes, lights and siren still wailing, got out and stomped back to the car, and yelled at the driver, "What are you thinking? You cannot follow us through traffic like that. It's dangerous and against the law. You are going to get yourself or someone else killed. I have law enforcement on the way as we speak, so I would suggest you take a side road and get off my ass! And you are personally responsible for a delayed response to someone having a heart attack." I got back into the ambulance and sped off to the call while he disappeared down a side road.

Well, it is dangerous and unlawful. Yeah, you never know who you will encounter doing that. Not real smart, but I'd had enough of this idiot driving like that. Fortunately, this is not a common issue, but sadly not unheard of.

"Does Anyone Know Who Shot This Guy?"

As I mentioned previously, early in my career as a paramedic, law enforcement was far and few between. We would run stabbings and shootings all the time without LE being on scene. We had no choice. One afternoon we ran a call for a shooting in a rough neighborhood to find a middle-aged man lying in the middle of the road with a gunshot to his chest. He was breathing, but unconscious. There was a rather large crowd surrounding him (looky-loos), so we had to wedge ourselves through the crowd to get to him.

As we did, I had to step over a revolver lying on the ground. I asked if anyone knew what happened and I was told he was shot. Duh. I then asked who shot him, and someone in the crowd said, "Yeah, I did." I asked everyone to step back so we could take care of the shooting victim and for the shooter to stand over by the curb. They all obliged, including the shooter.

A rescue unit showed up as we were loading the patient into the ambulance, and I asked them to secure the scene and not to move the weapon until LE got there. I have no idea if the shooter hung around long enough or not.

Chicken Wing

I wrestled throughout high school and then freestyle tournaments well into my thirties. I was nothing spectacular, but I was average. In my opinion, wrestling is the best sport of all time. It's a one-on-one aggressive hands-on battle with no team coming to help. Just you and your opponent. You probably don't care, but it explains this story a little better.

We were working a vehicle accident on a remote two-lane road with steep culverts about ten feet deep on each side. The driver was drunk and ran off the side of the road into the ditch. Of course, he had no injuries at all and was just belligerent. We were standing next to the driver while he was giving the sheriff's deputy lip service, when suddenly he pushed the deputy in his chest with both hands, knocking him to the ground.

Before the deputy hit the ground, I had tackled this guy around the waist and we both went down into the ditch. I pushed his face into the mud, applied a double-chicken wing to immobilize him until the deputy got down there with me. We both put cuffs on him and maneuvered him up the ditch to the back of his patrol car. I leaned into the patrol car and said, "Not a smart move, buddy."

Particularly when officers were responding without backup, we all had to have each other's backs. I just reacted. I know it was not in my job description, but I was not going to let the officer get into any trouble while on his own. Besides, it felt good too.

"I'm You're Worst Nightmare"

When I was working as a paramedic in the ER, I became good friends with all the ER staff and other hospital employees. They were all good people, and most people have no idea how much crap the nurses, doctors, and other techs get from patients and others. During my time in the ER, nurses were old school, had respect for all doctors, and dutifully followed the rules. This is not to say that isn't the case today, but they were more intimidated by the physicians back then.

I know you'll have a hard time believing this, but some doctors are plain mean and obnoxious. If a nurse did something to make a doctor mad, he had the ability to make their lives and their jobs miserable. They had the means to complain to the hospital administrator and nurses would catch flak without both sides being heard. The doctor always had the upper hand.

Well, I didn't have to worry about losing my job, as it was a part-time gig, and I was not going to take any crap from anyone. So when I saw some seriously bad behavior on the part of the doctors, I only had to see it once before I took it on as a problem to solve.

I saw a nurse come out of a treatment room visibly upset and crying. She walked to the breakroom and got upset over the way she was treated by the on-call doc. When I found out that this was not out of the ordinary, I started to keep an eye on a few specific docs who would treat the nurses badly.

On one shift, one of the ER nurses came out of a treatment room crying and mad at the way she was being treated by this doc. I told her, "I got this." I headed down the hall, opened the door and stepped in, closing the door behind me. There stood this obnoxious jerk of a doctor glaring at me, already mad at the previous nurse, opening and slamming cabinet doors, looking for something.

He looked at me and said, "Who are you, and what are you doing in here?" I replied with a smile and said, "I am your worst nightmare." He started to give me lip, but I interrupted him and told him that he would not act like a jerk anymore in this ER, and if he needed anything, I was going to be the one to get it for him. I assured him that I was there to assist, but if he continued to be obnoxious, he would be on his own. And I reminded him never to talk down to one of our ER nurses again. He toned it down a bit and tried to make an excuse for being mean, but I ignored him. He then apologized just before leaving and was not a problem anymore after that.

Flying by Instrument

While working as a flight medic on the EMS helicopter, we responded to a shooting on a remote island not far away from the bay. This was going to be one of those runs where there was no ground ambulance coming, and no rescue truck was available.

As we got close to the beach of the island, we saw someone in a four-wheeler flagging us down. We found a clearing on the beach and land. Keep in mind that sand is one of the worst things you can have blowing up into the rotor blades of a helicopter. It can cause some serious damage. We had no choice though.

As I stepped out of the chopper, I walked over to the four-wheeler and saw a male in his thirties lying in the dump bed, unconscious and bleeding from his chest. The gentleman driving the four-wheeler was a neighbor and witness to the shooting. He said the shooter left the island by boat, so he called 911 and drove out to the beach area to meet us.

Since I was by myself and there was nobody else around, the pilot shut down the helicopter and came over to me with a backboard and some straps. I intubated him and applied a Vaseline gauze dressing to his chest wound while he was lying in the back of the four-wheeler. We loaded him onto the backboard, moved him to the helicopter and locked him in. I planned on starting IVs on him and placing him on oxygen while en route to the hospital.

As we start to load up, we felt a cool, stiff breeze coming from the water. We looked up and saw nasty, dark, ominous clouds that built up quickly. It was going to be a classic hard-driving downpour. It looked like a wall of rain was moving toward us at a fast rate of speed. We got in, put on our seat belts, and the pilot started the engine and got the blades rotating.

He told me over the headset, "I'm not so sure about this rain. It may cause us some problems with visibility and possible downdrafts." I answered, "Your call, if we take off, he may die by the time we get there, if we don't, he *will* die right here. You do what you think you can do." All I got was, "Copy that."

The rain was now over us and we couldn't see the nose of the helicopter due to the amount of rain coming down. It was hitting the aluminum shell of the helicopter hard, making a loud enough noise that it was difficult to hear even over the headsets. As I started two IVs on the patient and placed him on an oxygen mask, the pilot said, "He we go!"

We lifted off the beach slowly, and the pilot's intensity and focus were clear in his expression. This was not routine. He turned the ship to the right and we started to go forward. It was a little unnerving as neither of us could see anything at all. In the back of my head, I visualized crashing into the water or into a building we couldn't see.

About five minutes into this nightmare ride, suddenly we went through the other end of the wall of water, and it was as clear as ever with the sun shining. And there, straight in front of us, was the hospital. We landed, took in the patient, and when I came back, the pilot was inspecting the helicopter for damage. We both were sure it sounded like we were getting pummeled by hail. He did not see any issues and we flew back to the airport. I told him I was impressed with that stunt, and he said it was all by instrument until we got out of the rain. He also admitted he was nervous and would not have lifted off in any other circumstance than life and death.

"Buck, You Need to Sit Down"

One of our paramedics with years of experience on the job got into the back of the ambulance with a medical patient. Just as I was about to close the door behind them and get in the driver's seat to go to the hospital, I suddenly noticed something was wrong.

I heard my partner, Buck, asking the patient some questions. His verbiage was garbled and slurred and made no sense. The patient looked at me as I stood at the door I was about to close with a puzzled look on his face. Buck talked again and it was the same thing, but this time he noticed his own voice was not right.

I jumped in the back of the unit and told Buck he needed to sit down right now. He had a look of horror on his face. Remember, he was a seasoned paramedic and knew what was going on. He was scared.

I immediately called for two ambulances, one for the original patient and one for Buck. Buck was having a stroke.

I laid him down on the bench, started an IV, and put him on oxygen. Buck complied, knowing the procedure. He started to tear up as I was treating him. It was a bit unnerving for me as well. Another unit came to take Buck to the hospital, and then another for the original patient, who was stable.

Sadly, that was the last call Buck ever ran as he had to retire due to his permanent disability from the stroke. It was a little unnerving to realize that we are just a vulnerable as the patients we see.

"You Can't Let My Kids See Her This Way"

Every so often you respond to a call that hits you in the gut emotionally. We typically just lock it in a little box and ignore it most of the time. And it does not necessarily have to be something crazy or out of the norm. It just hits the right buttons at the right time.

We were working a cardiac arrest on a young mother in her thirties with her husband standing next to us crying and losing it. She had a heart problem and was on a lot of medications for it. On the ECG monitor, she had flatlined (asystole). It's rare to be able to resuscitate someone that is in asystole; there is no electrical activity in the heart whatsoever, so it's difficult to successfully treat.

We worked on her with CPR, IVs, medications, intubation, and the like for about forty-five minutes with no response. We stopped the resuscitation efforts and told the husband that we did all we could, but she was dead. He obviously lost it emotionally, and we had a hard time consoling him.

A shocked expression overtook his face, and he said, "You can't let my kids see her this way!" I asked him what he was talking about. He told us their two elementary school kids would be getting off the bus in the next thirty minutes, and he didn't want them to come in and see their mom dead on the living room floor. He was freaking out and pacing around the living room, not knowing what to do.

My partner and I both had young kids, and it was tough seeing him hurt like this. I explained to him that we had to wait to hear from the Medical Examiner's Office before we moved her, and that could take a while. Feeling for the husband, I went outside and turned the emergency lights off the ambulance and moved it across the street and a few houses down. I then walked to the next-door neighbor's house and knocked on the door.

A nice lady answered, and I asked if she knew the family next door. She told me they were good friends and that their kids went to school together. I asked if she would mind meeting the kids at the bus stop, taking them to her house, and taking care of them until their father could come over. She was more than happy to do that, and the dad agreed.

His wife was released to the funeral home when her physician agreed to sign the death certificate, and we left while he waited for them to arrive and take her. Other than the dad worrying so much about the kids and his young wife, it was a typical cardiac arrest scenario. But for some reason, when we got in the ambulance and drove away, we both started crying as we talked about the call. We don't know why, nor did we question it. It just hit us the wrong way and it hurt.

"Did You See What He Just Did?"

With PCP being the popular drug in the '80s, it made things interesting. What is amazing is how strong people become when on PCP. On scene of a possible drug overdose, we saw a man in his early thirties, about 6'4", no shirt, and in good shape, screaming at a single-wide mobile home. We were there by ourselves initially and found out that he was screaming at his ex-girlfriend and was threatening her with bodily harm. He was banging on the door and kept trying to get in. Fortunately, it was a metal door, and it was locked.

As long as he did not gain entry, we decided we would wait for law enforcement. This guy looked nuts. A single deputy showed up, and as he approached the scene, the guy high on PCP started yelling at him too.

Since he was much larger than the cop and nobody was in harm's way yet, he backed out and waited for backup. Oh boy, this was going to be a show.

A rescue truck showed up with two firefighters on board along with two more officers. The three officers decided to approach him again, and he ran back toward the mobile home and grabbed the top corner of the metal entry door with his hands and peeled it down off the frame. My partner and I were glued to the action like a reality show. He kept grabbing parts of the door and was literally folding it in half. I yelled at my partner, "Did you see what he just did? That's crazy!"

The three cops got closer and tazed him, but it had no effect at all. He just got ticked off. They started wrestling with him and trying to cuff him, but the cops were losing. I was itching to get in the mix but waited to see if they could get him under control. One of the officers used pepper spray to his face, and all it did was make him madder.

Okay, time to get it on. My partner and I, along with the two firefighters on rescue, jumped in to assist. We finally got cuffs on him and strapped him to our stretcher with even more cuffs holding him in place. Once we got him in the back of the ambulance to take him to the hospital to be evaluated, I found myself all alone with this guy, and my eyes burned so badly from the pepper spray's off-gassing that I could barely see through the tears and the pain. This guy was still mad at everyone, and I asked who was riding in with me. The guys on rescue would normally send one of them to assist, but they were short-handed that shift. The officers rode by themselves and could not leave their car there unattended.

Great. I had this giant psycho lying on the stretcher in the back of this small box with only me in the back with him. And he was not happy. My eyes were burning really bad and I could not do much of anything for him anyway. It was a rough ride to the ER, and once we got there, I had to place my head under a sink in the ER and flush out my eyes and wash off my face.

Just the off-gassing of the pepper spray from the patient incapacitated me. I cannot understand how this stuff just made him mad and didn't bother him at all. As I was leaving, I saw the other officers with their heads under sinks doing the same thing.

"To Make It Easy to ID Your Body"

Our area is prone to hurricanes, and we've been through our share. The biggest problem was when an approaching storm made a last-minute turn and didn't impact the area as expected. This caused a lot of people to blow off the weather warnings and assume each hurricane would be no big deal. Ask anyone who has suffered through a major storm and they will tell you that's a mistake.

We were expecting a worst-case scenario impact from a Category 4 hurricane that would bring at least a thirty-foot storm surge that covered most of our response area. As most people evacuated to shelters or drove far away, there were others who were going to tough it out. We drove through the streets in the areas that were to be significantly impacted and knocked on doors, telling people they needed to evacuate.

Amazingly enough, we ran into about a dozen people who refused. We explained the storm surge expected and the damage that would occur, and they did not care. So I decided to ask people for their social security numbers. When they asked what I needed that for, I told them I would like to write that number on their forearms with a magic marker to make it easier to identify their bodies after the storm passed.

When I told them I was serious, some decided to leave, but still others decided to be tough guys. The hurricane ended up turning last-minute, and we got little storm surge and now a larger group of people who will not evacuate when needed. They'll tell everyone they survived a Category 4 hurricane, but the truth is they never did feel the real impact of a storm. Some learn the hard way.

We Cannot Wait for the Ladder

I responded to a medical patient on the roof of a local pharmacy. To access the patient, we had to climb through a scuttle hole in the roof and up a narrow, totally vertical ladder. Once we got to him, we realized he was having a seizure, and it appeared to be from heat exposure; it was extremely hot and humid that day, plus it was one in the afternoon.

Once an IV was started to give him fluids and medication to stop the seizure, we had to figure out how we were going to get him down to the ambulance. We figured the best way was to use one of our ladder trucks and move him from the roof with a harness and stokes basket made just for this situation. We called for the closest ladder truck with the harness and stokes, but it was on the other side of the city. They were en route, but I knew they were at least fifteen minutes away.

The man was still unconscious after the medication stopped the seizures, and I felt we could not wait for them to arrive, set up the ladder truck, set up the harness and basket, etc. Well, the worker was installing a new air-conditioning unit on the roof, and they had just placed this huge unit on the roof with a crane hanging from a set of slings. I decided that we should tie him into the basket we had with us and use the crane.

I know, for any of the technical rescue folks out there, you just popped a cork. *Never* use on-site equipment and only trust your own equipment. I get it. I was a technical rescue tech myself for many years and understand that sentiment. But sometimes you must think outside the box and do what's best for the patient.

Heck, the air-conditioning unit weighed over 1500 pounds according to the crane operator, and this guy weighed about 140 pounds. I thought the slings would hold him. And since I had been in construction most of my adult life, I knew that most crane operators were damn good and typically better than any ladder truck operator.

After tying the patient in the basket, I tied a tag line to the end to control the basket as it was raised in the air. The operator slowly and meticulously raised him off the roof and moved him down to a waiting stretcher. He set the basket softly onto the stretcher and he was transported to the ER. Quick, done, safe, no sweat. The only ones sweating were the rescue techs who did not get to play when they got there. Sorry about that.

"Don't Take This Personally"

Another situation where we had to think outside the box was at a commercial structure under construction. Construction site rescues are difficult as nothing is complete or safe to work around. You have uneven dirt ground, construction material everywhere, and safety railing to keep you from walking off the roof or falling down an elevator shaft. I had spent plenty of time working high-rise commercial construction, so I was familiar with the surroundings and what was or was not safe.

This construction site was only about five stories tall, and a worker had fallen from the fifth to the fourth floor and broken his leg. We stabilized his leg, started an IV, and placed him on a backboard. Getting him down to the ground to be transported was the issue. We got up to the patient by climbing makeshift ladders made of two-by-fours since no stairs had been poured and no elevators were in place yet.

I glanced over and saw a twenty-yard dumpster sitting on the fifth floor, hanging from a crane. I asked what they were using it for and was told that was how they got all their material to the upper floors. I asked if they would mind if we used it to get their worker down. They were more than happy to assist. The crane operator moved the dumpster to our floor on the other side of the building, and I went to inspect it. It was clean as it only carried lumber up to the floors. I got on their portable radio and asked the operator if he was comfortable moving the patient. He told me that he would do anything we needed to help.

We moved the patient over to the dumpster and placed him on the bottom. Three of us got in with him, and they closed the door on the end. I told the operator to go ahead and take us down when he was ready. I leaned over to the construction worker and said, "Don't take this personally that we placed you in a dumpster." He laughed along with the other crewmembers and started talking about nothing until we got down.

Everyone asked when the crane operator was going to move us, and just then the door opened and we found that we were on the ground. He moved us so gently and smoothly we had no idea we were moving at all. It was a smooth ride for the patient, as he was not jostled around, causing him pain. The ambulance ride to the hospital was much rougher than the crane ride. Having worked with many crane operators, I can attest that they can place a dime on top of another dime hanging from a fifty-foot cable. They are that good. Again, sorry, techy guys.

"Let's Go Old School"

While working a vehicle accident with significant frontal damage to a car pinning the driver in place, we had to figure out how to get this lady out as quickly as possible. She was injured badly, and we needed to get her to the hospital.

The dashboard and steering wheel had crushed into her chest, but we were able to force the seat with the jaws of life, allowing enough room to pull her out onto a backboard and the stretcher. As we tried to pull her out, it became apparent that her foot was trapped. I could barely reach under what was left of the dashboard and feel her foot, but I felt that the floorboard had wrapped around her foot. This was a rare issue, and we had no room to access the floorboard with hydraulic tools to free her.

I felt around to get an idea of how the foot was trapped, and realized the metal was pushed up on both sides of her foot. It dawned on me that we still had an old set of porta-power tools in the rescue truck. The four-ton jaws on the porta-power were the size of my hand. I had them grab the unit and I carefully maneuvered it under the dash and to her foot.

This unit operates with another person who manually pumps a handle at the other end of the hydraulic hose, forcing the small jaws open. I asked the operator to slowly pump it until I said to stop. When it got to just about the size of her foot, I placed it against the top of her foot and asked him to slowly pump it again until I said to stop. As it slowly opened, I slipped it in between the two pieces of metal and held it in place with my hand. I had the operator slowly pump it up again as it pushed the metal both ways off her foot. I was able to pull out her foot and finish moving her to the outside of the car onto a backboard.

We all enjoy the advancements in equipment and power tools at our disposal in this job, but sometimes you need to rely on the simple tools or equipment that you sometimes forget about.

Balancing Act

We had an emergency on a four-lane bridge over a river that had no middle divider, and there were head-on accidents all the time. Just below the peak of the bridge, a fully loaded dump truck hit an older large four-door sedan head-on, trapping two elderly ladies inside. The impact was impressive. The bumper of the dump truck ended up just above the dashboard of the car on the passenger side and over the lap of the driver, causing the dash to push down on their legs. The car was pushed up against the railing of the bridge, half of it scrunched in an upside-down V-like pattern. The bulk of the truck was against the driver's side of the car, making it impossible to gain access by crawling over the top of the car.

There was no way to access the patients from the driver's side due to the truck's location, which was practically sitting on top of the car, so we had to shimmy our way down the side of the railing, rubbing against the car on one side and the railing on the other side. The railing was only about three feet high, and it was a little unnerving looking over the side of the railing as we moved toward the patient in the passenger seat.

It took some maneuvering to lift the dashboard and get her legs out from underneath, but now we had to figure out how to get her out of the car. At the time, short backboards were the norm for immobilizing possible spinal injured patients, and that was what we used. We snuck the board behind the passenger's back and strapped her in. We then placed a long backboard on top of the bridge railing with a little bit resting on what was left of the car door. There was only room for two of us to work on her, making it difficult to lift her out of the car and onto the long backboard. We had pre-strapped the long backboard, so as soon as we got her lying flat on the board, we strapped her in tightly, being careful not to bump the board. If we did, it would have fallen into the river below.

Maneuvering patients out of a smashed vehicle is routine, but I have never been so nervous as I was with this accident. Once the patient was strapped in, I took a gorilla grip hold of one end of the board and my partner did the same on the other. We inched our way along, dragging the board and the patient along the railing, with barely enough room to get the board by the car, the other half of the long backboard hanging over the railing. It was not terribly hot that day, but I don't remember ever sweating so much moving someone from a vehicle.

We finally got her past the car and onto the roadway and transferred her to a waiting stretcher and into a waiting ambulance. Another medic had crawled past us to gain access to the driver and determined she was dead. It took a large wrecker to pull the dump truck away from the car to gain access to the driver. They have since installed a permanent Jersey barrier along the middle of the bridge to deter head-on accidents.

Someone Has to Make a Decision

I briefly mentioned earlier about the aftermath of a Category 5 hurricane I responded to with a toy drive for the misplaced children for Christmas. I will now detail the entire response and the overwhelming support that came from across the country. It was an amazing experience of witnessing people, corporations, and government all helping each other in a time of crisis.

The Trip to Total Devastation

In the early 1990s, a Category 5 hurricane hit a large metropolitan area located about three hours away, and it was unbelievable how powerful this storm was. Initial reports via our local Emergency Operations Center stated that the city was almost completely wiped out. It was obvious they would need assistance, even though they were a large county with numerous resources. An EMS Strike Team was assembled, and I had the honor of being the strike team leader. This consisted of a large Incident Command Bus, two ambulances, and my staff/rescue vehicle. There were two paramedics in each ambulance and a member of Emergency Management staffing the command bus.

We were given direction to stage at the command post at a county facility, check in, and wait for an assignment. Upon arrival, we saw a sea of emergency vehicles parked all over the place in a large parking lot and long lines of responders waiting to check in. It was a little frustrating knowing a lot of people were in dire straits and over a hundred emergency vehicles with firefighters and paramedics were all just standing around waiting for direction.

As the representative of our contingency, I stood in line to register with a young lady who was terribly overwhelmed with the sheer number of personnel coming her way. She had legal pads full of names of responders looking to assist in any way possible. The problem was that she handed the sheets over to someone in the command post to determine who needed to go where, and he was overwhelmed as well.

While listening to discussions among those in charge, it became obvious that they had no idea where to send anyone and there were no communications from anyone in the devastated areas. They were attempting to do recon to make those determinations, but it was taking too long to get information back as to what was needed. They were very frustrated as well.

I gave the staging officer a list of resources I had with me along with my cell number so they could call me and tell me where they needed us. The other problem was the cell towers that were still standing were being overwhelmed with traffic, making it difficult to talk to anyone. After going back to the crew that came with me and giving them an update, I walked back to the command post to stand in earshot of the staging officer in case they called out my name.

After about thirty minutes of watching a very unorganized mess go nowhere, I started to walk back to the crew and let them know that we were probably going to be sitting here all night based on what I'd heard. On the way back, the emergency management official who traveled with us in the command bus said he saw a gentleman who was obviously distraught and looked lost in the mess. He was wearing a suit and looked out of place. He had a look of hopelessness and was pleading for help with his facial expressions.

The emergency management official asked the man if he was okay, and the response he got was that his city was devastated, and nobody was willing to help. He said he was the assistant city manager for a small, poor city in the south end of this large metropolitan area that was hit by the eye of the hurricane, and he had been told it may be a while before someone gets there.

After he was introduced to me, I asked him what he needed. He told me no emergency responders had been to his city yet, and they had no plans on sending anyone any time soon, as they were focusing on the larger cities and urban areas. He had no idea if there were injuries or people trapped in debris since nobody was searching. He said the county fire rescue department had evacuated and was not coming back. City hall and the entire police department was destroyed, leaving no responders at all.

I told him what I had with me and that we were willing to help in any way we could. He almost started crying with relief that someone was going to assist him. I walked up to the staging officer and told her we were going to this city at the request of the assistant city manager. We walked back to where our crews were parked and I told them we would follow this gentleman to his city, start a search and rescue operation, and provide medical care as needed. The guys were more than excited to be of help to someone, and we started our caravan of emergency vehicles down the road with the assistant city manager.

The farther we drove, the worse the damage became. We started seeing trees down, buildings damaged, and debris everywhere. It was a little eerie driving down an interstate at around 45 mph with no other traffic and dodging debris the entire way. We finally started seeing commercial buildings just off the highway, and they were completely destroyed. Large commercial structures lying in a pile of building materials were becoming the norm. A large area of trees on the other side of the highway were all snapped in half and lying in the same direction. It looked like a forest of dominos. It was hard to keep your eye on the road as you could not stop looking at the devastation.

As we got into the city proper, it looked like an atomic bomb had gone off. There was almost nothing taller than five feet of debris. The few standing structures were made of concrete block, and even their roofs were completely gone. We pulled up to city hall and all we saw was a destroyed building with multiple police cars that were either flipped over or smashed into other buildings. I could now see why the assistant city manager was so upset. His city was wiped off the map.

Search, Recon, and Field ER

I had us split up and start searches in three different directions. As I was driving down the road, a couple flagged me down and said they thought their relative was trapped in their mobile home. I followed them to the mobile home park and all I saw was a sea of trailer frames. There were no homes or structures left. I went up to the home the couple said belonged to their relative and looked around. There was nothing to search. I could see through the frame to the ground and it was nothing but debris, like the rest of the neighborhood. For the next few hours, we all searched for victims but found nobody. There was not much to search in to begin with. We all met back at city hall at a predetermined time and concluded everyone must have evacuated to a secure shelter or had left the area.

I looked around and determined that we needed to set up a treatment area for residents that may have been injured from the storm. We cleared all the debris from the field around city hall and parked the ambulances facing the main road so people could see them. A few people at a time came by and asked us to treat some minor wounds, but not much else happened.

As word got out that there was medical care at city hall, more and more people started to show up. We were getting busy with either minor injuries or personal medical issues. Everyone who relied on prescription medication no longer had access to their meds, or anything for that matter. Diabetics were having issues, cardiac patients were complaining of symptoms due to the trauma of the event, and those who relied on meds for their hypertension, anxiety, etc. were all having problems.

I decided we needed to be more organized than just working out of the back of the ambulances. I took a crew and an ambulance to the other side of town, where I noticed a two-story motel that had significant damage and had lost most of the roof trusses. We went into the lobby and I visualized everything we needed to get started. We loaded up our vehicle with about a dozen chairs, some tables, and other miscellaneous items I thought we could use and took multiple trips back and forth to get everything we needed.

We took some caution tape I had in my truck and roped off a section of grass for a field emergency room. We set up some chairs just outside the tape for a waiting room and others inside for treatment areas alongside the two stretchers and portable cots we had on our ambulances. A small table and chair were used as check-in and triage. It was a little emergency room under the stars, and as word got out, it got busier.

The Incident Command Bus was situated just on the other side of the parking lot. I started to make some phone calls to the command post in the city we initially staged in to find out what resources were available. They were still overwhelmed, but I got a lot of phone numbers from them. I found out where the three closest hospitals were that were operating, and we started transporting some patients who needed further treatment and care. It was about a sixty-minute round trip depending on the location. Tying up an ambulance and two paramedics was going to be an issue.

Time to Get Organized

Once we found out what hospitals were taking patients and how to get there, we needed to be more efficient. I got the phone number of the county director of transportation and others from the assistant city manager and started to get things rolling.

I explained to the director what we had set up and the issue of getting patients to the hospital. He asked me what he could do for me, and I told him it would be great to have two transit buses at my disposal and kept on site. Within two hours I had two buses on site with drivers who told me they were committed to our location. As we got nonurgent patients that needed transport, I had them sit in the air-conditioned bus, and on an hourly rotation, the buses would transport whoever was on board. The other bus would then start loading patients and would transport once the other bus got back. The system was working well.

As a bus would leave, I would contact the emergency room to let them know what was coming their way. It was a hodgepodge of patients that included those needing stitches to needing insulin or even dialysis. It then became a concern about sending the right patient to the right hospital that could handle them. Trauma, dialysis, cardiac, and others needed to go to the appropriate facility. That would create a mess. I decided we needed to improve on our plan.

The first night we were there, we slept on a stretcher or the bench seat in the back of an ambulance, or on a cot under the stars since it was so muggy and hot. It was strange to lie in the middle of a city with no noise to speak of. The only noise we heard every now and then were of wild animals. You know, like lions, tigers, and bears. Not kidding. A large zoo in the big city just north of us was demolished. They were not able to move or protect all the animals in time. Many wild animals were running around loose. We were already tired and had to sleep with one eye open.

The next morning, I decided that we needed security and a better method to get patients to hospitals at longer distances as well as providing more advanced medical care. I got on the phone and called our Emergency Management Office and talked to our EMS director to give him a situation report. He asked me if I needed anything else. Well, they asked… Director von Hilton was extremely supportive and helpful during the entire event.

We had two helicopters that were owned and operated by the EMS organization I worked for. One was a backup for when the front-line unit was down for maintenance. I told them we needed one of the helicopters to be stationed here for emergency transports to farther hospitals. "Okay, what else?" was the response I got. I said that we had set up a field ER, but we were in the hot sun all day, plus it would not be a good thing if we got some heavy rain. I asked if we could get one of the huge tents that the county uses for special events to make an ER out of it and be protected from the elements. "Okay, what else?" was the response. I told him we would run out of food quickly and the snack bars and water were not only getting old but running low. He said he already had that taken care of and was sending some food along with the helicopter.

We found an empty flat lot across the street from city hall that we converted to a landing zone for the helicopter. It took us hours to clean up all the debris on the lot and surrounding area. It does not take much debris to cause problems with a helicopter, so we made it look nicer than before the storm and marked it off with scene tape. The EMS director called in the off-duty pilots and put them on rotation to fly over to our site. They came the next day with supplies and with the ability to transport patients. Each evening they would go back to our home county to refuel, swap pilots, and bring more supplies.

Gotta Do the Right Thing

I decided to drive around town to do more recon and see what was around. Just twenty minutes away I saw a McDonald's restaurant with smoke coming out of the kitchen vent on the roof. I almost cried tears of joy. *They opened a McDonald's already? This is awesome,* I thought. I pulled into the parking lot with visions of a Quarter Pounder in my head, and all I saw was an unbelievable amount of police vehicles behind the building stretched out into a large open field. I walked inside and saw nothing but cops sitting around in the booths eating burgers and fries, and cops behind the counter doing the cooking. To be clear, there were no donut shops in town.

I asked what was going on and they told me that all the law enforcement strike teams in the area were staged and deployed from there. Here we were, begging for law enforcement for our location at city hall, and they had about a hundred cops hanging out at McDonald's.

I then asked who was in charge and was directed to a tent in the field to the rear of the building. I found a police chief from an out-of-town location sitting behind a desk, looking like Patton. Large and in charge. I introduced myself and told him what our mission was and where we were located. I told him that if they need any medical attention while here to come to city hall and we would take care of them.

He chuckled and told me, "We're just fine, we have our own docs here." The surprised look on my face was probably obvious, as he then told me that there were two emergency room physicians on site from a naval base just for them. After composing myself, I asked who was in charge of the ER docs and was told their commanding officer was in the next tent.

I stomped over to the next tent and found an admiral sitting behind a desk, telling war stories to someone else already in there. I introduced myself to him and told him what we were doing at city hall. I asked why there were two ER docs hanging out with a bunch of cops at McDonald's.

He told me that they were dedicated to taking care of any cops that may get injured while deployed.

Now, to be clear, I am not always politically correct. This was no different. I immediately got irritated and said, "For what? In case a cop chokes on a Big Mac? That is bullshit! They need to be with us at city hall where we've set up a crude field ER to take care of citizens that have been injured or are in need of medical care."

The admiral stood up and poked out his chest (which still did not extend past his belly) and asked me who I thought I was. I responded by telling him that we were the only team available in the city to provide any medical care, and word was getting out to the citizens that if they need help they should go to city hall. I again stated that they belonged at city hall with us.

In a deep and bossy voice, he told me that the ER docs were assigned to the cops, and that was where they needed to stay. Wrong answer. I snapped back that we were all there to take care of the local citizens affected by this hurricane, and the docs would be better suited to work with us providing medical care.

He was not happy that someone was questioning him and asked me, "Who are you to question what I'm using my physicians for?"

I responded with, "I am your worst nightmare. I do not care how much gold you have on your uniform. If you refuse to give me your docs, I will make sure it becomes public that you refused to let them assist in treating the locals when they needed it most. How do you spell your last name again?" He asked me if I was threatening him, and I told him that I was not—I was promising to make his life miserable if he didn't help us out. I reminded him again what we were all there for, and that our purpose should make the decision easy.

The admiral thought about it for a minute and agreed that the mission was to provide assistance to the locals. He actually became pleasant to talk to. He just didn't like someone questioning him. And yes, I was waiting for him to call on some cops to come and place me in cuffs and escort me out of their command post (playground).

He took me over to another tent that housed the two ER docs, introduced them to me, and explained that they would be coming with me back to city hall. Being ER docs, they were more than happy to oblige and provide the help needed.

Before I left, I went back to the police chief in charge of the strike teams there and asked for a cop to be assigned to city hall for our protection. I explained the wild animals and the possibility of there being issues as more people started coming out from shelters or returning to survey damages. He was more than happy to oblige, and he sent a deputy from another county over to us.

The two ER docs, a male and a female, were eager to help. They loaded up their gear and supplies and followed me over to city hall. When we arrived, I introduced them to the rest of our crew and gave them a tour of our wonderful facility. I showed them our waiting room made of motel chairs and our treatment area made of more chairs, along with cots and stretchers from our ambulances.

It was getting late and we offered to let the two docs sleep in the back of our ambulances to be more comfortable. We also said we would provide them dinner for helping us out. We grabbed one of the tables and two chairs from the ER that we snatched from the motel and set it up like a fancy dinner table in the middle of the field. We took a stretcher sheet and draped it over the table, placed a flashlight in the middle of the table facing up, since we didn't have any candles. We had some paper towels from the ambulance that we used for place settings along with some plastic utensils.

We escorted the two docs to the table with cut-up pieces of stretcher sheet draped over our arms like maître d's, pulled out their chairs for them, and told them we had a special dish for them. Another medic came over and placed some snacks and cookies in front of them and another poured water from a water bottle into a couple of paper cups. We asked if there was anything else we could get for them. They looked at us like we were nuts but chuckled and chowed down for a quiet, not-so-private dinner by flashlight.

Here Comes the Cavalry

The next morning, more people were walking around, and more were coming to our field ER for assistance. This included minor cuts, diabetics having issues since they had no medication, and the like. Nothing too busy, but word was getting out that medical care was available.

Later that morning a large box truck and another work truck from the county we work in showed up, and they tracked me down to ask where I wanted the tent. We had cleared out a large open section of field for a tent, but it was not big enough for the tent they brought, which was huge. We moved everything away, broke down our field ER, moved the ambulances, and made space for this huge tent that would normally be used for large public events held by the county.

The delivery crew set this thing up in no time. It was like watching the circus set up the big top. Well organized and methodical. In no time, we had a field hospital with an entrance, a waiting room, and a treatment area, all under a large tent, out of the sun or weather. It was awesome. I thanked them and they took off back home.

So we had a large field hospital with limited supplies. Now what? Word had gotten out around the county that we had set up our field ER, and other areas were sending people to us. As other agencies started showing up at staging, some were directed to us. Just as I started to worry about not having the proper supplies to provide the medical care needed, three vans showed up from a hospital in another part of the state. They asked me if we needed any medical supplies. I told them that was exactly what we needed, and they asked me where I wanted them placed.

I asked them to put the supplies over in a corner of the tent that was easily accessible, and they started unloading cases of IV fluids and tubing, suture sets, medication, bandages, dressings, and whatever else you would see in an ER. They asked what else we needed, and I told them common prescription meds, a small refrigerator with insulin, and casting material. They said they would be back with more supplies the next day. We had ourselves a working field ER. It was awesome.

They came back the next day with everything requested along with a few nurses. You cannot beat that kind of assistance. As word got out how bad the damage was, more people and organizations from around the country started to mobilize and provide help. It gave you goosebumps. Everyone wanted to help with no questions asked.

Just then, a large caravan of camouflage-painted semitrucks pulled up, and an officer with the National Guard asked me where I wanted the supplies. As I looked down the road and saw at least six trucks waiting in line, I asked what they had. He told me it was one truck with nonperishable food and the other trucks had nothing but bottled water in them. He also said he had a contingent of people to manage and distribute them.

I figured this would be a nightmare to have a distribution center at the same location as our field ER. It would be too congested. I look around, and about three blocks away I saw a water tower. It would be a good landmark for people to find as they sought out food and water. I asked if he would mind setting up the distribution center under the water tower, and he said to consider it done and left. It ended up being the primary distribution center for food, water, and clothes.

The next person to show up was someone from the Red Cross asking where he could set up a cooking station. *Right here, right now!* I thought. I asked him to set up on the other side of city hall. He had a large grill and a cooler truck full of food. He set up and never stopped cooking.

We quickly went from a totally devastated small city ghost town to a crazy busy metropolis in only a few days. It was mind-blowing how quickly things expanded and how much assistance continued to pour in. There were military helicopters flying around, long lines of semis and delivery trucks showing up to my location asking for direction, hospital personnel and equipment showing up nonstop, and eventually ambulances from other jurisdictions and fire engines from our county all staging at city hall.

The two ER docs that I stole from the cops went back to their original staging area, as one of the hospitals not only showed up with medical supplies and nurses, but with some ER docs. The huge county tent could be seen for miles, and from the air it looked like the epicenter of the entire operation. Two semis from Anheuser-Busch showed up and the driver asked me where I wanted him to unload his truck. I laughed and told him that he needed to unload it all in our tent and not tell anyone else about it. He laughed back at me and told me that it was just water. They had shut down their beer production line and started canning emergency drinking water.

Then two semis showed up from Walmart and asked me where they should drop off their load of supplies. He told me it was loaded with diapers, clothes, blankets, flashlights, etc. It became nonstop with truckloads of supplies, equipment, and people showing up to help. I was dumbfounded by the outpouring of humanity all at once.

I stayed there for the first two weeks and eventually had someone relieve me, the other medics, and the emergency management personnel. I got into the helicopter to be flown back home, and as we flew over city hall, I got goosebumps again. It looked like a bustling city from the air with traffic as far as you could see.

Unfortunately, the people that lived through the storm had to deal with its devastation for years to come. We never forgot the people that lived there and what they went through. That had a lot to do with why we did the toy drive for the kids the coming Christmas.

Chapter 10

RANDOM CRAZY STUFF

T his is a list of some random calls or situations that don't seem to fit anywhere else. Some are funny, some are screwed up, some are simply crazy.

❖ Okay, That's Not Good

In my early days working with EMS, we had one exterior compartment that held our drug box that had all of our advanced medical equipment for intubating, administering medications, starting IVs, and the like. It was locked and the keys were kept by the medic on the passenger side, as he would be running the next call. We would take turns after each call as to who would be in the back during transport and who was driving.

It was a busy shift during the day, and in the early evening we ran a medical call for a patient with abdominal pains. We took the typical gear inside the house that included the drug box, heart monitor, and oxygen. After evaluating the patient, we told him that we felt he should be taken to the ER for further evaluation. He refused to go anywhere even though we were convinced he had a serious medical issue going on. We spent a little more time talking to him, trying to convince him to go. He was not a happy person and gave us a hard time even though we told him it was for his own good.

A rescue crew from the fire department was on scene with us, and they were nice enough to carry our equipment back to the ambulance for us as we talked to the patient. Neither my partner nor I paid any attention to what was taken back, but after exhausting all efforts to get the patient to go to the ER, we had him sign a waiver and we left.

We ran a few more calls that evening that consisted of a car accident with minor injuries and another minor injury from a bicycle incident. None of these ended up being transported to the ER. Lucky for us, the calls seemed to have stopped, and it was time to try to get some sleep.

At around 3 a.m. we got a call for a possible cardiac arrest in the southern part of the county and about twenty minutes away from our station. Upon arrival, my partner got out of the driver's side and grabbed the heart monitor and oxygen as usual, as I went to retrieve the drug box from the locked cabinet to the rear of the passenger's side. The fire department was already on scene and confirmed it was a cardiac arrest and was administering CPR.

I grabbed the drug keys from my pocket and unlocked the cabinet door, and as it swung open, I had a look of horror on my face. Aloud I said to myself, "Okay, that's not good". I was staring into an empty compartment. Nothing. I quickly jumped inside the back of the ambulance, thinking we may have left it on the floor by the side entry door. Nothing. I typically don't panic about anything, but in this case I may have panicked a bit as my heartrate was crazy fast.

I looked inside the drug box compartment one more time as if it could just magically appear. Nope. No magic tonight. I walked rapidly toward the home where I could hear them counting out loud as they did compressions and paused to ventilate with the demand valve. The demand valve was how we ventilated in the '80s, and it had a distinctive sound as oxygen under pressure was forced into the endotracheal tube to ventilate the non-breathing patient. *Seven, eight, nine, ten, pssshhh* was all I heard as I walked into the room.

My partner, Juan, told them to stop compressions so he could look at the heart monitor. I stepped in and was just about to tell Juan that we had no drug box when he said, "That's it, we can stop now. We'll call it at 0335 hours." I know it sounds callous, but I was relieved that he just called it and pronounced the patient dead. With or without the drug box, it was obvious that it was not a viable patient.

I pulled my partner aside and told him about the missing drug box, and he had the same look as I had when I opened the cabinet. We then started to backtrack calls we ran to figure out when we had it last and when we used it. We did the paperwork and made the normal phone calls to the Medical Examiner's Office as we tried to pin down the drug box at the same time. No idea. We were physically and mentally tired from a busy shift, and our brains could not place it.

As we cleared the scene of the cardiac arrest patient, we got another call for an injury that we ended up transporting to the ER. Now we were concerned that if we got another call that required the advanced equipment and medications, we would be in a pinch and need to manually grab backup equipment from the inside drug cabinet.

As we were getting the ambulance back in service, it dawned on us that it must have been left at the scene of the patient that was refusing service earlier in the night. We called dispatch on the phone, told them what was going on, and asked for the patient's phone number. They placed us out of service for the time being, and we decided to call and see if the drug box was there. Most of us road medics got along with various dispatchers well, and they had our back on most occasions. She agreed to keep it to herself, and we said we'd let her know by phone when we were back in service.

We knew this grumpy guy would not be happy with us calling at 4 a.m., but it was a serious situation. We called and the grumpy guy answered the phone. No surprise there. We told him we thought we left our medical kit there and asked if he would mind looking. He quickly told me that it was not there. I begged him to just look by the front door for us. He put the phone down and went to look. He picked the phone back up and says, "Yeah, you left it here." I asked if he could hang on to it until we got there, as we would head that direction right away and were about thirty minutes out. I asked him to keep it inside until we got there. He told us he would, and we took off.

It was after 4 a.m. and there was no traffic, so we decided to drive fast to get there as soon as possible. Traveling down the primary north-south road, we got up to 80 mph, trying to get back into service as soon as feasible. About halfway there we heard a familiar voice over the radio. "Medic 6, Med-Com 4?" My partner and I looked at each other with worried faces. It was the Gestapo.

One of our supervisors was a pain in the rear and was always on top of everything that was going on. He went out of his way to catch people doing something wrong. He even stayed up all night to sneak around the county, looking for things to complain about. This night he was up, and he saw us drive by him in the opposite direction at a rapid pace.

"Medic 6, go ahead," was our reply.

He responded with, "Call me landline when available." Great, we got busted. Figures, it was one of those shifts anyway.

We got to the house and saw our bright-blue drug box sitting on the front porch under a shining porch light. Good thing there were no burglars in the area that night. That would have been some serious paperwork.

We got our box, headed back to the station, and got back into service. After reaching the station, we called our supervisor and said, "Hey, how you doing? What are you doing up so late?" He responded with, "Cut the crap. Where were you guys going so fast away from your station?" We decided it was best to come clean, so we told him the whole story. Believe it or not, he just laughed and said, "Have a good night, what's left of it." Everyone has to be in a good mood every once in a while.

Proud Puppies

My partner and I responded to a possible heart attack at a condo that we were familiar with, as there was a large elderly population that lived there. Arriving on scene, we found an elderly lady sitting on her couch complaining of chest pain and shortness of breath. She told us the pain was only a four on and scale of one to ten and that she just had minor shortness of breath. She had a history of hypertension and not much else.

We started an IV, put her on some oxygen, and placed the heart monitor on her. We moved her to the stretcher and had her lie down so we could do a 12-lead ECG to help determine if she was having a heart attack. She was wearing a silk robe, and her nails and hair were done meticulously. She took care of herself. I explained to her that we had to get to her chest area to apply the electrodes and that we would be careful to keep her covered. She suddenly whips open her nightgown and exposes her bare breasts to us, saying, "Go ahead, do what you gotta do."

The first thing we noticed was that her breasts were standing straight up and firm. She was around seventy-five years old, mind you. I immediately tried to cover her back up, telling her that I just needed to get underneath her breasts for the electrodes. She pulled her nightgown back open and said, "That's okay, I'm proud of these puppies. They cost me a lot of money back in the day. I'm not ashamed."

I covered her back up again and told her that was not necessary but that she had every right to be proud. Good for her. She joked with us all the way to the hospital, even though we diagnosed her as having a heart attack at the time. You just never know what's going to happen next.

Thanks, But No Thanks

When Dr. Kurley was the medical director for our EMS department, it was a fun time. We had an aggressive ER doc who demanded medics working under his license be just as aggressive when treating patients. When I say "aggressive," it's not in a mean way, it was delivering emergency medicine as needed, when needed, without any question. You could not be afraid to rapidly assess a patient and provide whatever emergency procedures were necessary. You do not have time to lollygag around, thinking about what should be done, you know what needs to be done and do it. That is aggressive emergency medicine.

Dr. Kurley made sure we all knew what we were doing, and our protocols reflected that aggressive attitude. A majority of our procedures were on standing order, and we were not required to call the ER for advice. A lot of EMS agencies around the country at the time were required to call in and get permission to administer various treatments. There were rare times that was necessary while working under his direction.

I'm emphasizing how prepared we were as an agency with Dr. Kurley as our medical director. He had faith in our abilities, though we were always being tested. Every time we brought a patient to the ER when Dr. Kurley was working, we would not only give a patient report, which was normal, we then got the third degree about the details of what was going on with the patient. He would ask us what our diagnosis was, what further treatment we thought was necessary while in the ER, and then explain the pathophysiology of what is going on with the patient and why. It was always a challenge, and it kept us on our toes. We loved the pressure and we learned from it.

From time to time, while on a medical call in the public arena, a good Samaritan would either already be on scene or show up while we were doing our assessment or treatment and provide input. And usually in a condescending way. A typical example would be working on a cardiac patient when someone comes up and identifies himself or herself as a doctor and starts barking orders. Usually, these orders made no sense either.

We all handled these "doctors" differently, but for the most part it ended up with us telling them that we were following our protocol and operated under our medical director's license. We could not take orders from anyone else. The only time this would be possible is if it were the patient's personal doctor giving direction. That's a different story, at least until we get them in the back of our ambulance, and then they belong to us.

To be clear, most of these well-wishers were actually doctors. Some not. What typically happened was when a bunch of ridiculous suggestions came out of their mouths, we'd then ask what type of doctor they might be. We have had podiatrists, dermatologists, family practice docs, orthopedic docs, and chiropractors show up and start bossing us around. A large majority of these specialists had no clue how to deal with emergency medicine. And it showed.

Some would just walk off after our little speech, some would stomp off mad because we made them look bad in front of their significant other, and some would start arguing with us. They all lost eventually, but we should not have our attention diverted to a hero wannabe and away from patient care.

For some reason, there was a spate of these run-ins that lasted about a year. It was getting old. Understand, most of these docs had no clue what our qualifications were and what skills we had. After numerous stories of this getting back to Dr. Kurley, he came up with a genius idea. It was a laminated card the size of a credit card that took the argument we always had and put it on paper. We lovingly called it our "Dr.-Go-to-Hell" card. We all carried a copy of this on our person for these run-ins. We would just hand it to them and ask them to read it.

It was typed out in a few paragraphs, thanking them for stopping by to offer their assistance, but saying we were working under the direction of our medical director and were not able to take orders from anyone other than him or the on-duty ER physician. It stated that if we needed assistance, we would ask, and it would be to hold an IV bag or carry some equipment for us. It was then signed by Medical Director Dr. Kurley.

These were awesome. By the time they finished reading it, we were typically ready to load up our patient and go, or they would just leave without saying anything. Genius.

Always Bee on the Lookout

That is not a typo in the title. My longtime EMS partner, Juan, was driving lights and siren to a call during one of the busiest times of the day as we came up to one of the busiest intersections in the area. It's always scary driving through these intersections with cars flying every which direction. As Juan inched his way into the intersection, I looked to the right and gave the typical, "Clear right!", letting him know traffic was clear on our right. This allowed him to concentrate on traffic to the left and in front.

After telling him it was clear, I heard the driver's door open, the siren's blare increasing tenfold inside the cab. Juan was nowhere to be seen. Now picture me sitting in the passenger seat of an ambulance in the middle of a busy intersection, siren blaring, lights flashing, and driver's door open—with no driver. It had to look as weird as it felt.

Finally I saw Juan running around the intersection like a wild man. I screamed at him to get in the ambulance and asked what he was doing. He yelled back, saying, "Is it gone?" I had no clue what he was talking about. He slowly came back to the cab, looked inside, and asked me if the bee flew away. I never saw a bee and didn't know what was going on. He looked on the dash and did not see anything, so he got back in and continued down the road to the call.

"What the heck was that all about?" I said. He proceeded to tell me that he was terribly allergic to beestings and they may very well kill him. We finished the run we were making, and I got more detail. When Juan was a young child, he was stung hundreds of times by a swarm of bees and had a severe reaction. He typically carried an EpiPen with him just for that. I learned something about my partner that I never knew before. And he didn't care what the situation was, his first priority would be to get away from those things.

Nothing is Sacred

During the time when I served as a training officer, the county was in the process of replacing a drawbridge with a taller bridge to allow most boat traffic underneath without any problems. The department I worked for had this bridge in our district and our response zone. The construction company had a few large barges with huge cranes mounted to them, along with a lot of heavy equipment and material scattered around the causeway.

The neighboring training officer who worked for the department on the other side of the bridge and I decided we would preplan for any construction incidents that may occur during this two-year project. We both had fire/rescue boats, both had paramedics, and our departments had technical rescue training and equipment. After a two-hour walk-through of the site by the job superintendent, we determined the biggest issues we would face would be a worker injured while out on a barge, a worker falling in the water, or a crane collapse.

We spent a month planning a three-day training session for all three shifts that included all the scenarios we were concerned with. We had water rescue manikins in the water, we had rescue manikins on the barge and down a scuttle hole, down inside the barge. We had a section of crane that was lying on site to use to determine the best way to deal with either lifting or cutting the frame if it fell onto a vehicle or into the water. It all went well, and we all learned from the training.

Just weeks after the training, the tones dropped for a call at the construction site at the causeway for a crane collapse. At first, I could not believe what I just heard. It took a second to sink in. I jumped in my vehicle and raced to the scene along with an engine and rescue from our department and an engine and rescue from the neighboring department. We both had our rescue boats on standby.

Instead of the crane coming down over the roadway as we trained for, it fell parallel to the road and into the construction material storage area. As I pulled up, the job superintendent told me that there was one injury and one dead. The worker who had injuries was stable and transported to the hospital by EMS. We confirmed the dead worker after the superintendent showed us where he was located.

This poor guy was sitting in the port-a-john, going to the bathroom when the crane landed on top of his head and crushed him to death. After crushing him and the port-a-john, the crane fell to the side, so there was no extrication needed. All that was needed was the medical examiner.

I Hate Snakes

For all you reptile lovers out there, I apologize in advance. There is absolutely nothing good about snakes. I am afraid of them and I hate them. I have no idea why or what triggered it, but maybe it's because these things move about with no legs in the underbrush, unseen until you step on one, and then they bite you. Maybe it's just me.

While working a rather large wildland fire as a division supervisor, I was responsible for the tactics and strategies of containing this fire in a defined geographic area. I was in a staff vehicle and communicating with multiple brush trucks and a forestry tractor. Keeping track of the crews and the status of the fire takes your full attention.

I stationed myself in an open area not far from a residential structure and barn that we were protecting from the fire. I asked for one of the forestry tractors to cut a line in front of the house to slow down any fire that got that far. There was a lot of sand and low brush around the house and it was very dry. It would not take much for the fire to move quickly through this brush and threaten the house.

As I watched and directed the tractor in front of the house, I saw objects flying off the tracks of the dozer as he went by rather quickly; the fire was starting to move fast. He wanted to make at least three passes to make the fire break wide enough to be effective.

As he came by for his second pass, I walked in to get a closer look at what was flying off the back of the track and I saw that it was a swarm (pit, nest, whatever) of rattlesnakes flying in the air. Of course, they would be moving somewhere fast to get out of the way of the dozer and the fire. It made sense to me that they should come my way in the clearing.

I screamed like a little girl, ran back to my staff vehicle, and climbed on the roof of my SUV. I had my radio in hand as I talked to the other crews, but I was not getting down until I got an all clear. The forestry firefighter laughed at me but kept going. When a brush truck came back out to my location to get directions for filling his water tank, they saw me on the roof of my SUV. They looked at me like I was crazy. They told me I was not going to be able to see into the woods any better from that location.

I told them there were rattlesnakes all over the place and I was not getting down. They laughed at me as well. They took off for water after I gave them directions to the water source, then went back to the firefight. I stayed on the roof of my vehicle until we had the fire wrapped up and I had some of the crews tell me the ground was clear. I hate snakes.

Is It Rude to Wear Gloves?

During my time in the ER during the late '70s and '80s, and when I started at the fire department, then EMS, we never wore medical gloves for much of anything. It may sound crazy to some in today's world, but it would be rude to some patients if we wore gloves. Some would actually get offended. It was rare to wear a mask during an emergency run or even in the ER. I threw away more masks due to them being damaged in the med box than I did from wearing them.

The HIV/AIDS virus in the early '80s is what actually caused EMS and hospital personnel to start wearing medical gloves when handling patients, especially those that were bleeding. Up to that point we would have blood covering our entire arms and hands from working a trauma event and didn't think anything of it.

During most of my career, we did not have access to safety needles that would protect medical personnel from getting stuck. IV needles that either retract or get covered up are the norm now. It was not out of the

179

ordinary to get stuck by an IV needle that was used the shift before, placed inside the med box, and was forgotten about. It was lazy but not unheard of. Some medics would stick the needle into the cushion of the bench seat after starting an IV to keep from getting stuck, just to expose the next shift to contaminated needles.

Then the situation turned around and HIV/AIDS patients felt like they were being singled out by us wearing gloves when HIV/AIDS was suspected. So, to make it politically correct and simplified, it was decided that we should wear gloves for all patients.

Today, emergency responders and hospital staff have gone through hell dealing with the worldwide coronavirus pandemic. It had to be difficult dealing with the entire situation and being exposed all the time, plus the stress of personal family issues relating to the pandemic itself.

During my career, I saw many viruses wreak havoc on the medical system. I mentioned HIV/AIDS in the early '80s. Other diseases we had to deal with included tuberculosis outbreaks in nursing homes, common flu outbreaks, various strains of hepatitis, Severe Acute Respiratory Syndrome (SARS), and H1N1 or the swine flu. There will be a never-ending flow of various diseased or viruses for years to come, and emergency responders will still be there when you call.

"Just Don't Get Pulled Over"

As a hazmat tech, I spent a number of years teaching a class with a bomb squad tech at the sheriff's office about handling meth labs and patients on meth. We had a blast. I had my own meth lab. It was a truckload of props, and for each class I would set up multiple labs that went from the basic homemade setup to the extensive chemistry lab. Most of the precursors were empty containers used as props. It would also include booby traps that were common for labs, and paraphernalia used for abusing meth.

It usually makes for a good hands-on experience of what you would see if someone were either making meth for themselves or on a large-scale basis. We also discussed how patients strung out on meth may act, and how to treat them.

The deputy I taught with always joked about me traveling with my meth lab to classes. It's against the law to be in possession of all the equipment and precursors together. He told me it was fine, just don't get pulled over. I told him that I had him on speed dial just in case that happened. He would laugh and tell me that he would deny knowing me and let me rot in jail for a day before he got me out. Nice. But you must understand I would have it coming. I played a practical joke on him during one of our classes that embarrassed the heck out of him. You heard that right. I pranked a bomb technician. Probably not the smartest thing I ever did. He just promised to pay me back one day.

A firefighter who was also a hazmat technician took one of my classes and asked if he could use my presentation and the meth lab to put the class on for his guys at his department. I had no problem with that at all and gave him what he needed. As I loaded part of my meth lab into the back of his old, rusted-out, falling apart pickup truck, I jokingly told him, "Just don't get pulled over." He asked why and I told him that it was illegal to have this material, but if he was pulled over, to make sure to tell them he's teaching a class.

Sure enough, his truck broke down and he pulled over to the side of the road. He called for a tow truck. As the tow truck driver walked up to the truck to assess the situation, he saw the meth lab material in the bed of his truck. He asked the driver what that was all about and was told he was a firefighter teaching a class.

The tow truck driver told him that he was not allowed to tow the pickup and was required to call law enforcement. Any explanation did not matter. A deputy pulled in behind him to see what the issue was. Of course, it was a deputy he didn't know. He showed the deputy his fire department ID and explained the class again. The deputy asked for the fire chief's phone number so he could check it out.

The deputy called the chief and confirmed he was a firefighter for him and was teaching a class. He explained the same thing to him that I did. It was illegal to have possession of these items. The tow truck moved his vehicle and he put on the class. I'm glad he was the one who got pulled over and not me. If I'd made a phone call to the bomb tech, I would have been laughed at and sitting in the county jail for a while.

Mr. Hoover

This was one of the most bizarre calls I ever made and the most embarrassing for a patient. We responded to a personal injury at a mobile home park that had mostly elderly residents. As we walked in the door, we saw a gentleman in his '80s sitting at a small metal kitchen table. He was completely naked, and there was a pool of blood at his feet. A Hoover vacuum cleaner sat on the living room floor, but there was no hose connection to be seen. He looked disheveled and was slurring his speech. It may have had to do with the bottle of vodka that was on the table—and there was no glass to drink from.

He had a phone in his hand, trying to talk to someone, but it was difficult to understand what he was saying. As I got closer to investigate the origin of the blood, I looked above the clots of blood dripping down from his penis. The tip of his penis was mangled like hamburger and there was a baggie tied in a tight knot at the base. I looked over at my partner and said, "This is your call, I believe."

Since the bleeding had mostly stopped, we did a full body exam and found no other injuries or problems. We loaded him onto the stretcher, covered him with a sheet, and moved him to the ambulance. And then it was my turn, and he was my patient.

While riding to the hospital I asked questions to find out what happened. He told me the story. For some reason he had decided to place his penis inside the suction end of the vacuum cleaner, not realizing there were turning blades just inside to create a vacuum. As he pushed his penis inside, it tore it to shreds. It started bleeding and he couldn't stop it with paper towels, so he grabbed a baggie and tied it in a knot, like a tourniquet.

He told me that he drank almost an entire bottle of vodka before he called his wife to tell her what happened and that he would need to go to the hospital. He was known from that point on as Mr. Hoover.

Cannot Take the Heat

A call that I had never run before—or since, which was due to making a bad decision—was probably part of why certain products have so many safety warnings on them. A gentleman in his 30s had been suffering from back pain for a long time and tried multiple solutions to make it better. He was frustrated that taking over-the-counter pain meds did not fix the problem, and that heat and ice was temporary.

A day before he had to go to work, he was concerned that his back would be so bad he would have to call out again. He decided he would take some borrowed prescription pain meds and placed a heating pad under his back before he went to sleep.

The pain meds knocked him into a deep sleep and the heating pad was set on high. The next morning his wife nudged him to tell him it was time to get up for work. He didn't move. She shook him and got no response and noticed he wasn't breathing. She called 911.

When we arrived, we found this gentleman lying supine in bed and had the typical mottled look from being dead for some time. We got the history of what happened the night before from the wife. We declared him dead after a quick assessment showed he had been dead for a while.

We rolled him to the side and saw that his back had second-degree burns in the shape of the heating pad. I was not aware they could get this hot, but he laid on it all night without moving. Of course, his wife was hysterical and had a difficult time dealing with what just happened. It was not a pretty site. The Medical Examiner's Office wanted to come to the scene, so we waited for them and talked to the wife outside to keep her occupied.

The medical examiner called us the next shift to tell us that the heat damaged some internal organs, causing his death. His internal organs heated up to such a degree overnight that they stopped functioning. He had never seen anything like it in his thirty years as a medical examiner.

Chapter 11

YOU NEVER KNOW

I have always stood by the mantra that you treat everyone with the same level of respect and professionalism, no matter their background or status. If you treat the wealthy CEO of a large company that lives in a luxurious community different than the homeless guy living under the bridge, you are negligent in your duties. It is the right thing to do. There are times when you have no idea who you're dealing with, and it should not matter.

No matter what area you provide emergency assistance to, there will always be someone out there who may surprise you with their status. Granted, if you work in Los Angeles, you'll probably run into celebrities or famous people more often than in a small town in the Midwest. Keep in mind that even in small towns you may run into influential people or those with an interesting background. I will outline a few calls that surprised my partner and me.

Of Mice and Men

I responded to a possible Signal 7 in a hidden older section of town on the river. The house sat on the river with a breathtaking view, but the neighborhood was well hidden from the main road. We had never been back there before.

Upon arrival, we walked in with all our equipment, just in case it was a viable patient that we had to initiate treatment for. A pleasant elderly lady met us at the door and walked us into the bedroom to show us her husband, who had passed away. She told us it was expected. At the time, we would pronounce someone dead, document a time of death and contact the Medical Examiner's Office with detailed information so they could determine the patient's disposition.

As I sat at the kitchen table gathering information from the wife of the deceased, I looked up and noticed some pictures on the wall. I asked if that was her and her husband along with another couple. She said it was, and that they were all good friends. I asked about the pictures because standing next to them was Walt Disney and his wife. Yeah, the guy who made a fortune promoting a mouse at an amusement park.

Of course, I had to ask how they were friends with them, and I got an interesting story along with more pictures of the event. While Mr. Disney was in the process of building his theme park around a mouse, he was looking for a tree that would be fitting for the attraction that mimicked a family treehouse. He traveled the world searching for the right look, and lo and behold while traveling down the river next to their house, he saw a tree in this lady's backyard.

He found the house and introduced himself and asked if he could use their tree for the model he was needed. She said they took about a month to take pictures of every single branch from every conceivable angle of this entire tree. They then transformed this into what is now the tree at Mr. Disney's attraction. An exact duplicate. She said over time the two couples became good friends and traveled and took trips together. I never thought our little area of the world would have ties like that.

Pretty Sharp for an Old Man

Running calls to nursing homes is not typically on the top of the list of exciting runs to make. It can be depressing and typically falls into the category of a fall or a long-term illness that has gotten out of hand. Nonetheless, when you are of the age to be in a nursing home, you may have a medical history of some sort. Sometimes it's a challenge, other times it's routine.

Responding one day to one of our nursing homes for a transfer to the hospital for direct admit turned out to be remarkably interesting. In the early days at EMS, we would be responsible for these calls. Usually, the doctors' orders did not involve much from EMS other than transporting them, and this particular location was an almost forty-minute haul to the hospital, allowing time to talk to the patient.

I rode in the back with this gentleman in his early 90s and we carried on a conversation that was intriguing. Mr. Wiley talked politics, military strategy, and his personal feelings about women in the military or the workforce. He was old school but sharp as a tack on every subject he discussed. He was also very opinionated and stood his ground on every matter. I had a blast talking to this guy and was impressed as to how sharp and educated he seemed, even at his age.

As we dropped him off in his room at the hospital, we said our goodbyes and he thanked us for being so friendly and caring. He then asked us to stop in to see him next time we were at the nursing home, as he would have something for us. We agreed and parted ways.

About a month later we went to the same floor of the same nursing home for a fall. As we stepped into the room, we realized it was the same gentleman, Mr. Wiley. He had fallen from his bed to the tile floor and fractured his hip. He recognized my partner and me and welcomed us back with a chuckle. He was in a lot of pain but very cooperative and understanding. We gently moved his frail body onto a scoop stretcher that minimized the amount of movement to get him immobilized and on the stretcher. We started an IV and administered pain medication to make it tolerable.

As we were rolling him out of his room on the stretcher, he suddenly yelled for us to wait, stretching out his arms and grabbing the door frame like a dog avoiding a bath. We froze, thinking we'd jostled him and caused him some pain, and we apologized. He told us that he was fine, but he had forgotten to give us our gift from the last time we saw him. We told him there was no need for that and that our priority is getting him out of pain and to the hospital.

He insisted that we go into his nightstand and grab our gifts before we left. So, we found the bag he mentioned and placed it under his pillow on the stretcher and headed to the hospital. He told us that he would sign it for us when he got better and to bring it with us the next trip to the nursing home. We kept him as comfortable as possible and gave some more pain medication while en route. I told him to relax, and we would try to avoid any potholes in the road on the way.

After we dropped him off in the ER, we got the ambulance ready for the next call and left. Sadly, we knew that a fractured hip for someone that age was not a good thing. We were a little bummed out since he was a really nice guy who we got to know a little bit. That was a rare scenario where we get to know our patients at all. We shoved the bag into a compartment and forgot about it.

A few weeks later we went back to the same nursing home for a routine transfer, and while we were there, we thought about Mr. Wiley. Before we went into the patient's room on the same floor, we went a few doors down and poked our heads inside Mr. Wiley's room to see a freshly cleaned room with no pictures or personal belongings, and a freshly made bed. My partner and I looked at each other with sad expressions, and a nurse told us that he died at the hospital.

It was upsetting to hear that, but we were not surprised. We went on to the other room and completed our transfer. On the way back to the station we started talking about Mr. Wiley and how nice he was and how sharp he was at his age. That reminded us that we never looked inside the bag we placed in a cabinet in the back of the ambulance.

We got out the bag and opened it to find two copies of a paperback book. The book was written by Mr. Wiley. This made sense as to him wanting to sign it for us. It appeared to be about politics and military strategy. That sounded like a familiar topic from before. I flipped to the back of the book and saw a picture of three men on the back. The picture was of four-star General Wiley standing between President Eisenhower and General George Patton as he received the Congressional Medal of Honor.

Now it all made sense. We were in the presence of a historical figure who was tough all the way to the end. You never know who you will come across in this business. We were humbled.

World Champion

Sadly, we rarely get to know a patient's background or history, since we're with them for such a short time and they're typically not in the mood to talk about themselves when they're being treated for a medical issue. We rarely learn the outcome of a patient we drop off at the ER, never mind the personal side of someone.

Again we responded to a Signal 7 at a residence, and while talking to the surviving spouse, I noticed a number of plaques hanging on the wall in the living room with large belts that had large ornate buckles on them. I look closer and they denoted "Lightweight World Champion" in boxing. There were at least four of these. I asked the spouse about them, and she told me that her husband was a world champion boxer for many years.

When we got back to the station, we looked up his name and sure enough, this guy was a big deal back in his day. According to his wife, he was a fighter to the very end, as she expected him to be. It always amazes me how someone of great accomplishment moves to an obscure place in the country and lives out their lives in peace without all the stress or fanfare. It would have been nice to know he was around, but at the same time it was great to know that he was able to retire and enjoy life without all the attention.

Chapter 12

DARK SENSE OF HUMOR

Those who work in the public safety arena are known to have a strange sense of humor. Some would say it's a dark sense of humor. I believe it's in the eye of the recipient. This sense of humor is due to two things: time and exposure. There are times when things are just not happening, and it may be boring for a bit during a shift. In addition to that, the things we are exposed to throughout a career makes you a little darker and even more numb to things civilians would consider horrible. I believe this sense of humor helps you deal with both.

I will mention most, not all, of the crazy things I witnessed or was involved in during my time. I will also mention that we were not as politically correct then as we are in today's world. Some of these stories may offend you and some may seem cruel. I believe it got us through some tough times, and today there is more angst over what may offend others. We have lost a lot of that sense of humor. You are welcome to skip this chapter or to laugh along with the crazy antics.

Gotcha!

Hanging around a firehouse, you will quickly find that there are a lot of people busting each other's chops. Lots of good-natured fun to pass the time or get back at someone who pulled a prank on you.

Fried Eggs, Anyone?

Typically, while you are at the fire station you hang your fire coat on one of the handles on the cab of the engine with your helmet hanging on top of that and your boots by the doorstep of the truck. When a call comes in, you kick off your shoes, step into your fire boots, throw your jacket on, and jump in the truck along with your helmet and gloves.

It was not uncommon payback to place a raw egg inside someone's fire boots near the toe and just wait. Sometimes it was a day or two later, but when they stepped into their boots, they would crack the eggs and have a great gooey mess at their feet while fighting a fire or other emergency. It was always a hassle to clean your boots after that, but it was good payback.

You Rang?

While working as a county EMS paramedic, I was still a volunteer with a fire department in the same zone I covered. We would be invited to have dinner with the guys at the fire station at times, and of course the zingers would start. You always had to be one up on someone else.

Outside, next to the main entrance, was a "night buzzer" for anyone who had an emergency after the doors were closed and locked for the night. It looked like a normal doorbell, but it made an obnoxious sound when you pushed it in, and it buzzed for as long as you held it in. This was to make sure the crew would hear it if they were sleeping.

There were many nights when we would run a medical call, and after transporting to the hospital we would drive by the station on the way back to our EMS station. We would pull onto the ramp just outside the bay doors and aim the ambulance toward the road with the engine running and in drive. The passenger would jump out, press the emergency buzzer, and jam a penny in the side to keep it in. We would then run to the ambulance and take off. It would cause the buzzer to go off continuously until they took the penny out. Of course, they knew who did it, but it was worth the effort.

Can You Check My Blood Pressure?

It doesn't take long for payback, and it's not like we didn't deserve it. I happened to be stationed at a free-standing EMS building just at the base of a busy bridge. We were typically busy at that station and were gone quite a bit.

After coming back from a call just before noon, we got a knock on our station door. When we answered it, an elderly gentleman asked if we could take his blood pressure since he was taking medication for high blood pressure and wanted to keep track of it. Of course, we had no problem doing that and invited him in, took his blood pressure, and wrote it down for him. After a few minutes of friendly chat, he thanked us and left. Not five minutes went by and there was a knock on the door again.

Another couple asked if we could take their blood pressure. We happily obliged and made small talk, and they left. Well, this continued through lunchtime and after the fifth person stopped to have their blood pressure taken, we asked if someone told them to come by. They told us nobody had talked to them, but they saw the huge sign outside the station and thought they would take advantage of it.

We walked outside, and on the outside wall facing bridge traffic, there was a huge (and I mean *huge*—4'x16' banner) stating "FREE BLOOD PRESSURE CHECKS. TODAY ONLY." We doubled over laughing and realized we had been paid back for messing with their night bell. All in good fun, and we met some nice people.

My Patrol Car's Possessed

As I mentioned earlier, everyone from fire, law enforcement, and EMS all worked together and relied on each other many times. We all became good friends as well. For a large county there were a lot of small fire departments, not very many EMS ambulances, and even fewer law enforcement available to cover such a large area. We dealt with city police, the county sheriff, and highway patrol primarily.

One trooper would come by the station for a bathroom break or lunch break and he was welcomed. In the beginning of my career, it was not uncommon to have one state trooper cover the entire county by himself. The sheriff's office would typically only have three deputies covering the entire county as well. One north, one central, and one south. They were busy and typically ran most calls alone. They felt some relief if we happened to show up, depending on the call, and they knew we had their back.

Trooper Rick Shake would come in, bust chops, and go use the bathroom. He would usually take off his gun belt with tons of gear on it and place it on a bed just outside the bathroom. Of course, we would move it and he would come out confused as to what he did with it. We even put a banana in his gun holster one time. He was ticked off with us for messing with his gun. I get it, serious stuff, but we were professionals.

After laughing it off and pledging payback (there was a lot of that), he would go out to his car to leave, and when he turned on the ignition, all of his emergency lights would come on, the siren would blare in yelp, the radio volume was as high as it goes, the heater was on full blast, the windshield wipers were on full speed, and his four-way flashers were on. We would always get a warning with a chuckle and a reminder that he knows what vehicles we all drive. He drove around all day by himself, so he needed the humor break. We all became good friends as well.

The Bunk Room from Hell

When stationed at a firehouse with seven crewmembers, there are a lot of practical jokes going around. We all had to share one bathroom and shower that you had access to from the large bunkroom. The bunkroom was exceptionally long and narrow. There was enough room for five beds on each side with ample room to walk between them. The beds were all metal framed beds that were donated by a local nursing home. They'd just bought new mattresses to go on top.

The Ice Storm

A couple of common and often repeated pranks involved late night showers. While someone was in this small shower with a shower curtain, someone would fill a five-gallon bucket with ice from the ice machine, then fill it with water and let it sit for a few minutes. Someone would sneak into the shower on his tiptoes, being careful not to be heard, and would dump the ice bath over their head and run back into the bunk room and jump into bed like nothing happened. Of course, the loud scream from the bathroom woke everyone up, so we were all curious as to what happened. You would eventually see a very mad face poke around the corner swearing to get payback or someone in the bunk room laughing and admitting they got caught. All in fun.

Splish Splash

After everyone went to bed (or pretended to be asleep), every once and a while someone would place saran wrap tightly around the bowl of the toilet, close the lid, and sneak back to bed. This was good whenever there was one of the crew who had a routine of getting up in the middle of the night to urinate. So, half-asleep, a member would stagger into the bathroom in the middle of the night while everyone else was pretending to be asleep. We sounded like a bunch of little girls on a sleepover giggling about what was about to happen. Like clockwork, we would all hear the guy screaming and cursing at the top of his lungs, calling us all names I can't mention here. And of course, nobody had a clue who would do such a thing. At times it meant they required a new shower, and they had to keep an eye out for pranks while taking a shower. Makes for a nice, relaxing evening.

Scrubbing Bubbles

If you haven't figured it out yet, it was a challenge to take a shower in this firehouse. The best part was you never knew who was going to prank someone and when. Another crowd favorite was when a crewmember naively placed his shampoo, soap, towel, etc. in the shower to get everything ready. All it took was for an emergency run that didn't require everyone to respond and it was free game. One would replace the shampoo with some prank shampoo that turns dirty black as it foams up. The more you scrubbed it in, the more it foamed up into black bubbles. Lesson one, *never* leave your shower amenities alone and leave the station.

Dress to Impress

This same crazy firehouse just so happened to be right next door to a popular nightclub with music, drinking, women, fights, etc. There were parking spaces that nosed right up to the fire station, and the station also conveniently had an exit door right into the parking area where everyone walked by to get into the club. On a Friday or Saturday night we would line up folding chairs on the apron and enjoy the free entertainment.

Rule number two was to never walk by this door in your underwear after taking a shower or changing into a jumpsuit for runs at night. If this was seen, there was a silent sign language among everyone else that it was door time. At least three guys would nonchalantly walk near the guy in his underwear standing by the door. One would quickly swing open the door to the outside while the other one would grab him in a bear hug and another grabbed his legs. They'd carry him outside into the parking lot. The door automatically locked from the outside, so you couldn't get in that way. Someone else would make sure all the bay doors were down and other entrances were locked.

197

You now had one of the crew walking around all these night club attendees in their underwear, banging on the door, screaming for us to let him back in, running around the station trying to find a way in, and threatening all of us. We would usually let it go on for a few minutes, or until we got an emergency call and had to leave.

Chainsaw Massacre

We took the pranks to such a level that you would even get payback on other shifts that just so happened to mess with you. Yep, some would come in on their days off just to prank someone at the station. It took some planning and dedication, but it was one of the best.

You always had at least one guy who had a key to the side door I previously mentioned. At least three, if not four guys who were off duty would come wearing creepy-looking Halloween masks, all carrying chainsaws (with no chains), between 1 a.m. and 4 a.m. when they were in a deep sleep. They would quietly open the door, start their chainsaws, and run around the bunkroom, holding the chainsaws up to the crew sleeping and yelling at them. They would all wake up screaming like little girls, crawling backward on the bed to get away and generally freaking out. They would then all leave quickly at the same time, run to a car that was hidden behind a neighboring building, and leave. The terrified guys would never have a clue who the attackers would be as they had masks on, and no car was ever seen. They would spend weeks trying to figure it out and would never know who did it.

Nice Smile

Typically, the best practical joke is done without the recipient having any idea who was behind it. And most of the time they'll never know.

A particular lieutenant was mean to his crew and didn't treat them with much respect. This played into why he was the butt of a lot of practical jokes without anyone ratting out the instigator or accomplices.

An engineer/driver on our shift had a partial upper denture he wore due to his two upper teeth being knocked out when he was in his teens. He was always taking them out and misplacing them, and we would take them and hide them from him from time to time.

One of the guys was cooking chili for the entire crew in a huge pot on the stove. As was demanded, the lieutenant had his designated seat, and he expected his food to be placed on the table before he showed up in the dining room. As we started to eat, the engineer started complaining how he'd lost his dentures again. Of course, we gave him a hard time about losing them on a routine basis.

In a rare moment, the lieutenant took a bite of his chili and complimented the chef for making such a great chili. The chef thanked him, and the conversation went on around the table. When the lieutenant took a third spoonful of chili, lo and behold, he let out a few curse words while staring at his spoon, looking at dentures covered in chili. He dropped his spoon into his bowl, jumped up from his chair, and demanded to know who put the dentures in his chili.

Of course, we were all just as shocked and guessed out loud that the engineer, who would typically steal a sample of any food being cooked during the day, took a bite of chili, and lost his plate in the pot without knowing it. The lieutenant did not believe it for a minute and demanded to know who put this upper in his bowl. We all denied any knowledge of who was behind it and were all laughing at the same time. It was pretty funny. The lieutenant stormed off without eating, we all had extra chili, and the engineer found his dentures.

Everyone was happy, except for the lieutenant. But he was never happy.

Hey, Beth, Are These Yours?

Karma is a bitch. Throughout my career, I have participated or played many practical jokes on many coworkers, and eventually it comes back to bite you. If I were keeping count, I think I'm still ahead though.

I don't believe I'm alone in there being times when you wish you could swallow your words back as soon as you say them. There are times when you speak before you think. Yeah, that's probably more common than most of us want to admit. This was a situation where I made a really stupid comment before thinking. I must admit this was one of the best practical jokes played, even though this time I was the recipient.

Typically, when we go to work our twenty-four-hour shift, we pack a rather large bag full of stuff to last through the shift. It would include a ditty bag with toiletries, a change of underwear and socks, a towel, maybe a spare uniform shirt, etc. When you get home after a shift, you go through your bag and toss some clothes and your towel in the wash, replace things you used, and restock for the next shift.

One morning after getting home and going through my bag, I found a pair of female thong panties under my towel. I was confused as to how they got into my bag (and they were not mine, by the way), and the first thing that came out of my mouth was, "Hey, Beth, are these yours?"

Think about that for a minute. Go ahead. Well? Pretty stupid statement, huh? The second I said it I regretted it and reprimanded myself. What if they weren't my wife's? Yeah, not too smart.

And of course, my wife is always inquisitive about everything and can't stand not knowing about something. Her immediate reply was, "Is what mine?" Now, normally she would not answer me so quickly, or not at all. But this time, she came right back. Imagine that.

"Never mind," was my response back to her. And of course, she came to the bedroom to see what I was talking about. Not looking good, huh? "Is what mine?" she asked. I held up the panties and asked her if these were hers, thinking they got stuck to the towel in the dryer.

She grabbed them out of my hand and immediately told me that they were not hers and demanded to know who they belonged to. Of course, I had no idea who they belonged to. I quickly thought about how they could have gotten there, and I recalled messing with a few guys the shift before. I started laughing nervously and told my wife it had to be payback for a practical joke I played on someone at work.

She was not laughing. She was mad. I finally convinced her it was payback for a particular joke I played on someone, and then she decided to be my partner in a revenge attack. She was used to me playing practical jokes, so it made sense.

I decided it was Lt. Kizzy, who I played a joke on the shift before and figured it was payback. Our little scheme was going to be epic. Or so I thought. Beth and I were friends with one of the dispatchers, and we told her what was going on and how we wanted to get him back. She thought it was a great idea and was in.

This lieutenant would come into dispatch each morning at a particular time each shift, and this time the dispatcher would call Beth and let her know. While he was there, Beth called her and explained that she found the panties in my bag and got so mad that she had kicked me out of the house and was talking about divorce. As she relayed the fake story, the dispatcher played it up with gasps and OMG comments loud enough that the lieutenant could hear the one side of the phone conversation. This lieutenant was very nosy, so it was an easy hook.

When the dispatcher hung up, the lieutenant asked a million questions about the phone call. The dispatcher looked visibly upset and told him what was supposedly happening. We were trying to make him feel bad for the practical joke of messing with me like that. He came off as concerned about what was going on and left.

I saw him later in the shift and he asked me if everything was okay. I told him that someone was messing with me and it went so far that it to cause problems at home. I was trying to get him to feel bad and apologize. He told me he would help me find out who did it. I told him in an angry tone that he knew who did it and that he needed to apologize. He was perplexed and got defensive and then left.

He came back to my station to see me later in the day and stirred the pot again, making snide remarks and getting me riled up. This time it started to get real. He told me that if I was unable to keep things right at home, I shouldn't bring it to work. He then left me again. Now I was really upset and mad at his attitude.

A full shift later (three days) another medic came to me with a smirk on his face and asked if I found my little surprise. Of course, I had no idea what he was talking about. He asked again if I ever found anything odd in my overnight bag. Then it clicked. Okay, I can be a little slow at times. To clarify, I asked if he was the one who put the panties in my bag. He started laughing and admitted to it and was disappointed he didn't hear anything about it.

Just then, the lieutenant came into the station and he started laughing as well. I came to find out that when he left after seeing me the first time that day, after I confronted him, he ran into the other medic who actually messed with me and told him the story. That was why he came back to wind me back up, since he knew the real story and realized I was trying to pin it on him.

To summarize, not only did I get paid back for playing a practical joke on someone, but I also got a double whammy by getting a joke pulled on me while I thought I was pulling a joke back on them. Bottom line is sometimes practical jokes can go too far and have the potential to cause serious problems. I don't regret pulling any of the practical jokes I played on anyone or any that were pulled on me, it just needs to be kept toned down at times.

"It Was a Wonderful Flight"

I had the most fun working with Juan. I think I mentioned already that we were always in sync with each other and worked seamlessly together. This included horsing around.

During the early part of my time with EMS, we were responsible for transferring patients from one facility to another. Typically, it would involve transferring a nursing home patient to the hospital for admission by their doctor if they were having medical problems. Later on, they had separate crews and private companies take care of those calls so more ambulances would be available for emergency calls.

The units we worked out of were either a van chassis with a van cab and box on the rear frame or a pickup truck cab with a separate box on the back. The unit I worked on the most was the latter. To communicate between the driver and the attendant in the rear, there was a radio system that allowed the driver to monitor all sound in the rear, in case the medic in the rear needed something, or there was a pressing issue they needed help with. In return, the driver also had the ability to talk into a microphone, allowing their voice to come over a loudspeaker in the patient compartment. It allowed us to talk back and forth.

During one such transfer of a dementia patient, I was driving, and Juan was attending in the rear. We were in a good mood that day and were having a lot of fun. I know that sounds weird to some civilians, but it can't be doom and gloom all day every day. You would not last.

Remember, this was an elderly dementia patient who had to go to the hospital for some x-rays and lab work. He was otherwise doing fine and was conversing with Juan all the way to the hospital. Nice guy.

I decided to get on the loudspeaker and spouted off, "Good afternoon, ladies and gentlemen, this is your captain speaking. Welcome to Flight 123, nonstop from the nursing home to the hospital. The weather ahead is good, therefore we should have a smooth and uneventful flight. Now sit back and relax." Juan was losing his mind; he laughed out loud. The patient looked over at Juan and said, "Is he a good pilot?" Juan assured him the pilot was a good one.

About halfway to the hospital I continued with, "Folks, we have reached our cruising altitude of 20,000 feet, so I'm going to switch the seat belt sign off. Feel free to move about as you wish. If you look out of your right side, you'll see the Atrium high-rise, a beautiful site to see, and if you look out your left window, you'll see a new condominium project under construction."

A few minutes later I came back with, "Ladies and gentlemen, we will be arriving at our destination shortly, so make sure your seat belts are fastened and the table in front of you is stowed away."

As we arrived at the ER entrance, I got on the intercom one more time. "Welcome to Southeast Hospital. As we taxi to the gate, please keep your seat belts fastened until we come to a complete stop. We hope you enjoy your stay here. We hope you had a great flight."

After I parked the ambulance, I got out, went to the rear, and opened the doors to the patient compartment. We pulled the stretcher and patient out and raised it up to waist level so we could start moving him to his room. As we walked toward the door, family members showed up and grabbed his hand, asking if he was doing okay. He responded, "It was a wonderful flight." Their response was, "We're glad it went well for you." She looked at us and whispered, "It's okay, he has dementia." We smiled and had a chuckle as we moved into the hospital.

Irritating Hospital Personnel

"Operator, May I Help You?"

I wish I could take credit for this one, but I've seen it play out a number of times. In the hospital, any department can dial zero for the hospital operator and ask for someone to be paged (yes, pagers were a big deal then). An example would be calling the operator from the ICU and asking for Respiratory Therapy. The operator already saw what department you were calling from, and in a few seconds, over the loudspeakers throughout the entire hospital you would hear, "Respiratory Therapy, call extension 357; Respiratory Therapy, call extension 357." And they would call to see what you needed.

Obviously the same is true of the ER. It got so aggravating at times, that an ER nurse would march over to a particular phone and scold the medic and laugh at the same time. A typical call went like this.

The operator would simply answer, "Operator."

And Tom would respond in a serious tone with, "Could you page Dr. Dover, please? His first name is Ben. Thanks."

In a few seconds you heard over the entire hospital, "Dr. Dover, Dr. Ben Dover, call extension 432." Then there was the classic, "Paging Dr.

Butts, Dr. Seymour Butts." The list goes on, and the nurses all knew what phone to run to for catching this guy in the act.

"Does the Doctor Know?"

This is one of the funnier stints I saw was while I was working in the ER. Dan, who was always busting chops with someone, decided to stir the pot and run. Dr. Chad Westup was an ER doc who had a limited and dry sense of humor. He always took the job seriously and was always the ultimate professional when he dealt with any patient in the ER.

Dan brought in a patient, and as he was leaving, he saw Dr. Westup placing sutures in a laceration on a young lady who cut herself on some glass. He was focused on what he was doing, when suddenly, Dan leans in with a look of horror on his face, and in a loud and inquisitive voice says, "Chad! Does the doctor know you are doing this?" Dan then quickly walked away.

Dr. Westup had a stuttering problem when he got stressed or upset, and he started stuttering as he stood up to chase down Dan. The patient had her mouth wide open in shock, not knowing what to believe. Dr. Westup saw that Dan had already walked outside, so he stomped back into the treatment room to finish the stitches. I overheard him assuring the patient that he was, in fact, the ER doc, and that Dan was just horsing around. I think Dan gave Dr. Westup ulcers over time.

"Sorry, There's Nothing We Can Do"

One shift working with EMS, we had a three-person crew. I had already been working in the ER and knew everyone well. I was working with two rookies since I was an FTO, and I had a difficult time convincing them to go along with me on playing a practical joke on the ER staff, but eventually I talked them into it.

We were standing by at the ER to help cover a few geographic areas that were busy because the hospital was in the middle of the coverage area they needed us in. I convinced them to let me lie down on the stretcher and have them cover me up with a sheet. They rolled me into the ER and started rolling down to the end of the hallway toward the last room on the right. This was where we placed people who died, either en route or in the ER, to wait for either the medical examiner or to stage until other arrangements were made.

As they wheeled me down the hallway, several nurses were curious as to why we were bringing a dead person into the hospital, especially since they weren't notified that we were coming in. Right on cue, they responded with, "There was nothing we could do. We tried everything and decided to pronounce him dead as we arrived." This, of course, would be odd, and the nurse's curiosity got the best of her. As I expected it would. She pulled the sheet back off my head and I grabbed her arm and screamed at her. She screamed extremely loud and I'm sure she cursed a bit. I got a well-deserved punch in the arm and a, "That's not funny!"

Everyone else in the ER, including the doc, were all laughing out loud, and the nurse was just a little embarrassed. Unfortunately, I knew payback was coming next time I worked in the ER. They were just as brutal as we were.

Okay, That's Pushing It

Now, some of you will think that I went over the line with some of these practical jokes. I get it. It was all in fun, and it was a way to redirect all the negative things we had to deal with daily. We had to find a way to laugh it off, if you will. I told you in the beginning that we had a dark sense of humor.

"You Gotta Know How it Feels"

While at EMS, at times I would work with a relatively new girl who was a little naive. She would fall for practical jokes all the time. You couldn't help but pull pranks on her. It was just too easy. The best part was that she had a great sense of humor and usually laughed along with you.

We were at the county gas pumps filling up the ambulance. It was me, Terry, and Emery as a crew. Emery was always trying to protect the rookies from abuse, as he went through it himself.

No hazing or anything crazy or immoral (my definition) was ever done to new hires, just fun stuff.

We carried body bags in our units for the obvious reason, and being an FTO, it was my job to make sure everyone knew how to use all the equipment on the ambulance. I pulled out a body bag and laid it out on the ground. I asked Terry if she had ever laid down in one. With a confused look, she told me she hadn't, and she had no intentions of doing so. I explained in great detail how important it was for her to know how a patient felt when we applied certain equipment or items to them. I asked her if she had ever lain down on a backboard, and she said yes. I asked her

208

if she had ever had a splint placed on her arm, and she said yes. I told her that was a good thing and said, "You gotta know how it feels when we use these items on them."

She nodded in agreement. I pointed to the body bag and ask her to go ahead and lie down inside. This way she'd know how it felt to the patient. Most of you already know the patient that gets put into a body bag is not feeling anything.

She hesitantly stepped into the bag and started to lie down when Emery grabbed her arm and yelled, "No, I can't let you do that. That's too much. I cannot watch you do this!" Terry stepped back out, gave me the evil eye, and said, "Are you messing with me?" Of course, I was. I told her I would not let her actually lie down in it anyway, I was just seeing how far she would go. We all had a laugh, and Terry questioned everything I said for the rest of the month she was stationed with me.

"What Do We Do Now?"

Working with an EMT named Norris while I was with EMS was always fun. He was always a little spooked by dead people and didn't want to have anything to do with them. He wasn't comfortable touching them, moving them from our stretcher to the table in the county morgue—nothing.

In the early years with EMS, we were responsible for taking patients directly to the funeral home or the morgue if they couldn't arrange someone to pick the body up. We had a patient who was found dead at home and was released to the funeral home since it was an expected death.

The funeral home was in an old Victorian house built in the early 1900s, and it was rumored to be haunted. It was a beautiful place but a little spooky at night. And this call occurred in the early evening hours, just as it was starting to get dark. Did I mention he was also afraid of ghosts?

Norris was a good EMT but had no ambitions of becoming a paramedic, and that was okay. He had no interest in knowing much more than he needed to. He knew how to attach the electrodes on a patient for a three-lead ECG and how to set up IVs for me to start. He was good at supporting the paramedic he was working with.

We backed into the dark parking space in the rear of this funeral home. We were under an overhang made to protect us from rain and sun, making it darker than on the street. As I opened the rear doors to the ambulance to pull the stretcher out, I stared at the stretcher and paused. Norris was already nervous, since we were dealing with a dead person and possible ghosts.

He immediately asked, "What's wrong?"

I responded with, "Did you just see the patient's chest rise? I swear he's still breathing."

Norris stepped back and with a shocked look on his face said, "No way! What are you talking about?"

I had a fake look of horror on my face and repeated, "I swear, I saw his chest rise. Oh my God! We just pronounced this guy dead. What do we do now?" Norris was now frozen in fear and was just standing there, staring at the patient.

I jumped in the back of the ambulance, grabbed the heart monitor, and placed it on the bench seat. I pulled out the wire leads that attached to the electrodes you would place on a patient's chest. I grabbed the positive and negative lead in each hand, pressing them together between my thumb and index finger without Norris seeing, and pretended like I was placing the leads on the patient.

With the sound set on high, you saw an ECG on the screen and a heart rate of eighty beats per minute. I yelled back to Norris, "Dude, he's still alive. We are in so much trouble. What do we do now? I can't believe this is happening!"

I saw Norris wandering around in circles with his mind racing, not knowing what to say or do. He was starting to panic, so I told him I was just messing around and there was nothing going on. He pointed to the monitor and asked why it was showing an ECG rhythm on the screen. I raised my hands and showed him what I was doing and told him that the ECG he saw was mine.

Now Norris was really amped up and more nervous than ever going into the funeral home. He took two steps inside and asked if I was okay by myself. Since the patient would be slid over to a funeral home stretcher just inside, I told him I would take care of it and do the paperwork. I went back outside and see him sitting on the back bumper of the ambulance, waiting to let me have it. He had a nervous laugh as he admitted that he fell for the prank, and it didn't help much when I told him I heard voices while I was in the funeral home.

Chapter 13

MANY FIRSTS

I was fortunate to have been in a lot of the right places at the right time. I was always striving to improve my skills and was aggressive in applying my skills. I will outline a number of situations when I was lucky enough to be in a position to be the first to apply a skill or be involved in something that has not been done before either in the county or quite possibly even in the state.

❖ First EMT

When the first fire department I worked at was mostly volunteer, we did not respond to medical calls at all. Fires and vehicle accidents were the only responses made. I was the first volunteer to get my CPR and Advanced First Aid certifications. This is what led me to talking the fire chief into letting me purchase and place some basic medical equipment on our quick-response/brushfire vehicle. When I was at the station, I was able to respond to some medical calls either in the quick-response vehicle or the chief's car that was parked outside the station.

Eventually, I became the first state-certified EMT in the department. I was able to get more medical equipment for the vehicle and eventually more personnel went to EMT school, making it routine to assist on medical calls.

Competition Team

As a volunteer firefighter in the mid-'70s, I was a member of our fire competition team that did well during state-wide events. As a paramedic I was part of the first ever competition team that our EMS department put together. We competed at the state level, and just prepping for the competition made us sharper with our skills. The competition would involve patient assessments, treatment using our actual equipment, and teamwork evaluation. We were judged by esteemed doctors and paramedics from around the country. The competition not only improved our skills, but we also learned from other teams from around the state. We ended up doing okay, landing in about the middle of the rest of the competition. We learned a lot from that experience and went on to do other competitions in the following years. Once again, learning with and from other medics and doctors from around the state was remarkable.

Full-Time Firefighter

As I mentioned in the beginning of my time at the local volunteer fire department, there were two guys who worked part-time during the days and the rest of the department consisted of volunteers.

One of our volunteers was a fire commissioner and was interested and learned in local and state politics. He personally wrote a state charter creating an independent taxing authority for the fire department, allowing the district to procure tax money from the residents of the district instead of relying of donations. He petitioned the state, and we became the first independent taxing authority for a fire district in the state, thanks to his hard work and persistence. Numerous other fire districts in the state followed suit over the years.

This allowed a steady revenue each year, allowing the department to purchase needed equipment, a new engine, and a new station, along with full-time firefighters. I was one of six people hired to be the department's first full-time firefighters in its history. The station was now staffed around the clock with full-time firefighters and, shortly after, a new station and engine were opened in the southern part of the district, allowing quicker response times to that area.

Most Dramatic Response to Treatment

The EMS system I worked for was fortunate to have aggressive medical directors that had full trust in the paramedics working under their license. Dr. Kurley and Dr. Best went to the same medical school together and were one of the first doctors to have emergency medicine as their specialty. They had similar respect for all the paramedics they dealt with and were aggressive in their treatment philosophies. While most paramedics around the country were required to call in to the hospital to get permission to implement various invasive medical procedures, we had standing orders to treat patients as necessary based on our assessment. It was rare that we were required to call in first.

I was working with two rookie EMTs at one point in the '80s and enjoyed working with them, as they were excited about the job and learned quickly. One eventually became a paramedic and the other a paramedic/supervisor. We responded to what dispatch called a "personal injury" in a residential neighborhood. Upon arrival, I noticed a car sitting in the driveway that had a slope to the road, the hood up, and two car ramps in front of the car.

Upon entering the house, family members were freaking out, crying, and trying to comfort a gentleman in his early '30s who was sitting on the couch, slumped down in the seat, trying to catch his breath. The information we got was that the man was working under his car while it was up on the ramps, with his young son sitting behind the wheel. He did not have blocks behind the rear wheels. His son leaned on the gear shift lever and it popped into neutral, causing the car to roll down off the ramps, allowing the driver's side tire to roll over his father's chest before stopping on the driveway. The weight of the car crushed his chest, fracturing multiple ribs and causing him to have a difficult time breathing.

Looking at the father, it was obvious that he was having a hard time breathing. He was literally purple from his upper chest to his head. His neck veins were dramatically distended, and his eyes were bloodshot and looked like they were going to pop out of his head from pressure. He was conscious and could not talk and had a look of doom in his eyes. He knew he was dying right there. I mentioned to my partners that this was classic out of the book traumatic asphyxia. It always stood out in the textbooks with the illustrations they had, but this was the first and only time in my career that I had run into this type of patient with the classic symptoms.

215

What had happened was the pressure on his chest caused multiple ribs to fracture, which in turn ruptured one of his lungs. There was no open chest wound, leaving his skin intact. As he breathed in, the air would escape from the ruptured lung into the pleural space (his chest cavity), and when he tried to exhale the pressure would build up in his chest because it could not escape out of his damaged lung. Each breath would make the situation worse to the point where all of this air pressure in the chest starts pushing on the heart, making it difficult for the heart to efficiently pump blood.

Once this happens, as the heart contracts to circulate blood throughout the body, the air pressure would exert more and more pressure on the heart with each breath and with each contraction. For each contraction, the heart is unable to fully relax and fill completely with blood to prepare for the next contraction. It gets to the point where the heart cannot pump out enough blood. The blood returning to the heart gets backed up, causing the neck veins and blood vessels in the head to build up pressure as well. Along with this, there is no circulation of oxygen to this area either. Thus, the bulging neck veins, bulging eyes, and purple color. This is a life-threatening situation that will not last long before dying.

He also had classic vital signs fitting the description of traumatic asphyxia. His heart rate was around thirty beats per minute, he had no blood pressure, along with very labored breathing. He was suffering from a tension pneumothorax, which was one of the issues causing the traumatic asphyxia. The only way to stop this progression was to remove the air under pressure from the chest. The procedure for this is called chest decompression, and the technique we were just trained in performing about a week prior to this call was called a needle thoracentesis. Fortunately, this was a standing order and did not require contacting the hospital for permission to perform. Time is of essence in this situation.

My partners were very routine and quick to place him on a heart monitor, take blood pressure, pulse, and respirations as I did a quick assessment. I immediately pulled out the long needle set aside just a week ago specifically for this procedure, located the landmark on his chest, and told the patient that he may feel the needle but would be able to breathe better after I place it in his chest.

I punctured the chest wall with the needle attached to a syringe and advanced it into the chest. The pressure caused the plunger in the syringe to push out of the barrel. I then heard a loud hiss of air coming out of the needle for a few seconds. As this air was escaping, we watched his color change from purple to pink, working its way up from the chest to his head, his neck veins started to flatten out, and his eyes stopped bulging out and looked normal. His heart rate slowly went back to normal too as we listened to the beep of the heart monitor get faster and faster until it stayed at around eighty beats per minute. My partner took his blood pressure, and it was now normal. This was probably one of the more dramatic responses to treatment I have ever seen in my career. The patient was then able to talk to us and explain what happened.

To be clear, as time went on throughout my career, we ran across many patients with a tension pneumothorax that had to have a needle thoracentesis performed, but typically these patients were unconscious from a traumatic event along with other traumatic injuries. Having a patient with traumatic asphyxiation looking at you and begging with his eyes to help him is rare. It ranks among one of the most memorable calls I responded to in my career.

You're Putting that Tube Where?

One of the basic procedures a paramedic performs is endotracheal intubation. This entails placing a tube into a patient's airway through their mouth to facilitate breathing. It typically requires the paramedic to place a laryngoscope into the patient's mouth to visualize the vocal cords and pass the tube between the cords into the trachea, or airway. This will allow you to manually ventilate someone who's not breathing or assist breathing in someone who is breathing very shallow or slow. Paramedics typically become good at this procedure as it is almost always done while a patient is lying on the floor or ground, in a ditch, in a car, etc.; it's never ideal, like in a hospital at waist-level with good lighting.

If a patient has trauma that may cause them to clench their mouths closed, you are not able to place the laryngoscope in the mouth to visualize the vocal cords. If a patient with congestive heart failure (CHF) needs assistance with breathing, placing a laryngoscope in the mouth will typically cause them to gag and vomit, making it more difficult and dangerous to place and endotracheal tube. Emergency room physicians with patients in this situation would place the tube by inserting it through the nose and passing it into the airway. It took some finesse to "feel" the tube and to hear the breathing from the tube as you got closer to the vocal cords before pushing it the rest of the way in.

This procedure was not in our routine yet, and while working in the ER in the late '70s and watching the doctors perform this procedure, I inquired as to why we couldn't learn this technique. They agreed that if a patient needed a breathing tube, they needed it in the field and couldn't wait until they got to the hospital.

Within weeks of getting the training, I responded to a pedestrian hit by a car who not only had internal injuries, but also had head trauma. He had labored, shallow breathing and needed to be intubated. His mouth was clenched down tight, not allowing us to place it through the mouth. I passed the tube through his nose using the techniques I learned and watched while working in the ER. We were able to successfully breathe for him until we got to the hospital. I can't say for sure that this was the first nasal intubation, but at this point I had not heard of it being done in the field, and usually word gets out about things like that. Nobody was aware of it being performed as of yet.

Human Suffering and Nightmares

I mentioned in the beginning of this book that it takes someone special with the ability to handle the day-to-day exposure to human suffering to work in the field of public safety. I discussed how important it is to have empathy for every patient you're called on to assist and that you should make the attempt to avoid becoming personally involved or emotional, as difficult as that may seem. In my entire thirty-eight years running calls, I only had one that caused me to have nightmares. I have seen a lot of brutal things and a lot of human tragedy, but for some reason this one hit me without expecting it.

I was working with the same two EMT rookies in the '80s, and we had just backed the ambulance into the station at around 3 a.m. after a call, with the engine still running, when we got toned out for a vehicle accident only about four blocks away. We were still in our seats, so we just put it in drive and took off. While en route, dispatch told us a vehicle was on fire with someone trapped inside. We got there in under a minute, and as we pulled up, we saw a vehicle totally involved in fire, with another vehicle upside down on top of the burning car. Nobody else was on scene yet due to us getting there so quick. The fire department and the sheriff's office were on the way.

We went straight to the car on fire, since dispatch told us someone was trapped. It was difficult to get close, but we found a young female driver sitting behind the steering wheel with her arms out in front as if to shield her from the flames with her body totally charred and still smoldering. She was frozen in char and obviously dead. There was nothing we could do for her. The other car on top was just catching fire, but we couldn't see anybody inside from where we were.

About that time a fire truck and deputy showed up on scene. The fire department started attacking the fire, and the deputy came running over to us with a look of horror on his face, telling us there was a victim lying in the middle of the road on the other side of the vehicles. We followed him to find a young male in his '20s with one hundred percent of his body burned and still on fire. He was lying there screaming in pain, and I directed my partners to grab an armful of normal saline IV solution bags right away. When they came back, which seemed liked seconds, I cut them open one at a time, pouring the saline over him, putting out the fire and stopping the burning the best I could on the rest of his body.

The patient looked up at the deputy and begged him to shoot him and put him out of his misery. The deputy was stressed, understandably upset, and felt helpless. He looked at me with a face that was asking for direction. It was almost as if he was asking permission to go ahead and put him out of his misery. Believe me, if I were in the same situation, I would wish the same thing. I cannot think of anything that causes more pain than burns. This was not a burned finger or an arm, this was his entire body.

Quickly surveying the patient, it was horrible to see that he had one hundred percent second- and third-degree burns to his entire body, with all his clothes completely burned off. His entire chest and torso had third-degree burns, and as the burned tissue started to cool a bit, his chest got tighter and tighter. He was trying to breathe but couldn't expand his chest at all due to the eschar, or burned tissue, covering it. Palpating his chest was like pushing on leather that was as stiff as a table.

We tried to ventilate him with a bag-valve-mask device, and we could not squeeze the bag to force air into his lungs due to resistance. His chest would not expand at all. He needed to be intubated. I got out my laryngoscope, and when I placed it in his mouth to find the vocal cords, I saw that his entire airway was burned and cherry red. His head did not tilt back at all due to the burns and eschar, making it difficult to see his vocal cords. I knew the vocal cords were just above what I was seeing, so I guided the tube to that general area, and it passed through. We tried ventilating with the bag attached to the endotracheal tube (breathing tube) but to no avail. Still no chest expansion. He needed an escharotomy.

Once again, we had just added this to our protocol and were trained via pictures and lecture on how to perform an escharotomy on patients that fit this scenario. This had never been done in the field before in our county, and as far as I could find out, even in the state. This was not a standing order but had to be called in to the hospital for permission to perform. This was one of the more aggressive procedures in our protocols at the time. Because the eschar was so tough and nonelastic, there was zero lung compliance.

I directed my partners to get a backboard and stretcher and load him into the ambulance as soon as possible. While they were setting that up, I got into the back of the ambulance and contacted the emergency room on the telemetry radio to request permission to do an escharotomy. Thankfully, Dr. Best was working. We had a good working relationship not only as medical director but working together in the ER. He trusted me and I trusted him. I told him I had a burn victim with one hundred percent second- and third-degree burns and needed permission to perform an escharotomy to the chest due to zero lung compliance. With no other questions or hesitation, he said to do it and that he would see me in the ER when we got there.

Just as I finished talking to Dr. Best, the crew rolled the stretcher into the back of the ambulance and I grabbed a scalpel and started the procedure. This consists of cutting through the eschar to where the skin is able to expand when we ventilate with the bag attached to the endotracheal tube. As I cut into the eschar, the skin popped open like a Ball Park Frank to around an inch wide. Not to be graphic, but that is exactly what it looked like. I cut a square around his upper chest, and when my partner squeezed the bag to ventilate, the section I had just cut expanded, allowing ventilation to occur. There was no need to even attempt to start an IV as both his arms and neck had third-degree burns.

As we were about to leave, a firefighter leaned into the back of the ambulance and yelled that there was another patient found in the ditch on the side of the road. We were the only ambulance on scene, and I was the only paramedic on scene at the time, so I told my partner to keep

221

ventilating. I told my other partner to ask for another ambulance to respond and said I would be right back. I grabbed the medical kit and followed the firefighter to the ditch.

When I got there, I saw another male in his twenties moaning in pain, having difficulty breathing with third- and fourth-degree burns over his whole body. The skin and hair on his head were burned off and all I saw was skull. Some of his extremities were burned down to the bone. But he was still alive and trying to breathe and in a lot of pain. I knew he had to be intubated and an escharotomy performed as well.

I laid down in the ditch with him to place the laryngoscope in his mouth to visualize his vocal cords and place the endotracheal tube in the airway. All I was able to visualize was a lot of burned tissue inside his mouth. I noticed two swollen and burned pieces of tissue that looked like little round balls moving away from each other every time he tried to breathe. I figured this had to be his vocal cords that were burned and swollen, so I slipped the tube in between these two swollen balls of tissue and tried to ventilate with the bag. You could see his chest trying to rise with each squeeze, so I knew I was in the right spot.

As I was securing the endotracheal tube the other ambulance showed up, and I gave the guy a quick report and told him I got permission to perform an escharotomy on my other patient and that this one needed it to be performed as well. Fortunately, the paramedic who showed up was Mike Elder, one of our most knowledgeable and most competent medics in our department. I left with my patient, and Mike ended up performing an escharotomy as well on the patient in the ditch. This was the first and second time an escharotomy was ever performed in the field in our county. Thankfully, this is a rare scenario.

My first patient that we transported lost his pulse while en route to the hospital, so we pronounced him dead before we got there. Personally, it was a relief that this happened, as I would not wish that level of suffering on anyone. Statistically, he had a zero percent chance of survival due to the amount and severity of his burns. Upon arrival we moved him to a remote room in the back of the ER for further investigation by the medical examiner.

The second patient that was found in the ditch was transported to the hospital and survived long enough to be flown to a burn hospital. The sad part is he survived long enough to have his legs amputated and an arm amputated, then died from infection almost three months later. He suffered way too much in my opinion.

We stayed up the rest of the night for that twenty-four-hour shift as nobody could sleep. We met up with the firefighters at the fire station and talked about the call until we had a shift change at 7 a.m. I was exhausted from a busy shift anyway, but that last call was both exhilarating and depressing at the same time. That's where it's tough to deal with all the competing emotions you encounter at times. It was exciting that I had the chance to perform an aggressive procedure never done in the field before and had recognized it quickly and without hesitation. It was depressing thinking about the young girl frozen in time in the car that was on fire, the young man begging to be put out of his misery, and the other young man suffering in the ditch with so much pain.

All was good when I got home. I told my wife about the call and went to take a nap since I got no sleep that night. I then went about my business for the rest of my day like normal. That evening, in the middle of the night, I apparently had a nightmare and screamed at the top of my lungs and sat straight up in bed, scaring my wife to death. I was sweating like I had just run a marathon in humid weather, and the bed was completely soaked like someone threw a bucket of water on it. I had no idea what happened and had no recollection of any details of a nightmare. I think we had to replace the mattress after that night. I never had issues like that before or since that night. It was obvious to me what caused it, but it was never an issue again. I always took pride in the fact that no matter how crazy, scary, or violent of a call I ran, it never bothered me. These experiences affect everyone differently and it does not reflect on how good or bad a medic or firefighter you may be.

The Inaugural Paramedic Program

I had been a volunteer firefighter since 1975 between three different departments. In the late 1990s, the assistant chief from the department I first started with met with me for lunch and asked if I was interested in leaving EMS and coming back to the fire department to initiate the first paramedic program there and become the first full-time fire training officer.

I have been forever grateful for him making that move and asking me to be a part of what I consider one of the most rewarding parts of my career. There were already a handful of paramedics working there, but they were not allowed to perform paramedic duties since the department did not have a medical director, paramedic equipment, paramedic training, and nobody was credentialed to work as a paramedic under a physician's guidance.

The job made me responsible for acquiring all of the necessary Advanced Life Support (ALS) equipment, hiring a physician to be our medical director, acquiring vehicles to accommodate ALS response, and providing the necessary training to prep them all for sitting in front of the medical director to prove they were ready to work on their own. It took about a full year of getting everything in place to get at least one paramedic rescue truck up and running, along with the required state inspection and licensing.

It progressed into all stations having paramedics responding to calls, along with extra paramedics rotating their time on rescue. As more departments got involved in running paramedic non-transport service, we worked closely with the county EMS to write common medical protocols and guidelines. This allowed us to all be on the same page working together. It was uplifting to see so many agencies and multiple medical directors working together to agree on treatment modalities and how best to serve the public throughout the county.

A Quiet and Peaceful Learning Space

As a long-time instructor, I was always looking for ways to make training realistic and to get as much hands-on as possible. I had gotten to know one of the investigators who worked at the county morgue very well. His name was Sid, and we became good friends. It made it easier to communicate with him when I had to call them while on scene of a Signal 7, trying to determine if the medical examiner or investigator needed to respond to the scene, have them taken to the morgue, or just released to a funeral home. He trusted my instincts and I tried to help him out as much as possible.

After a patient from a vehicle accident was transferred over to the medical examiner, I asked Sid if I could sit in on the autopsy because I was interested in seeing what the cause of death was. He called me back and told me that Dr. Tombstone was more than happy to have me and that he enjoyed teaching while doing an autopsy. I went the next day on my day off and was hooked from that point on.

I would call almost every day I was off duty to see if they had any cases I would be interested in. I attended autopsies regularly, and as I got into the routine, they started having me assist with weighing various organs, assisting in removing organs, and eventually even dissecting coronary arteries to see if I could find arteriosclerosis (hardening of the arteries) or atherosclerosis (plaque forming inside the arteries) forming in any of the vessels. If so, I would cut out a piece and place it in formaldehyde for further testing and examination by the medical examiner.

An interesting side note was that I found while dissecting coronary arteries on various patients, from teenage years to the elderly, almost all had some arteriosclerosis or atherosclerosis. There were elderly patients that died from trauma and had complete occlusion of major coronary arteries with no history of heart problems or symptoms before the traumatic event. At the same time, I found numerous younger people had either blockages or hardening of the arteries as well, with no symptoms or medical issues. Dr. Tombstone said that we naturally start to accumulate plaque at an early age, and it increases as we age. That was interesting and concerning at the same time.

I then asked if I could practice performing various invasive procedures on some of the cadavers as most of them may never be performed in the field, or at least rarely. It made sense to me to get the feel of it now instead of in the field. Depending on the patient, I was able to perform multiple cricothyroidotomies, needle decompressions of the chest, intracardiac injections, intraosseous needle insertion into the bone marrow of the tibia to get fluid access if a vein was not attainable, and multiple central line IVs such as subclavian, internal jugular, and external jugular.

Doing these procedures routinely made me proficient and confident in performing any of these methods in the field while on duty. Since I was an FTO, I then asked if I could bring in various paramedics with me for the same training. The medical examiner was supportive of paramedics, so he allowed me to rotate crews in, and I would demonstrate a procedure, explaining step by step how to do it, then would allow them to repeat it. They all said it was some of the best training they ever got.

One of the procedures we performed allowed me to do a study, the results of which caused us to change our protocols for performing it in the field. Our routine procedure for intracardiac injections was to inject the needle in the subxiphoid area. In certain cardiac arrest situations, it was common to inject one or two medications directly into the heart if an IV could not be established. The procedure was thought to directly inject the medication into the left ventricle.

After each injection we administered in the morgue we would then look at the heart to see exactly where the puncture was from the needle to see how consistent it was. After about thirty injections it was determined that they consistently were injected into the septum between the left and right ventricle and not into the chamber itself. This would render the injection useless and could possibly make the situation worse if the patient was in ventricular fibrillation. Based on this training and nonscientific study, our protocols changed to performing all intracardiac injections with the anterior approach.

Emergency Room Paramedic

At the time I started working with EMS as a paramedic, one of the only three hospitals in the county handled most of the major trauma cases and cardiac patients. It was the only hospital to perform open-heart surgery. The best part of this hospital was that the ER physicians were focused on emergency medicine as opposed to it being a part-time job for doctors from other specialties, including family practice.

Emergency medicine was in its infancy. The emergency medicine residency program started in the early '70s. In 1979, the physician in charge of the ER was one of the first to go through this program. He was aggressive in treating patients and loved paramedics. He even made a comment that went over like a lead balloon that he would prefer to see the entire ER run with paramedics instead of nurses. There was no such thing as a specialty for nurses to work in the ER. These were nurses who either liked the action, or ICU nurses who would fill in for vacancies. They did not have any training specifically for emergency medicine.

That same year, I asked this ER doc if there was any chance of getting to work in the ER as a part-time job. His face lit up and was excited about the prospect. He asked me to come in the next day after I got off shift to discuss it.

After meeting with him for about an hour in the doctor's lounge, we marched up to the hospital administrator and he told him that he wanted to hire paramedics for the ER. After a little pushback, the doc convinced him it was the right thing to do, and the administrator asked for a job description. We went back to his office and wrote out a job description in about two hours. It was basically performing paramedic duties, along with anything the ER doc allowed with supervision. This was about to tick off some nurses.

That same day, as I was leaving, a firefighter I knew rode into the hospital with EMS to assist. He had just become certified as a paramedic, even though the fire department did not provide that level of service. It was a similar situation I went through when I went to EMS.

After talking to him for a few minutes and telling him about the possibility of working in the ER, he got all excited and wanted to do the same. He felt it would be the only way to keep up his skills. The next week, we both met with the ER doc in charge and went over the final version of the job description. We all liked it and took it to the hospital administrator. In about a week, we were both working part-time in the ER.

We were the first paramedics to work in the ER as paramedics in our county. About a year later, they opened up more positions and other medics came on board and loved it. The nurses we worked with were awesome. We learned from each other on many aspects of emergency medicine. We all got along well, and it created a better working relationship with all medics who came through the doors.

First CEN Class

As I mentioned above, there was no focused training for nurses working in the ER at the time. When the nursing credentialing body approved a certification for a Certified Emergency Nurse (CEN), I was asked to assist in teaching a few modules for the course.

My background working in the ER and as a paramedic instructor made it a good fit. That was one of the more enjoyable classes I ever taught. That certification eventually became the standard for nurses working in the ER and it became a recognized specialty.

Chapter 14

MY DAY OFF?

T he one thing that seems common with firefighters, paramedics, and law enforcement is that you always seem to encounter emergencies when you are off duty. It is common for the neighbors who know you are a first responder to rely on you for help. And for all of us, it is a call to duty that we react and assist without hesitation. We just happen to be at the right place at the right time. I have had numerous incidents I found myself in the middle of while off duty and will detail some of the more memorable ones.

Are You Guys Really Paramedics?

I was visiting a friend out of state where I grew up. I went with her and her one-year-old daughter to see her family. I was driving down a two-lane country road at night when I got hit broadside at an intersection with impact into the driver's door by a pickup truck traveling 55 mph. I was in a rental car and nobody was wearing seat belts, except for me. When this occurred, there were very few seat belt laws around and my friend never wore one. She didn't buckle her baby in, so I didn't make a fuss over it. I was wearing mine due to it being a good habit as it is required at work and I have seen the difference it makes.

The horrifically loud bang that I heard upon impact was deafening, followed by screeching tires that lasted about fifteen seconds. This was us sliding sideways down the road at least seventy-five feet into a ditch. The truck that hit us went off the road and crashed into a parked vehicle.

The silence following the accident was equally deafening. Then I heard the baby screaming in pain, lying on the floorboard, and I saw her mother sitting silently and staring blankly out the windshield. I was feeling firsthand what a lot of my patients involved in vehicle accidents go through, including the confusion about what happened along with concern for everyone else.

The driver's window was shattered and the door was smashed in. I could not open my door due to the amount of damage. I immediately went into medic mode and started to assess my friend and her baby. I asked her if she was okay, and all I got was her asking what had happened in a dazed fashion. I did a quick survey looking for obvious injuries and there were none. The baby was still screaming on the floorboard and I quickly determined that she had a fractured leg and felt it was best not to move her. I crawled over my friend and crawled out the window to find the driver of the truck. He had a fractured leg as well but was conscious and alert. The witness who called for EMS said he was told they were sending two ambulances since there were four patients. I went back to my friend and she was still conscious and asking questions but not acting appropriately due to the circumstances. She just sat there, blankly staring out the window and repeating questions.

When an ambulance pulled up, I gave them a patient report detailing what I had found for injuries. I told the paramedic that my friend was the priority patient with a possible internal bleed and the other two had fractured legs. He told me they would take care of them and to walk with him over to the ambulance. I insisted that they attend to my friend first, but he grabbed my arm and walked me to the medic unit and started to bandage me up. I apparently had a lot of blood on my face and my left arm and hand. He was focused on the obvious and not the serious. I started to get mad and told him I was a paramedic from another state and knew what I was talking about and that he needed to leave me alone and treat my friend.

A sheriff's deputy walked up and convinced me to stay seated on the bench seat in the ambulance. In a few minutes they walked my friend to the ambulance I was in and had her sit down at the other end of the bench seat. I was very mad now. I explained that she should not be walking to begin with and should be on a stretcher with IVs started and supplemental oxygen due to her possible internal bleeding. They got tired of me second-guessing them and moved me to the other ambulance. They put the baby in with her and put me with the driver of the truck. We all went to the same emergency room.

When we backed into the emergency room entrance and I got out of the ambulance, I saw that they walked her out as well and into a wheelchair. No IV and no oxygen. I was not happy at all with their treatment and let them know about it. I saw on their patches that they were paramedics, but I asked, "Are you guys really paramedics? Did you guys steal those patches on your shoulders?" Now, dealing with my share of obnoxious patients and outsiders, I got that they were not happy with me and I was just making them miserable, but they sucked.

I quickly told them that she had all the signs of an internal bleed and if she died, it would be on them. Well, I was still amped up from the crash and witnessed horrible medical care and had to say something. They moved me to a room that had four stretchers in it separated by curtains and they left.

While the nurses were attending to my friend, I heard everything that was going on, and having worked in the emergency room, I knew what they were talking about. They started two IVs, put her on oxygen and called for the lab and x-ray. Duh. One nurse put a urinary catheter in place, and I heard her state that it came back with nothing but blood. She had an internal bleed. That was a surprise. Not!

She ended up going to emergency surgery for an internal bleed and fortunately came out of it fine after a long recovery. The baby was in a cast for a long time but recovered as well. Yeah, I was that pain-in-the-ass patient, but it was personal, and it was obvious that they missed the big picture. I was in paramedic mode the entire time. That is the way we think all the time.

My God! Did That Just Happen?

My wife and I were traveling down the interstate through one of the busiest interchanges in the area at around 60 mph when I noticed a lot of brake lights coming on at the same time and cars coming to a stop. A few seconds later I noticed a little girl lying in the middle of the interstate unconscious with multiple injuries. She was in a car that had broken down on the side of the highway, and she bolted into the road and got hit. Traffic was at a stop and people were getting out of their cars and freaking out.

I got out of my car with a basic medical kit I always carry with me and went over to the little girl. She was unconscious, her breathing was shallow, and she had an obvious broken leg, bleeding about her head, and chest trauma. I inserted an oropharyngeal airway to keep her airway open and did a quick head-to-toe exam to find injuries. I instructed a bystander wanting to help to hold on to her leg to keep it from moving and asked another bystander to hold her head still in case there were spinal injuries. As I finished my evaluation a medic unit from the area showed up and I gave them a report. I assisted them in placing her on a backboard, putting her on supplemental oxygen and moving her to the ambulance. I got back in my car and we wormed our way around the accident scene that was blocked off by the highway patrol and continued our trip. I never found out what happened to that little girl.

Is That Smoke?

I was visiting my family in my hometown one winter. There were about two inches of snow on the ground and the temperature was below freezing with piles of snow curbside from the snowplows clearing the roads. I was driving with my sister up to an overpass that spanned some railroad tracks and looked up and saw what I thought was smoke. My sister and I agreed something had to be burning. As we crossed the overpass, we were staring straight at a two-story Victorian house with dark black smoke pouring from the eaves of the second floor. There was nobody around, no fire trucks, and light traffic.

I immediately pulled over and told my sister to start pounding on doors to get someone to call the fire department (we didn't have cell phones yet). I ran up to the front of the house and started pounding on the front door to see if anyone was home. I got no response. I then walked around the entire house to see if I could determine where the seat of the fire was. Looking in windows was useless due to curtains and shades. Windows and doors were all locked. Looking in the window on the front porch, I could see a glow and some smoke. The only other smoke I saw was out of the eaves of the second floor. The fire appeared to be just inside the front door in the living room and I assumed smoke had spread to the upper floor and into the attic.

I could hear sirens blaring not far away so I went to the road to flag them down and give them a size-up report and see if I could assist in any way. The first on-scene engine only had two firefighters and as they jumped out of the truck, I told them I was a firefighter from another state and gave them a size-up report, telling them I believed the seat of the fire was just inside the front door in the living room. One of them thanked me and he grabbed a hose line off the truck and started to stretch it to the front door. I assisted by pulling the rest of the hose off the truck and spread it out on the front lawn, taking out any kinks. The firefighter then started putting on his mask and turned on his breathing apparatus to go in. I told him I would feed him hose as he went in. Just then a second fire engine arrived with two more firefighters, and one of them came up to the front porch to go inside with the first firefighter to make an attack on the fire.

They forced the door open with a Halligan bar and axe and started to enter the home with me feeding them hose line. I could see the fire straight ahead of us through a moderate amount of dark gray smoke and thought they would be able to quickly knock it down. The firefighters disappeared into the smoke, then suddenly I heard some noise followed by some muffled screaming through the breathing apparatus air mask. Then the backup firefighter crawled back to the front door and screamed to me "He fell through! He fell through!" He then disappeared back into the smoke going after his partner. None of this made any sense to me at the time.

I screamed back to the engineer pumping the fire engine and told him what happened. As I was about to enter the house to assist, they both came crawling out toward the front door and I assisted the first firefighter out the door. He collapsed onto the porch with his bunker pants all charred up and still smoking. I assisted in taking off their air masks and tried to figure out what had happened. Two medics put him on a stretcher and took him to the hospital with second-degree burns to his legs.

Two more firefighters made entry and they eventually put the fire out. As they came out, I assisted in pulling the fire hose out onto the front yard, and I grabbed the nozzle from them and told them to get a breather. I stretched the hose out across the lawn and laid it down. Then one of the engineers from the engine yelled at me asking me what I was doing and telling me to open the bale on the nozzle. I had no clue what he was talking about. I thought he said the bale was open, and I said that it was okay, the bale was closed. He walked over and cracked the bale open, giving me an irritated look, allowing a small amount of water to flow out of the nozzle.

As a reminder, it was below zero and there were two inches of snow on the ground. Closing the bale would allow the water in the hose to freeze if it were not flowing. Duh! Also note that my entire career as a firefighter was in a location that rarely had snow and it was never below zero. It was a habit to close the bale and I did not think anything about it.

To add to the dumbass move on the hose line, I also found out from the firefighter who went back in to put out the fire that the first guy had fallen through the floor and caught himself with his arms and his air-pack to keep from falling into the basement. The fire was in the basement and while his legs were dangling, they were getting burned. Also, the house was an old Victorian house with balloon construction framing that allowed the smoke to travel from the basement all the way to the roof unimpeded. That was why there was smoke in the second-floor eaves.

Basement? What the...? As I mentioned early in the book, every geographic area has their unique issues to deal with. Well, not only do we not get snow and freezing weather, but we also don't have basements. That was why it wasn't even a thought during my size-up. Hey, I tried to help.

236

They were horribly undermanned and needed the help. They just probably needed competent help.

If that was not embarrassment enough, I put my foot in my mouth again two years later with the same fire department. During a family visit I stopped by a fire station to see a friend of mine who was a firefighter in that same department. Of course, we talked shop about fires and the like. He mentioned the fire at the two-story Victorian house that I ran upon and remembered that call from the news and from the other shift that ran the call. He remembered I was on scene that day. I responded with a snarky remark that the guys that went into the fire, went in standing up instead of crawling like they should, and it probably contributed to him falling through the floor. I made the remark that he probably learned a hard lesson. Then I heard a remark from one of the firefighters sitting in the living room. "Yes, I did." Yeah, it was the same guy. And yes, I was embarrassed and apologized for opening my mouth. He told me not to worry about it and that I was right, and he learned his lesson. After that, we had a friendly BS session between all of us for a bit before I left.

Right Place, Right Time

I was a member of a local gym that I went to each morning before work. Coincidentally, one of the fitness trainers mentioned to me the day before that they had CPR and AED training last week and just received a new automatic external defibrillator (AED) for the gym. I asked where it was kept so I knew ahead of time in case it was needed. She said that it was kept behind the desk and all fitness trainers got the certification.

I was on a treadmill in the back row getting warmed up when I noticed a lot of members looking to the left in disbelief. Of course, I had to see what I was missing so I looked to my left to see an elderly member of the gym collapsed on the floor where you check in.

I hopped off the treadmill and approached the gentleman and found him to be unconscious, not breathing and without a pulse. I immediately started CPR and the same trainer I talked to the day before came over and I asked her to get the AED, that he was in cardiac arrest. She was a little frazzled but got the AED and brought it back. She was shaking like a leaf and nervous, as this was the first time she had to deal with a medical emergency at work.

I calmly told her to place the pads on the patient and hit the "analyze" button. The AED read the rhythm and advised to shock. I told her I would stop CPR and make sure nobody was touching the patient and for her to push the "shock" button. She nervously hit the button and it caused the patient to jump with a jolt, and I think she jumped just as much. I continued CPR and told her to hit the analyze button again. It advised to "shock" again and we repeated the process. This time I reached down to feel for a pulse, and it was strong and bounding. The patient started to regain consciousness as the fire department paramedics came in.

I knew all the firefighter/paramedics well and told them what had happened. They started an IV and put him on oxygen, and I set up a lidocaine drip while they administered a lidocaine bolus. I assisted him onto the stretcher when EMS showed up and he left sitting up and talking. I told the fitness trainer that she did a great job and that she just saved someone's life.

The gym owners came over to ask questions and I told them that she put her training to use and saved the gentleman's life. There was a front-page article in their monthly newsletter with her picture and it made the local newspaper. You could tell she was proud of herself, as well she should be.

Always Prepared

I have always carried a basic medical kit and a fire extinguisher in all my vehicles. I have had too many incidents that I have rolled up on in my life for which I want to be prepared and not feel useless when it is needed.

While driving through the other end of the county in my personal vehicle on a day off, I saw a column of smoke appear out of nowhere. It was a dark, thick smoke, which was concerning. I was heading that way anyway, so when I saw the smoke appeared to be coming from an abandoned commercial structure in the rear, I pulled in to investigate. As I pulled into the rear of the structure, I noticed there were two old mattresses that were leaning against the building and on fire. The fire was beginning to lap up the side of the wall and was getting more intense. I used my cell phone to call 911 and told them the situation at hand. I pulled out my fire extinguisher and put it almost completely out before the first engine showed up. Of course, they busted my chops for taking away their fire, but it was close to getting into the eaves of the structure and out of hand. I told them they were welcome and left.

A few years prior, I pulled up behind a car that had its hood up with black smoke pouring from under the hood. The driver was on the phone calling 911 and there was nobody else in the car. I was able to knock the fire down considerably, but not completely. Car fires are difficult to put out with just an extinguisher. It can take a good amount of water and it is difficult to find all the hidden fires around the car. After the fire was put out by the fire department, they were nice enough to fill and recharge my extinguisher for me back at the station.

"Do I Look Surprised?"

My wife and I were running errands in my pickup truck when I got a call on my cell phone. It was a buddy of mine who was a battalion chief and on duty. He stated he was on scene of a possible chemical suicide with the hazmat truck and a few hazmat techs but was short one tech to be able to make entry into the scene. He asked if I was able to respond to the scene to assist.

We happened to be only two blocks away from the scene so I obviously said I could assist. I told my wife what we were doing, and she looked at me and circled her face with her hand, as if to say "look at my face" and then said, "Do I look surprised?"

I pulled up to the scene and went to the command post to be briefed, then started getting dressed in a level A hazmat suit. My being on scene gave them enough techs to continue with the entry and investigation. My wife put her feet up on the dash and just started reading emails on her cell phone like it was a routine thing for her. She was used to it by then.

All went well as nobody was found in the car and the chemical smell was from something unrelated. Chemical suicides were a trend for about a year. A person wanting to commit suicide would place a mixture of chemicals on the floorboard of the car and when they mixed, it would off-gas deadly fumes and asphyxiate them. Most of the time the windows would be fogged up from the off-gassing and they would leave a sign on the car warning first responders not to enter due to chemicals. At least they were concerned about someone else.

"C'mon, I'm Retired"

Since I have been retired, it just hasn't stopped. But that's okay. If I can help someone, all the better. Most firefighters, medics, or cops will tell you that your neighbors know what you do or did and you become the first to call if a situation calls for it. That's typical because we tell our neighbors if they need anything at all to call. And we don't mind at all.

"Did You See That?"

Just randomly looking out into the backyard one day with my wife, we saw a car drive off the road one street over from us. It was traveling at a fast rate of speed and ran into two trees, ending with a loud bang. My wife looked at me and said, "Did you see that?" I told her I did and had my wife call 911 while I jumped into my truck and went to check on the driver.

He was an elderly man who appeared somewhat confused as to his whereabouts, but otherwise there were no obvious injuries. After getting more information from him, it was obvious that he was a diabetic and had become hypoglycemic and passed out at the wheel. He said he was a few blocks from home and going to get something to eat but did not make it. After giving the rescue crew and EMS a report, I assisted them in moving the stretcher to the street through the dirt and brush.

"Is That My House?"

Again in my neighborhood, as I was driving down our street to go to the store for old people medicine, I saw someone lying in the ditch in front of a neighbor's house. Of course, I stopped to see if everything was okay. I didn't recognize him and when I got closer, I noticed that he was wearing filthy clothes, his hair was all matted, and he wreaked of alcohol. He was lying there unresponsive and when I lightly shook his shoulder, he moaned. I got on my cell phone and called 911 and told them what the situation was, and they sent fire/rescue, EMS, and law enforcement.

When the fire department showed up, we were able to get more of a response out of him and found out he had been drinking and was lost trying to find his way home. When we got an address as to where home was—he was about two miles off. He had defecated in his pants and could not stand on his own. EMS eventually took him to the hospital for evaluation.

Stay With Me, Fido

My wife got a frantic phone call from our next-door neighbor stating that one of her dogs was choking on something and stopped breathing and asked if I could come over. This neighbor had a heart of gold for animals and took in strays, fostered animals until an owner is found, and adopted others.

I ran next door to find her upset and crying, saying she thought the dog was choking on a toy and she couldn't get it out. The dog was making attempts to breathe but couldn't due to a stuffed toy jammed in the back of his throat. I opened his mouth and stuck my hand down his throat, hoping he wouldn't chomp down on me, and felt a fuzzy toy stuck in the back of his mouth blocking his airway. I tried to grab it, but it was too slimy to grab. I asked her to try to reach it herself since she had smaller hands while I pried the dog's mouth open. It was just too far back and slippery. I told her to keep her hand back there while I did chest compressions to see if it helped. The compressions caused just enough pressure to force the toy out so that she could grab it and pull it out. The dog slowly recovered and did fine.

"I Don't Want to See It"

My wife and I retired in a beautiful community with some acreage and just a handful of neighbors. We all help each other out as needed. I was assisting one neighbor in placing a tarp over a storage building that had just been built next to his house but had no shingles on it yet. The wind was blowing hard and I saw that he was having a hard time putting it in place, so I went over to help.

We had just gotten it to stay in place when my wife drove up and said another neighbor had fallen from a ladder and was injured. I jumped in my truck and went to my other neighbor's house to find Bill standing next to a mangled stepladder and holding his hand. He was in pain and looking away, stating that he did not want to see it. He didn't like the sight of blood or injuries, especially to himself. He had been standing on top of the ladder working on his house when it twisted and collapsed, causing him to fall to the ground. When he tried to break his fall with his hand, his finger was injured. One of his fingers was bent at a 45-degree angle at the joint. Other than that, there were just a few scrapes. He told me to just straighten it out for him and he would get back to work. He was a hard worker, but he wasn't as tough as he thought he was when it came to being in pain. On top of that, he didn't want to pay for an emergency room or doc-in-the-box clinic. That was the main reason he wanted me to fix it right there.

I told him that with the injury being in the joint, it could have chipped a piece of bone when it bent and if I straightened it, it may not heal correctly or function properly. I told him I felt he needed to get an x-ray to see if it was safe to straighten it out. After a long verbal battle about the cost of doing that, he agreed to go in to get it looked at. And yes, it had a small chip at the joint and the x-ray showed them how to manipulate the finger back without causing damage. All went well except for the bill he got later from the clinic.

"Do You Know What Year It Is?"

Another neighbor called my wife and asked if I could bring my medical kit and check out her husband. She said he appeared to have fallen and had a cut on his head and was bleeding badly. I jumped into my vehicle and headed over there, arriving in about thirty seconds. I saw my neighbor sitting in a chair with his wife holding a dressing to his head.

I asked what had happened and she stated that she was inside and had no idea what happened other than finding her husband standing there staring into space and bleeding from his head. A stepladder that he was using to sand down some wood on a porch was standing upright under the porch, appearing undisturbed.

I had BJ sit down in a chair and I looked at his scalp injury. It was just an abrasion that was still bleeding, but minimally. There was also a moderate-sized hematoma where the abrasion was, so I asked his wife to get a cold pack or some crushed ice in a baggy and hold it on his head to reduce the swelling.

I asked BJ what had happened, and he said he had no clue. I asked him what year it was, and he told me it was 1990-something. I asked him who was president, and he had no idea. He was getting flustered trying to find the answers, as he felt he knew but it could not come out.

244

We looked around and saw a portable sander on the ground at the base of a tall post, and when I looked up it appeared it was only partially sanded. He must have been working on the stepladder and fell and apparently moved the ladder back under the porch without realizing it.

My wife walked up to see what was going on, and he immediately said, "Hi, Beth." She said hi and asked him what happened. He had no idea. As I checked the rest of him out, I found he had significant swelling and tenderness to his right upper leg as well. He then said, "Hi, Beth." She acknowledged him again.

I told him that he needed to go to the ER to be evaluated and suggested he get a CAT scan (computer assisted tomography) to make sure there was no bleeding going on around his brain. After about ten minutes of him refusing to go, I convinced him that it was in his best interest, as he had multiple concussions in the past and the cumulative effects of concussion can result in serious long-term problems.

I walked him to my vehicle and drove him to the ER. They took him in and did a CAT scan, applied a dressing to his head as the swelling was down by now, and his leg was just bruised and swollen from the fall. I took him home and he took a few days to recover. He still cannot remember what happened that day.

Chapter 15

PERSONAL

The following are a few scenarios that are a little more personal.
They may be related to how I dealt with certain people or unique
situations that were a bit more personal.

❖ Right Place, Right Time, Right Doctor

As I already mentioned, I worked in the ER part-time as a paramedic
for ten years. It was probably one of the most rewarding jobs I ever had.
There is no place in the entire hospital that I would consider working other
than the emergency room. It is the perfect environment for a paramedic
since it encompasses everything we do in our profession. You never know
what is going to come through the doors, and it goes from zero to a
hundred in a matter of seconds. Just like working in the field as a
paramedic. Love it.

Since I typically would handle most cardiac and trauma patients that came into the ER, it just sharpened my skills more for the field. One particular shift in the ER was fairly slow and a cardiac patient came in with significant chest pain and shortness of breath. The medics who brought him in diagnosed him with having a MI (myocardial infarction), or heart attack after administering a 12-lead ECG at the patient's home.

Another ECG done while in the ER along with cardiac lab work confirmed the diagnosis. I transferred the patient over to radiology for an emergency heart catherization and stayed with him during the procedure. It was always amazing to watch as the dye was injected and the blood vessels of the heart lit up on the screen showing where there was a blockage or good circulation. This patient had significant blockage in three places and had little circulation to his heart. No wonder he was short of breath and had chest pain. His heart was not getting much oxygen at all.

I brought him back to the ER and based on the results, the ER doc called for the heart surgeon on call. I kept the patient as comfortable as possible with oxygen and pain medication while we waited for him to come in.

Fortunately for the patient, bursting through the ER doors was the best cardiac surgeon on staff. He was well known for his expertise and loved to teach whenever he had the chance. Our agency would have him come in for lectures for the paramedics at times because he was so detailed and excited about teaching. And he had a passion for sharing his knowledge.

After I gave him a quick patient report and he looked at the ECGs, x-rays, lab work, and the Cath Lab results, he arranged for emergency bypass surgery. Since I was with the patient from the beginning and I knew the surgeon, I told him that I would take him to the OR personally. He then scurried down the hall heading to the OR to get prepped.

I was not far behind him and as I moved the stretcher to the doors of the OR, I gave a quick report to the OR nurse and started to leave. The surgeon walked up to the patient just before he went into the OR to assure him everything would be fine. As they wheeled him through the doors, the surgeon looked over at me and asked, "You wanna go in and watch?" Duhhh. I responded with a "heck yeah" and told him that I needed to let the ER know what I was doing.

I called the ER charge nurse and told her that I was sitting in on the surgery and would be back when it was over, stating I was keeping her up to date on what I was doing. I decided it was best not to ask, but instead to tell her what I was doing. In a nice way, of course. See ya, bye.

I turned around and a scrub nurse told me to follow her. I went into the scrub room and she walked me through the tedious process of scrubbing in. She then put gloves and a gown on me along with a surgical mask and hat. Yeah, I got to walk into the OR with my hands in the air, pushing the door open with my backside, like I was somebody special. Pretty cool so far.

As I walked in, the surgeon said, "Come on over here. You get to stand opposite me at the operating table so you can see really well." There I was, belly up to the operating table and right up against the patient's chest, just opposite the surgeon. The patient was already out from anesthesia, and there was a lot of commotion among the nurses setting things up around us. I could not have been more excited.

More IVs had been started, the anesthesiologist was at the head monitoring the ventilator that was breathing for the patient along with his vital signs, there were trays of surgical instruments lined up to the side, and a rather large contraption I was not familiar with was at the foot of the patient. The ECG monitor was beeping loudly at a normal pace, and after a few nods to each other, a nurse injected some medication to stop the heart from beating. The nurse then opened a few valves and blood started moving through some large tubes and through a visible pump that kept the blood moving.

He was now on a bypass machine. When you are connected to the heart-lung machine, it does the same job that your heart and lungs would do. The heart-lung machine carries blood from the upper-right chamber of

248

the heart (the right atrium) to a reservoir where it picks up oxygen. The blood then travels through a plastic tube to the aorta. From the aorta, the blood moves throughout the rest of the body.

The surgeon then started cutting into the chest with a scalpel and a cauterizer, then he took a jigsaw (carpenter speak) and started cutting the sternum in half. A retractor was put in place to spread the two sections of the sternum apart to allow access to the chest cavity. I swear, I did not think one's chest could be spread open that far. After a little more work with the scalpel, I could see the heart lying in the open chest cavity. Now this was getting really cool.

Another surgeon had been cutting veins out of the patient's legs to be used for the bypass and placing them in a container. The heart surgeon reached in and grabbed the heart, rotating it around looking for the specific arteries he planned to bypass. As he rotated the heart away from him, he mentioned that he wanted to replace a particular artery first. He looked up at me and said, "Can you reach in here and pull the heart back toward you and hold it in place while I work on it?" Darn right I can.

Without hesitation, I reached inside this man's chest and gently pulled his heart toward me and held it still. I was in paramedic Disney World. This was an E ticket ride[1] that I will never forget. Here I was, with both hands inside this guy's chest while the surgeon cut and sewed in bypass vessels. He explained everything he was doing during the entire procedure, and I could tell he enjoyed teaching and loved his profession.

After what seemed like a full night of surgery, he reached inside with two small paddles on long handles attached to a defibrillator. Way smaller than the paddles we used on the ambulance for defibrillating patients. The electricity used to shock the heart was miniscule compared to what we used

---

[1] Disney originally had ticket books labeled A-E for attractions. "E" tickets provided admission to new attractions, along with other Disney favorites that were upgraded to the prestigious level. The "E" ticket was a term signifying the ultimate in thrills. It was phased out in 1982.

in the field, but there was nothing to impede the flow of electricity to get to the heart. The paddles were directly in contact with the heart. The shock was just enough to barely see the heart jump from the electricity, and then I heard the beeps on the heart monitor again slowly getting back to a normal rate.

He had the other surgeon close the chest with wire and staples, and he left the OR. I hung around long enough to watch him complete the task. I then went into another room to decon myself and get dressed to go back to the ER for the rest of my shift. I thanked the surgeon for allowing me the experience, and I think I floated back downstairs to the ER with a permanent grin on my face. Then the charge nurse said, "Did you have fun?" It was obvious. She then handed me a chart and said, "Here is your next patient to bring back, a broken arm."

"You Can't Tell Anyone I Let You Do This"

Throughout my career with EMS, we would typically rotate through different stations over the year. I always liked being busy, so they put me at busy stations most of the time. The most fun I had was working as the paramedic on our helicopter. I worked there quite a bit for about five years, and then as a fill-in when needed.

I enjoyed this station because it was a challenge and fun at the same time. I was the lone paramedic along with the pilot. That was all. In the early years on the helicopter, it was not unusual to be a first response unit and sometimes the only response unit due to the large geographic area we covered and a lot of remote locations including islands only accessible by boat.

The pilots were exceptionally good at their job, as most were Vietnam vets who flew helicopters in various capacities. Flying me around the county and to the hospitals was a walk in the park for them. What impressed me was how good they really were. Some calls will be discussed elsewhere detailing just how good they were.

After about a year of flying on the EMS helicopter, off and on I got to know the pilot's strengths and weaknesses and they got to know me better as well. We had a mutual respect for each other's jobs and tried to assist each other when possible. My job was to assist in picking out a good landing zone (LZ) that was safe, watching for power lines, and keeping them informed on how close we were to touching the ground when landing. I would open my door and lean out a bit, communicating back and forth with them over the headset. We trusted each other.

Other times, while working a call by ourselves, the pilot would assist when possible. Their priority always is the helicopter and the safety of everyone around it. In a remote area with no other help coming, sometimes they jumped right in to assist. If the helicopter was safe, they would help set up an IV, hold the bag up while I administered medications, carry equipment for me, etc. We got to know each other's jobs fairly well.

Responding to a call from the airport, my seat would be on the driver's side (of a car) and the pilot would be on the so-called passenger's side. When transporting a patient to the hospital, I would be in the back on a seat facing the patient who is lying in line with the helicopter, with their feet barely accessible as their legs were somewhat into the tunnel toward the rear.

On the way back to the airport I would be back up front. In the earlier years, when I flew, there were dual controls on the floor. They were two large pedals that controlled swinging the helicopter left and right along with a collective that sat between the two seats that controlled the speed and the pitch of the blades. It was a long bar-shaped lever you would twist and/or lift for the response you wanted. Operating a helicopter is like tapping your head, rubbing your belly, and tapping your feet all at a different cadence. Not easy.

One afternoon on the way back to the airport from the hospital, the pilot asked, "Wanna fly it?" Of course, the answer was "heck yeah." He then said, "You can't tell anyone I let you do this." I immediately responded with a motion going across my lips as if closing a zipper and a "Do what?" I had a grin on my face like a kid about to open a really cool Christmas present. He then proceeded to tell me why he wanted me to know how to operate the basics, and it made sense.

He told me a number of stories of helicopters going down due to the pilot being incapacitated for numerous reasons and everyone on board, including the pilot, ended up dead from the ensuing crash. He mentioned that bird strikes were common, and if a bird were to impact the plexiglass in front of the pilot and render him unconscious, we would both die. The only difference was that he would have no clue and I would watch it happen. Other scenarios included medical issues that would impede the pilot. All made sense to me. Now let me play.

I listened intently as he explained all the controls to me, even though some were obvious since I watched him fly so many times. The first thing he let me do was control the joystick on the floor that sat between my legs. This allowed the ship to rock left and right, forward and back. That was going to be the first lesson. That was straightforward. I got to fly back to the airport from the hospitals using the joystick for the next few shifts. Of course, he had his hands on everything just in case.

Next, I got to use the floor pedals that operated the tail rotor that would swing the tail end of the ship side to side. As long as we were moving, operating the foot pedals and the joystick (cyclic) was pretty easy as well. Now we were having fun. I did that for a few shifts.

He then decided to see if I could hover. Sounds easy. It was not. I didn't realize how sensitive the foot pedals were that kept the ship from just rotating in a circle like circling the toilet. That was an exceedingly difficult task. He then explained and demonstrated autorotation. That was no fun. He demonstrated that maneuver by disengaging the engine and autorotated for a bit before re-engaging. Okay, that scared me a bit. I got the point, and at the time I figured if we were in that situation, it would be a rough landing or we'd simply die.

The best part was after taking a patient to the other side of the state to a specialty hospital, I got to fly most of the way home. That was about a two-hour trip over nothing but bare land. I got in some fun time though. The best part was when he got bored and decided to show me how to do crop dusting and strafing runs. This nut went straight up toward the sky with our backs to the ground (I did not know a helicopter could do this) and then for a moment we sat perfectly still, then slowly started falling, tail first. As we fell toward the earth butt-first, he slowly rotated the ship so that we were facing the ground and traveling at a good rate of speed. As we got close to the ground, we curved upward back toward the sky and repeated. He explained this was how crop dusting with helicopters was done and to some degree how strafing in Vietnam was done.

He tried to scare me, but it was too much fun. It was a long trip in a helicopter, and I cannot blame him for breaking it up a bit to stay awake. Glad he did.

"Enjoy Your Time Off"

Early in my time with EMS I worked one station on a fairly regular basis for years and got to know all the EMS and fire crews from all three shifts really well. We all became good friends over time. One lieutenant with the fire department who worked the shift prior to mine was always busting chops as he left each morning, but it was all in fun. One morning as he was leaving, we told him, "Enjoy your time off." He planned on taking a vacation day that would give him several days in a row off work.

About three hours later we got a call for a cardiac arrest at the gym across the street from the station, so we got there in seconds. It was a two-story complex with racquetball and handball courts along with a weight room. We were directed to one of the racquetball courts to find someone administering CPR to his buddy whom he was playing against. We went into our routine cardiac arrest mode where everyone had a job and knew what to do. One of the firefighters with us took over compressions and I told the bystander to continue mouth-to-mouth as I gathered my intubation equipment to secure an airway.

When I asked the bystander to stop giving breaths so I could intubate, I froze for a second. "Guys, this is Wilt!" We all stared at him in disbelief for a second, then we went back into cardiac arrest mode, but with a bit more aggressiveness. We talked in disbelief among ourselves in between procedures. The heart monitor showed Ventricular Fibrillation. The best way to treat this is to deliver shocks with the paddles as soon as possible.

I held the paddles upside down while my partner squirted conductive gel on one of them. I rubbed the paddles together to spread the gel around and placed them on his chest while my partner charged the paddles. You could hear the high-pitched whirl get louder as the numbers increased on the screen of the defibrillator. Then a solid tone screeched out letting us know it was ready to be discharged. I pushed the buttons on each paddle at the same time and Wilt arched his back and all his muscles tensed up as the electricity shot through his chest and across his heart. No change. We repeated the shock two more time with more energy each time. No change.

We then started an IV, intubated his airway, and we pushed multiple medications in between shocks. We got him loaded onto a backboard and then onto a stretcher and continued CPR while taking him to the ambulance. One of the firefighters rode in the back with us to the hospital to continue compressions while I pushed medications and ventilated with a bag-valve-mask around more shocks.

When we got him to the ER, we told them this was a firefighter we worked with. The ER doc and nursing staff worked with more fervor and commitment as if it were one of their own. We all took turns doing compressions while on the ER stretcher to free up the nurses to do other things. They worked him longer than most. They saw the look of grief on all our faces and knew it was personal. They gave him every shot at recovery that they could. They stopped working the code and called him dead about forty-five minutes later.

"It's Okay, You'll Be Fine"

I cannot count how many times I have said this to patients who looked scared, sick, concerned, or even embarrassed. It is part of the job to assure them they are in good hands and we are going to help them out in any way we can. It really does help when the patient is reassured that they will be taken care of.

While working as a paramedic with a local fire department, we got a call to meet the Coast Guard cutter at their station to respond to a boater in distress. When we got there, I was informed that the captain of a commercial fishing boat was having a heart attack and he was two hours away from shore. The problem was that he was by himself on this boat and there was nobody with him to bring him to land.

We loaded up all of my paramedic gear onto the cutter. This included the heart monitor/defibrillator, oxygen, drug box, and some morphine that I took out of our lock box. I went by myself as my EMT partner had to take the ambulance back to the station and then work off one of the engines while I was gone. This was protocol due to a shortage in staffing, and taking my partner out of the station for around four hours was not necessary.

We headed out on the water in a rather large Coast Guard cutter at a decent speed. I was thinking it was going to be an exciting trip. I knew most of the crew because we had done training with them in the past. I stood next to the pilot as he navigated into the abyss. We started shouting back and forth about nothing in particular, just to pass the time. We were shouting because the huge engine on the cutter was extremely loud.

In short order it became a monotonous repeated motion that lasted two long hours. Hitting the waves, bouncing up, then crashing back down, and repeating for two hours along with the sweet smell of diesel fuel was anything but awesome.

It was amazing how they found the fishing boat out in the middle of nowhere without looking around for him. The Coast Guard knew their stuff. We pulled alongside the boat and they tied both boats together. Another crew member and I stepped over onto the fishing boat to evaluate the captain with the medical emergency.

He was lying down on a bench and obviously in a lot of pain. After a quick assessment it was determined that he was passing a kidney stone and not having a heart attack. I have never had stones, but any patient I took care of with kidney stones was in more pain than most heart attack patients. Looks miserable. He claimed he knew he had a large stone but didn't think it was going to cause any problems for him. Good time to take a boat out in the middle of the ocean by yourself, right?

We transferred him over to the Coast Guard cutter and had him lie down on a couch below deck. Another crew member got on board the fishing vessel and was assigned to pilot the boat back to shore. I started an IV and gave him some morphine for the pain. I titrated it a little at a time until he was comfortable. As the pain subsided, we all just sat down there and started a general conversation to pass the time.

As we pulled away and started to head back to the Coast Guard station, the patient looked at me and asked if I was okay. I told him that I felt like I was sick myself and was very nauseated. He said I was pale and looked like crap. I told him that breathing diesel fumes and bouncing in sync for two hours made me sick.

The patient, who was now feeling better due to the morphine, told me to lie down in the middle of the ship where there was minimal bouncing and to try to take a nap as I was obviously seasick. He leaned over to me as I was lying down and said, "It's okay, you'll be fine."

Now I had the patient taking care of me. How embarrassing. I made it back to shore without losing my lunch. I radioed in to the station and had the ambulance meet us back at the dock. We loaded him into the ambulance and took him to the ER. I took care of him in the rear of the ambulance and when we got to the ER, he thanked me for taking his pain away. And I thanked him for keeping me from puking my guts out.

"Get in the House, Now!"

When I was a training officer with the fire department, I had a take-home vehicle because I was on-call for major events and at times would go straight to meetings or trainings. One afternoon I was on the way home from work and I saw a large column of smoke coming from the general direction of my neighborhood. This was concerning because we were in the middle of a very dry spell and just a fart would start a brush fire. Due to this environment, the local department in the city where I lived had a first response of two brush trucks, two engines, a water tender, and a battalion chief ready for any brush fire call.

I saw no fire apparatus anywhere and heard no sirens. I figured they were already on scene and taking care of it, but the smoke was getting darker and larger. As I turned down my street, I saw the smoke off in the distance. It was in my neighborhood, so I wanted to check it out and possibly call it in myself. As I got closer, I realized this brush fire was in an empty field across the street from my house. Then it got crazy.

As I pulled up, I saw my younger son frantically stomping on five-foot-high flames with his shoes. His buddy pulled a garden hose that was on a hose reel and attached to a water source across the street, but he was pulling the entire reel, not just the hose. It caught and snapped the connection from the source. He fell to the ground while water was shooting up in the air in my front yard. Another buddy was running around in circles not knowing what to do. They all looked panicked as the fire was approaching a neighbor's house that was surrounded by a lot of landscaping and mulch. The fire was now around a half-acre in size.

I pulled up in my fire department staff vehicle, walked over to my garage and opened the door. I reached inside and grabbed a water extinguisher I keep charged inside. I walked over to the fire and as I walked around the perimeter of the fire, I put the fire out, leaving just some blackened grass and brush inside the perimeter. I heard numerous sirens in the background as I finished putting the fire out. In no time, four fire apparatus, a battalion chief, and a fire marshal showed up. They hit all the hot spots and made it safe.

As they did this, all three boys were breathlessly trying to tell me what happened at the same time. The short answer was they were playing with fireworks in the open field. Yep, on one of the driest days of the year. I looked at them, pointed to my house, and yelled, "Get in the house, now!" My son started walking home with his head hanging low while his two buddies started to walk away. "You too!" I yelled, pointing to them. I told them I would be there in a minute.

I went over and talked to the fire marshal and the battalion chief, both of whom I knew well. I told them what happened, and they had a muffled, toned-down laugh. This could have been a serious issue with it being so dry. The fire marshal asked me if I would handle it. I told him I would but asked if he could read them the riot act first. He responded with, "Of course. It would be my pleasure."

I went in the house and my wife had all three sitting on the couch and was reading them the riot act. But they hadn't seen anything yet. I told them the fire marshal wanted to see them outside. I stood away but stayed within earshot of the discussion, and it was epic.

He told the boys what the consequences could have been if the fire impinged on the neighbor's house, if someone had gotten burned or even killed. He mentioned that he could charge them all with arson, which is a felony, and they would have to do jail time. Even though they were juveniles in their mid-teens, they would have a permanent record. They were all very apologetic and almost in tears. As they started to walk away, I told them, "Now it's my turn. Get back in the house. All three of you."

Of course, I gave them a stern lecture and told them how they embarrassed me in front of my peers. I then proceeded to tell them if something like that happened again (and it better not), to be calm and think about what they needed to do. I explained how stomping on flames that are taller than you is not a good idea, and if they took the time to pull the hose out of the reel, they could have put the fire out themselves. And I commended them for being honest about how it started.

"Can You Hold My Hand?"

While working as a paramedic in the ER, a local fire department ambulance brought in a gentleman in his early thirties with a possible spinal injury. He'd traveled to the area to take advantage of the great fishing opportunities. He flew down by himself for a short break from the hustle and bustle of work back home. He was married and had a young son around five years old, but they were back home in another state, thus he was in the ER by himself with nobody else there with him.

We transferred him over to the ER stretcher on the backboard that he was carefully strapped to along with a cervical collar with tape holding his head against the board to keep him from moving. Until x-rays were done to determine the extent of injury, if any, he would stay strapped down and be kept from moving to minimize any further damage.

This patient was going to be mine to take care of since I took care of most of the trauma victims. I got a report from the medics that he was at a popular fishing pier and decided to dive into the water to cool off. Not being familiar with the water in that area, he found out the water was only a few feet deep where he dove in headfirst. He remembered hitting the bottom with his head, causing it to flex forward in a violent fashion. At that moment he noticed he couldn't move his legs to stand up. A bystander went over to him and kept him still in the water until the medics showed up and placed him on the backboard and immobilized him.

After getting some basic vital signs and asking questions, I took a pinwheel that has sharp spikes on the ends and started to roll it across his skin asking if he felt me poking him. As I rolled it up and down both legs, he had no feeling at all. I moved it up to his torso and still nothing. I moved to his arms and still nothing. As I went up to his shoulders, he started to feel slight pressure around the upper part of his neck. That was it. I was really concerned for this guy. I had never seen someone this bad at that point in my career.

He had diaphragmatic breathing[2] and was starting to work hard at it. He was obviously scared to death and very worried. He knew things were not good. X-ray came over with a portable machine and took lateral C-spine films to see if there was any obvious injury. I stood at the foot of the stretcher and holding onto both of his hands, pulled down his arms to lower his shoulders so they could get a good look at the entire cervical spine.

---

[2] The higher the level of injury, the greater the impact on breathing. With a high cervical injury, you will get partial function of the diaphragm. The intercostal and abdominal muscles do not work at all, thus all you will see is belly breathing, caused by the diaphragm working.

The x-ray tech came back in and slapped the film up on the lit-up viewing board, and the ER doc and I stared at the board shaking our heads. It was horrible. He had a serious fracture and dislocation of the cervical spine at the C-3-4 area. It was so out of whack that it was obvious there was a spinal cord transection[3]. The ER doc got in touch with the on-call neurosurgeon. He said he would be there in short order.

When you come into the ER and need to be referred to a specialist, you get the on-call physician if you do not already have a specialist that you see. Over the years we all knew the various physicians on rotation and who was the best and the worst. In this case, there were mixed feelings. The doc on call had the absolute worst bedside manner of any doc I had ever seen. He was rude, impersonal, mean to the nurses, and even cursed bedside at times. That was the last thing this guy needed. On the flipside, he was also the best neurosurgeon. If I ever needed to have surgery like this, he was the one I would want. Good bedside manner does not necessarily make for a good surgeon. We had mixed emotions about him coming in.

The automatic doors flew open and in walked this wonderful human being, dressed like he was ready to go work outside at a construction site and talking in a loud voice. He yelled out, "So, what do we have?" The ER doc gave him a quick report and walked him over to the x-rays on the lit-up board. He glared at them for a minute and then walked over to the patient. He took the pinwheel I used earlier and quickly moved it around the patient's shoulders and neck, asking what he felt. He looked down at the patient and said, "Looks like you f**ked up, buddy. You will not survive this injury. I will be surprised if you make it through the night. I'll get you admitted, and we'll see what happens by morning." He then walked out of the room and started the paperwork for his admission, then left.

---

[3] Spinal cord transection is a devastating condition, leading to permanent disability. It is a complete interruption of the spinal cord and compromises normal blood supply and cerebrospinal fluid circulation.

Well, that was a comforting way to tell someone bad news like that. The rest of the nursing staff and I all rolled our eyes in disgust over his wonderful bedside manner. I went back into the room to stay with my patient and continue to monitor his vital signs.

I looked down at him as he stared at the ceiling (that was all he could see while strapped down) and assured him that the staff in the ICU where he was going were sharp, and he would be in good hands. I couldn't tell him that everything would be okay, as I refused to lie to any patient I dealt with. That's just not right. You can be honest and caring at the same time.

I saw tears start running down his face. He was scared. His mind was racing. He looked into my eyes and asked if I could make a phone call for him. "Of course I can. Give me the number to write down and I'll grab the phone," I said. Just around the corner of the room he was in was a phone on the wall with an extremely long cord just for this purpose. I wrote down the number on a piece of paper and then asked who I should ask for. He told me it would be his wife.

Up to this point I had no idea he had a wife, as things were so hectic up to this point. As I punched in the number on the pad of the phone, I noticed my hand was shaking. My God! This was awful. My mind was visualizing so many bad scenarios in just the time I was punching numbers, I almost forgot who I was asking for.

The phone rang and a female voice answered. I asked if this was Jennifer and she said it was. I introduced myself and where I was at, explaining that her husband was in the ER, and that he wanted to talk to her. I told her that when they were done talking, I would give her more details as to what was going on.

As I walked back into the room with the phone, I suddenly realized that I couldn't just hand the phone to him because he was paralyzed. I had to hold the phone up to the side of his head so he could hear and talk. I had to listen to that entire horrible conversation. I was not looking forward to it.

The conversation went like this. "Honey, it's me. I really messed up big time. Yeah, I dove into the water and broke my neck. I can't feel anything. I'm scared. I need to you call my mom and dad." The conversation went on for a few more minutes as he asked her to make more calls for him and him trying not to scare her too much. Then it got even worse. "Hey, I need to talk to Timmy. Okay. Hey buddy, how are you doing? Hey, I want you to know that I love you very much and that I am proud of you. I need you to make me a promise, okay? I need you to promise me that you will always take care of Mommy. Be her little helper as much as you can. Always remember that I love you. Let me talk to Mommy again." He told his wife that he was sorry for being a dumbass and loved her very much. He said to take care of Timmy for him. He then told her that I would take the phone from there.

I picked up the phone and heard a sobbing wife on the other end as I walked back to the other side of the wall. I explained to her that it was serious, and she needed to make arrangements to get here as soon as possible, even that same night if flights were available. I gave her all the information and the address and a number to call into the ICU. I then hung up the phone with a shaking hand. That wore me out. Nothing compared to what that couple was going through, but it took a lot out of me. Enough of being selfish.

I went back into the room and started talking to him. Just general conversation to keep his mind off the situation as much as possible. I asked about Timmy and his wife, what kind of job he had, just small talk. The backboard under his head was all wet from tears running to the back of his head, so I took a towel and dried it up a bit for him.

As I stood there after taking another blood pressure reading, he looked over at me with his eyes and asked, "Can you hold my hand?" I hesitated for a minute, not knowing how to respond. This guy was around my age, and to ask that was kind of weird to me at the time. I said, "Absolutely." I reached down and held on to his right hand and continued to talk some more. As we were talking, he said, "Are you holding my hand?" I responded with, "Yes, I am. See?" I held his hand up with mine so he could see that I still had his hand. I knew he was paralyzed and couldn't feel anything, but it hit me hard realizing again that he had no clue I was holding his hand. He needed human interaction and he couldn't feel it. I wanted him to feel my hand so badly so he would know that I cared. It would never happen.

I rolled him up to the ICU on the stretcher after the paperwork was complete and a bed was ready for him. As we went down the hallway, we talked about silly stuff. I apologized for being the one taking care of him and not one of the pretty nurses. We laughed for a second. As we were going down the hallway, I realized that all he was seeing was the lights on the ceiling. Nothing else. How boring. That should be fixed. When we got to the ICU and transferred him over to the bed, I gave a quick report and handed them the paperwork. I held his hand one more time and wished him luck. I then joked that he finally had some pretty nurses to take care of him and left.

I got off work at 11p.m., as I typically worked the three to eleven shift. Before leaving I called the ICU and asked about his status. I was told he was sleeping, but his breathing was becoming more shallow and respiratory therapy was setting up for a possible ventilator to be used.

The next morning, I called the ICU again to check on him. They told me that he had died overnight and that his wife and son were not able to get there in time. She told me the wife called them and said the earliest they could fly in was the next day. He died without any family or loved ones around.

There are calls made throughout my career or patients seen in the ER over those ten years that will always have some type of impact on me. While seeing thousands of patients in the field and the ER, most just start to run together as routine. Others, like this gentleman, stick with you forever. I have told this story to fire and EMS recruits, various classes I have taught, and during commencement speeches at the academy. Even while writing this story, I get emotional. I am not sure what it is, but it pokes its head out every time I bring it up.

Too Close to Home

During my time as a training officer, I was sitting in my office doing office stuff when one of our administrative personnel came running in and yelled that Carlton had collapsed in his office and was unconscious. Carlton was the on-duty battalion chief, and his office was just down the hall from mine. I ask the office staff to contact the rescue crew over the intercom and tell them to bring their medical gear.

As I stepped into the battalion chief's office, I saw Carlton lying on the office floor, unconscious. I dragged him into the hallway where there was more room to work on him and check for breathing and pulse. He had none. I initiated CPR and waited for the paramedics on duty to come over. Fortunately for Carlton, it was two of our best paramedics with the department. They did a quick check with the heart monitor and found him to be in ventricular fibrillation. This was a shockable rhythm which has a better chance of being converted than others.

The crew delivered a few shocks via the pads placed on his chest, another started and IV and delivered some medication, and then they intubated him to protect his airway and breathe for him. We worked on him for about fifteen minutes on the floor when suddenly we got a normal rhythm on the heart monitor and felt a pulse in his neck.

The crew kept breathing for him through the endotracheal tube and we loaded him onto an EMS stretcher for transport to the ER. One of our paramedics rode into the hospital with him to assist EMS. Not long after being in the ER, Carlton started breathing again. They removed the breathing tube, and he was able to talk.

Carlton had everything on his side by being in a fire station full of paramedics and had CPR started within seconds of collapsing. He recovered following bypass surgery and eventually came back on duty as a battalion chief. He stayed in that position until he retired.

My Two Angels

Later in my career I was working as a training officer and part of that job included prepping new employees for being released to work at one of our stations. I was lucky enough to have acquired a two-story home in the city that we kept for many months just for training. We were able to work with the new hires on deploying hose lines, search and rescue, ladder work, and survival training.

One particular day we were conducting survival training and going over various procedures that could be used to survive when things go bad. One of those is called a bailout procedure where you would exit a burning room out an upper floor window if you had no choice other than to bail out. All employees were issued a bailout bag with a length of rope and a carabiner in it just for this maneuver. There were numerous ways to utilize this rope to slide down to safety, including wrapping it around a door frame, some furniture, or in the corner of the window sash.

We had reviewed all the procedures above and decided to show them that even in a pinch where you had no tools or other items to tie off on, you could always place the carabiner around and item and place it in the corner of the window, keeping tension on it, and roll out the window. You would then slide down the rope to the ground or lower floor.

To show them that they could make most anything work, I rolled up some paper really tight and placed it in the corner of the window with the carabiner hooked onto it. They thought I was nuts. I was just trying to prove a point, and I personally had done this maneuver dozens of times with no issues. Until today.

All of the orientation training with these recruits had been performed by me so far. We had FTOs who worked at various stations, but it was difficult to get them free to assist most days. Fortunately, this day one of our FTOs had asked if she could leave the station to come assist, as she enjoyed the survival training. Misty showed up around an hour into our training and started assisting with our bailout scenarios.

Anytime we had anyone jumping out windows or the like, we had a safety line attached to a safety belt that all personnel would wear. If someone were to fall, a device that the safety line was wrapped around would catch and lock in place to keep them from falling. Otherwise, it would just feed out normally as long as there was no quick descent.

As I rolled out the window showing off how to use rolled up paper as an anchor point in a pinch, Misty was handling the safety line and feeding it as needed, while the recruits watched. That is all I remember.

The next thing I remember is seeing the ceiling lights in the back of an ambulance go by me as I was being wheeled in on a stretcher. I had no clue where I was or what was going on. Then suddenly I heard a familiar voice, "Scooz, are you okay? Can you hear me?" I replied, "Bindi, is that you?" Hearing a familiar and comforting voice eased the panic of being confused. Bindi then told me she had already called my wife and she would meet us at the ER. I didn't see Bindi, but I heard her. I assumed she was in the back of the ambulance at the time trying to get my attention.

I then realized I was wearing a cervical collar; the medic in the back told me to relax and try not to move around. The doors closed, we started going down the road, and the next thing I knew I was being wheeled into the ER. As I was placed on an ER stretcher, I heard another familiar voice. "Hey, Scooz, I'm going to stay with you the whole time you are here. The ER doc will be right in." I looked up and staring back at me was Scout. He was a firefighter/paramedic that I worked with at my previous fire department, and he was working part-time in the ER. Knowing he was one of the best firefighter/paramedics in the department made me feel more at ease.

The ER doc came in and did a quick assessment, and then Scout proceeded to remove my fire boots and bunker pants that I was still wearing. I had no clue where my helmet and fire jacket were. After a quick set of vitals, Scout got a mirror and placed it in front of my face and laughed. Apparently, I was not as pretty as normal. I had abrasions down the entire side of my face from slamming into the wall. He then took me over to x-ray for an MRI of my head.

As he was wheeling me over there, I asked him if he knew what happened. He laughed again and said, "I already told you what happened, want to hear it again?" I told him to humor me and tell me again. It appeared I had hung myself, and it almost worked.

When I rolled out the window, the paper gave way and I quickly plummeted down the outside of the wall, and then the safety line caught in the safety device and snapped me to a halt. The safety line got hung up underneath the back of my helmet and pulled up so hard, it almost pulled my helmet off. The bad thing with that was I also had my helmet chin strap in place, and the weight of my body pulling up on my helmet was also choking me out by my chin strap.

Misty looked down when I fell and saw me hanging there unconscious. She told the recruits to run downstairs to assist me down as she fought with the safety device to free up the rope. She lowered me down to the ground and the recruits took my helmet and jacket off. By the time they did that, Misty was down there with me and did a quick assessment.

I supposedly regained consciousness and became a little combative when I stood up against their direction and tried to walk away. They sat me down inside the house and Misty had called for an ambulance and for rescue to respond. She told me I was a bit of an asshole, telling them that I had to get back to training and to leave me alone. At times they had to restrain me, not knowing what I was going to do.

A fire department engine, rescue, battalion chief, and an EMS ambulance had arrived on scene, and I was refusing to go to the hospital. Someone finally convinced me to lie down on the stretcher and go. As I said before, my memory is blank from the time I rolled out of the window, to seeing the lights in the back of the ambulance. I had lost that time in my memory forever.

I felt horrible that I gave everyone a hard time. I was not happy scaring the heck out of the new recruits like that. My being combative and argumentative makes sense. When I was literally hanging myself, it shut off oxygen to my brain and I became hypoxic. It is common for someone who is hypoxic to be combative. Even though I was carrying on what appeared to be normal, or in this case, obnoxious conversations with personnel on scene, I have no memory of any of it.

The moral of the story is this. If you ever have a medical or trauma patient who is combative, do not assume they are just being nasty and obnoxious. Evaluate the possibility of them being hypoxic. And I will always remember my two angels, Misty and Bindi.

The Most Stressful Part

I know this will sound weird, but the most stressful part of the job is driving lights and siren to a call. I'm sure most think that is the best part of the job. That's what I thought when I started out as a volunteer back in the '70s. It didn't take long to figure out that just the act of driving to a call with lights flashing and sirens wailing wore me out more than working a fire or a cardiac arrest. Way more stressful, in my opinion.

I would rather pull up to a scene with flames out of each window with people screaming for help, a multiple-vehicle pile-up on the interstate, or even in a structure fire with flames rolling over my head (which is actually pretty cool) than running lights and siren.

It doesn't matter if you're driving a large engine or ladder truck, an ambulance, a police car, or a staff vehicle. You have the same issues. Vehicles do not pull over and get out of your way, they slam on their brakes in front of you when they see you, they run through intersections without looking, and pedestrians walk in front of you in a crosswalk.

I personally have been involved in two accidents, one being my fault, and numerous close calls. When I would drive the 100-foot ladder truck, it was hard to miss and the difficult part was making turns at an intersection because I would have to take up three lanes of traffic to make the turn. But I would take my time, and people get out of the way. Not as bad for an engine, but drivers can see it pretty well.

Driving an ambulance is much smaller and more difficult for some to see. Responding in a staff vehicle is the worst-case scenario since you are at the same level as everyone else and most people do not see you. Short runs were not bad, however runs from one end of the county to the other was stressful. By the time I would arrive at some locations, I was worn out.

No matter what you were driving, we should stop at all intersections and proceed cautiously until through, especially if you had the red light or stop sign. And sometimes that just does not matter. The accident that was my fault was at a busy intersection that had five lanes in all four directions. Two turn lanes and three throughway lanes that always had traffic backed up.

I had the red light as I approached, I came to a stop with the siren blaring and lights flashing and looked at all three feeds to the intersection. As people stopped for me to the left and the turn lane and two throughway lanes to the right had stopped. I inched my way through the intersection and when it looked clear, I accelerated through the intersection.

Yep, here comes a van in the faraway throughway lane on the right flying through the intersection at a high rate of speed and broadsides me. There was significant damage to both vehicles. I was not injured as the impact was on the passenger side. I jumped out to assess the driver of the van, and he had minor injuries. As I said before, inching through this intersection was more stressful than fighting a fire or making a life-or-death decision on a medical call.

And it does not stop once you get on scene. If you responded to a vehicle accident or working a wildland fire on the side of the road, you now have to be concerned about being hit by those not paying attention to you but are looking at the scene (rubber necking).

Fire department vehicle collisions rank as the second leading cause of on-the-job deaths for firefighters. In 2017, 15,145 fire department vehicles were involved in collisions nationwide, leading to 1080 injuries and 18 deaths. Up to 25% of annual line-of-duty firefighter fatalities are attributable to motor vehicle crashes and collisions. More than one police officer per week was killed on average from a collision or from being struck directly by another vehicle. More than 10,000 ambulance-related collisions occur annually (Hohs, 2019).

Do you see where I am coming from now?

"Where Were You on September 11, 2001?"

You do not hear that question asked much today. In my opinion, that is sad. We can never forget that day in history, and to never let our guard down. It hit those of us in the fire service especially hard since of the 2,977 victims killed, 412 were emergency responders, of which 343 were from the Fire Department of New York (FDNY) alone.

I was not one of the brave responders that who worked the rubble pile for months on end and for years I was ticked off that I was not there. I cannot imagine the nightmare of being on scene during the initial phases of the tragedy or even being there after the fact, working the rubble pile for recovery operations.

I was a member of our state Urban Search & Rescue (USAR) team and was one of two rescue managers. Bill and I were assigned this position due to us both having a background in construction. Structural collapse is one of the disciplines USAR teams are trained for. Our team was new and still in the process of getting various certifications.

Bill and I were sent to Texas to become certified structural collapse instructors. It was to be a week-long course, with mostly hands-on training. In our class were USAR members from around the country who had been on federal teams for years and had multiple deployments under their belts. We were the rookies in the group but were excited about picking the brains of those with a lot of experience and taking it back to train and certify our team.

We got to the training facility on September 10, 2001. We got situated in our dorm room for the week and spent the day scoping out the training facility. It was an amusement park for first responders. There were multiple buildings that had been purposely collapsed for training on shoring and tunneling operations, there were actual trains on railroad tracks to simulate train crashes, and just about any other large disaster scenario you can imagine. We were pumped.

The morning of September 11, 2001 we were all in a large classroom and the lead instructor was the gentleman in charge of all federal USAR teams and coordinated their responses both domestically and internationally. He was the big cheese in the USAR arena. We recognized a few faces from some of our large state teams that were also federal response teams. It seemed like every state was represented in this huge class. We were going to suck as much info out of these guys as we could while we had the chance.

Class started at 8 a.m. with introductions of students and instructors, followed by a review of the curriculum. We took a break at 9 a.m. before we resumed the classroom portion of the class. As we all worked our way back to our seats, the lead instructor came out with a horrified look on his face. He told us that a plane had crashed into the

World Trade Center in New York. He turned on a television nearby, and we all looked in disbelief at what we were seeing. The tower had a gaping hole in the side with heavy smoke pouring out of every window on several floors.

We all started speculating what the tactics and strategy would be for FDNY to fight a fire of such magnitude and height. There was a lot of chatter surrounding the work that department was about to endure. At 9:03 we all saw a second plane hit the other tower. We all looked at each other trying to figure out what was happening.

Our lead instructor's pager went off and he left the room. We were all glued to the TV trying to figure out what was going on when he came back in and turned the volume off on the TV. He had a serious look on his face and said that we were under attack. He said that most of us would be going to New York to assist. Just then, about fifty pagers all went off at the same time at different cadences. It was a deafening and freaky sound. Every student in the class was an elite member of federal resource USAR teams, except for Bill and me, and they all got pages explaining that they were to deploy to New York.

There was a frenzy among the group members, trying to gather their belongings and figure out how they were going to get back to their teams to deploy with them. It seemed like everyone disappeared in a matter of minutes. Bill and I were kind of lost and had no idea what to do. The team we are part of was not a federal resource, but a state resource. We felt like we needed to go with the rest of the class somehow.

The local team was an elite federal resource, and we went to the location where their team gathered their equipment for deployment hoping we could help in some way. They were like a well-oiled machine getting pallets of equipment loaded onto semis and other pallets staged for military aircraft loading. We were out of place and were politely told that we would just be in the way. We watched for a while and as they started moving, we decided to leave the campus. We walked a few blocks away to a bar and grill for lunch and to watch the events unfold on their TVs surrounding the dining area. We had no rental car as a shuttle had taken us from the airport to the academy. We both talked about how let down we were that we couldn't go to assist. We contacted our team back at home and were told that all state teams were on standby and that we needed to get back home.

By that time, all domestic flights were grounded until further notice, and airports were shut down. We called the local car rental agency at the airport, only to be told they were closed as well and were not renting cars. Our USAR team at home had to fax a letter to the rental company's corporate office stating that we needed to get back home for possible deployment.

About an hour later we got a phone call stating someone would meet us at the rental counter at the airport so we could get a car. We walked about five blocks to the airport and had to show ID just to get into the airport proper. It was locked down tight. As we made our way down a long, dark hallway to the rental counter, all we could hear was the echo of our shoes hitting the tile floor. There was nothing going on in the entire airport. No personnel, no vehicles, no planes, nothing. An agent was waiting for us at the entrance to the rental counter and unlocked the door to the kiosk.

We did some paperwork and were directed to our vehicle. He locked the door behind him and left. We took the car to the academy, loaded up our personal items and started driving. It would take us about twenty hours to get home between the two of us driving. It was an eerily quiet trip since there was minimal traffic on the interstate and absolutely no air traffic at all. We got home and gathered our USAR equipment just in case. Of course, we didn't go anywhere. We were a new state team that only deployed within the state.

To this day I feel like we should have been there, but as time goes on, it is devastating to see how many firefighters, cops, and medics who worked the rubble pile are now dying of various cancers due to the exposure of God knows what while digging for survivors or remains. Odds are fairly good that some of those in our class had become sick or died from that response.

Your Witness

One of the more interesting aspects of the job as a first responder is being witness to all these crazy things. We may witness something happen, what people said, verify extent of injuries, or confirm treatment given. A majority of the time our part in the legal process is either writing a statement for law enforcement or doing a deposition with attorneys. There are other cases where you testify in court. What else can you do on your day off for five dollars a day but sit in a secluded room for hours, waiting to testify for five minutes?

I have had my share of depositions, statements, and testifying throughout my career. The one case that stands out for me was not even a call I ran. I wrestled in high school and competed in freestyle wrestling tournaments well into my thirties. I was a high school wrestling official for fifteen years, and when a local school lost their coach just prior to the season, they asked me to be coach. I loved the sport.

A few years later after I had gone back to officiating since they found a replacement coach, a student was seriously injured during practice in the wrestling room. The attorney for the school board asked me to testify as a wrestling expert and as a paramedic. Just to be clear, I am not an expert in either field. He just wanted it to sound that way for the courts.

The fun part was me being approved to be an expert witness on two levels. Wrestling and paramedic skills. I spent almost two hours sitting there listening to two attorneys argue back and forth about whether I was at the level of expert or not. Long story short, I was approved as an expert in both. This designation allowed me to give my opinion. Otherwise, you are not allowed to do that as a witness. It worked for the school board since my testimony and my opinion made the difference in the outcome. It was a different experience not referring to a run report I had written on a call I made, but just giving my opinion.

Chapter 16

MOST IMPORTANT

❖ My Best Partner

Anyone in the public safety arena will tell you that you need a support system to keep you sane and in tune with yourself. That usually is your spouse. My wife has been my best partner throughout my entire career. I cannot emphasize how important it is to have that support. He/she must get used to you being gone for a twenty-four-hour shift, or a forty-eight-hour shift if you take overtime or are paying someone back for a shift swap.

If you are on any specialty team you will be gone for even longer periods of time for either training or deployments. I was on our county Urban Search & Rescue (USAR) Team, hazardous materials team, technical rescue team, Incident Command response team, dive team, competition team, softball team, and I was a paramedic. All these teams required time spent on training or response, some of which occurred on your days off.

If you loved the specialty teams like I did, and you were excited about going to training or responding to events, that made it more difficult for your spouse to understand. It is sometimes hard for a spouse to understand why you are excited about leaving the family for another day for training after you just got off a twenty-four-hour shift, or why you were pumped to respond to another part of the state and be gone for two weeks at a time or respond to a large wildland fire and be gone until dark and typically head back the next day to help gain control of it.

Some would speculate that the divorce rate for first responders is high. There are studies all over the place that show that rate to be lower than the general population, while others show it to be near normal. My personal explanation is simple. Being gone for that twenty-four-hour shift gives the spouse a much-needed break. At least my wife looked forward to it. "See ya, love ya, bye." I believe they like the alone time and when we were together, we spent more time enjoying it. There was no time to get on each other's nerves. That's just my opinion.

Your spouse also must get used to the dark humor and the relentless practical jokes. We need to understand that what is funny among other first responders is not necessarily funny to family members. "That's messed up!" or "Not funny" seems to be the normal response. Eventually, they get used to it and just ignore it. They may not necessarily laugh at it, but they ignore it.

Heck, they should have known what they were getting into, right? Maybe. Some have no clue what kind of craziness first responders are exposed to. Most of the general population has no clue. That's why I am exposing some of it.

There are many calls and experiences my wife never heard about while I was on the job. She will see some of it for the first time in this book. At times it is better to just try to forget some of the experiences; at other times you need to unload on someone and get the mess off your chest. You just need someone to share it with. It could be something you were proud of or something that will give you nightmares. Sometimes you just keep it inside.

I blame my wife for not picking up the clues that we are a weird bunch. Now she has to suffer the consequences. We met while I was working as a part-time paramedic in the emergency room. She would type up and register patients as they came in. If someone came in by ambulance, she would have to come out to the ER to get the information she needed to type up a chart.

Here I was working my typical three-to-eleven shift and I spotted a new girl working in registration. She was a hottie, and I was going to check her out. Cute as a button, long brown hair, long beautiful legs, and deep dimples when she smiled. This was going to be trouble. Not necessarily with me, but with my competition. All afternoon, as medics came in the doors with patients, they saw her too. Game on! Everyone asked about her. I told them to back off, she was mine. One of the local medic hound dogs made a bet with me as to who could get the first date.

Spoiler alert, I won. It was not easy. All the other girls in registration told her to avoid all the hounds that came through the door as they were all the same, and there was nothing to like. Now, I have an advantage. I worked with her in the ER. She automatically thought I was a typical first responder, but the girls already knew that I got along with everyone in the ER, including registration. They knew I was a nice guy, so they lightened up on me a bit.

Of course, she could feel me checking her out all day, so she was a little intimidated. However, she had the task of taking the jewelry and personal property off people who died in the ER, then logging it and sealing it in a bag for family members to get later. This was going to be her first one. She shyly asked me to help her get the jewelry off a dead gentleman in the trauma room. Absolutely.

I went in the room with her and I took off some rings, his watch, and pulled his wallet from his pants. I handed them over to her one at a time as she logged them onto a form and on the envelope, then it was all sealed in. She thought it was kind of gross handling a dead person and taking things off him. I reassured her it was not a big deal and would help her. This was the first conversation we had, and it was over a dead body. It was a busy shift and I didn't have the time to strike up a conversation beforehand. Kind of romantic, huh?

She quickly found out that I had a weird sense of humor, but I was a nice guy. She held her own and punched right back with the humor. We hit it off well. We dated for over a year and eventually got married. You would have thought there was a medical conference going on during our wedding. It was full of nurses and doctors who were all friends of ours along with all the crazy firefighters, cops, and medics. What a fun bunch.

She stuck it out with me, and I am a better person for it. She was always there when I needed to unload and always willing to assist with anything the department was involved in. Fundraisers, building department floats for parades, softball tournaments, Christmas parties for employees' kids, you name it, she was there.

Here I am finally retired, and she gets excited when she goes back home to visit the kids or when I plan a day trip. I guess she will always need that alone time. Now I know why she smiles when I go down to the basement to work on this book.

My Sons

As you can tell by now, I kept pretty busy with my career. But you must know that I still made time to do things with my two boys. I was a baseball coach for both, from T-ball to Babe Ruth. I would go to the field and practice with them and would schedule my part-time jobs around their baseball game schedule as much as possible.

I remember going on a long road trip family vacation, and to keep the boys from fighting over who was looking out each other's windows, I gave them both a copy of the Emergency Response Guideline (ERG), or Orange Book, for hazardous materials. You can look up hazardous materials by name, number, or category with this book. We had a fun game. Every time we saw a truck with a hazmat placard on it, they had to race to see who could find it in the book first. And when they did, they had to read out loud the name and properties of the chemical. I sound like a fun dad, huh?

When they were still in elementary school, I brought in a cow's heart that I acquired from a local butcher shop and dissected it in front of the class, explaining how the heart works. I was the coolest dad for years. I had the attention of every kid as I took a scalpel and cut it open, showing the heart valves, the arteries, the chambers, and plenty of blood. Even when some of those kids were in high school with my boys, they still remembered that day.

They both grew up knowing what I did, and I hope I made them proud. One of the proudest moments of my life was watching both my sons graduate from the fire academy and become EMTs. My oldest son is currently a firefighter/EMT working at a local fire department, along with being a hazmat technician and a member of the same USAR team I was on. My youngest son is an EMT working for an ambulance service. Maybe it goes back to my opening statement that a certain degree of exposure leads to a certain degree of contamination. That's not always a bad thing.

REFERENCES

CareerCast.com. (2017). *The Most Stressful Jobs of 2018*. Retrieved from CareerCast.

Cooper, G. E. (2018, April 19). *The 25 Most Stressful Jobs in America: Is Yours on the List?* Retrieved from MoneyTalksNEWS: https://www.moneytalksnews.com/slideshows/25-most-stressful-jobs-in-america-is-yours-on-the-list/

Fahy, R. F., & Molis, J. L. (19, June 19). *Firefighter Fatalitites in the United States*. Retrieved from National FIre Protection Association: https://www.nfpa.org/News-and-Research/Data-research-and-tools/Emergency-Responders/Firefighter-fatalities-in-the-United-States/Firefighter-deaths

Lulla, A. M., Tian, L. M., Moy, H. P., Mueller, K. M., & Svancarek, B. M. (2020, February 1). Retrieved from EMS World: https://www.emsworld.com/1223779/ems-suicide-threat

Ruderman Family Foundation. (2017). Retrieved from White Papers & Research: https://rudermanfoundation.org/white_papers/police-officers-and-firefighters-are-more-likely-to-die-by-suicide-than-in-line-of-duty/

Stanley, I. H., Hagan, C. R., Hom, M. A., & Joiner, T. E. (2015, July 10). *www.elsevier.com/locate/jad*. Retrieved from Journal of Affective Disorders: https://www.suicideinfo.ca/wp-content/uploads/gravity_forms/6-191a85f36ce9e20de2e2fa3869197735/2018/06/Career-prevalence-and-correlates-of-suicidal-thoughts-and-behaviors.pdf

U.S. Fire Administration. (n.d.). *Resources for the Volunteer Fire Service.* Retrieved from U.S. Fire Administration: https://www.usfa.fema.gov/operations/ops_volunteer_fire_service.html

Made in the USA
Las Vegas, NV
18 June 2021

25005212R00166